Desert Islands

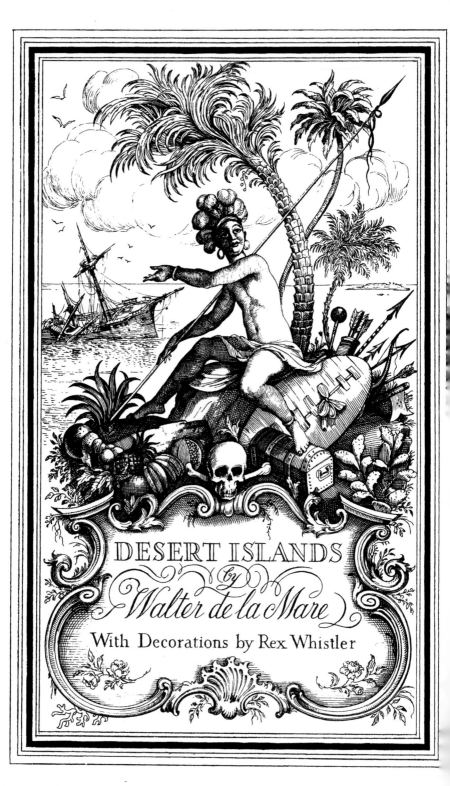

DESERT ISLANDS

by

Walter de la Mare

With Decorations by Rex Whistler

Desert Islands

WALTER DE LA MARE

With Decorations by Rex Whistler
Foreword by Michael McKeon

PAUL DRY BOOKS
Philadelphia   2011

First Paul Dry Books Edition, 2011

Paul Dry Books, Inc.
Philadelphia, Pennsylvania
www.pauldrybooks.com

1 3 5 7 9 8 6 4 2
Printed in the United States of America

Library of Congress Cataloging-in-Publication Data
De la Mare, Walter, 1873–1953.
  [Desert islands and Robinson Crusoe]
  Desert islands / Walter de la Mare; [illustrated by] Rex
Whistler; foreword by Michael McKeon.
    p. cm.
  Originally published as: Desert islands and Robinson Crusoe:
London: Faber and Faber, 1930.
  Includes index.
  Summary: "'A vast treasure chest, a bewildering collection . . .
to dazzle and fascinate everyone who lifts the lid.' – Geoffrey
Grigson"—Provided by publisher.
  ISBN 978-1-58988-067-2 (pbk.)
  1. Defoe, Daniel, 1661?–1731. Robinson Crusoe. 2. Robinson
Crusoe (Fictitious character). 3. Islands. 4. Fiction—History and
criticism. I. Title.
  PR6007.E3D4 2011
  823'.5—dc22

                                              2010051016

Contents

Foreword

by Michael McKeon

Desert Islands aims to capture the aura of an anomalous genre, and it shares much of that genre's anomaly. In the disarmingly candid words of its author, "there is no more sense in treating the fiction that has desert islands for theme as a branch of literature than there is in classifying the drama under the headings of plays that contain fat characters and plays that contain thin." We're all familiar with the idea of the desert island, if only from *New Yorker* cartoons or the challenging puzzler: "If you were stranded on a desert island and could choose only one book [type of food/companion] to accompany you, what would it be?" The question lingers in our culture as an amusingly superficial and short-cut route to ultimate judgments, the vestige (even the adjective is archaic— not "deserted" but "desert") of a problem whose scenario technological advance has long since outmoded but whose philosophical weight persists undiminished. How much of my life have I chosen? Do my desires express my needs? In extremity, stripped of my friends and things, by what am I defined?

Desert Islands, however, is not philosophy. It was written eighty years ago by the Englishman Walter de la Mare (1873–1956), midway through a notable career as novelist, poet, and short-story writer. His was surely a far different era than our own, and our distance from it—a time and place when stylish *belles lettres* that wore their learning lightly commanded more attention—may begin to explain the affecting sense of belatedness that now colors *Desert Islands*. The book has the fascination of one of those cabinets of curiosities, filled with randomly juxtaposed artifacts and devices rare and wonderful and far-flung, which long ago graced the homes of the Renaissance patriciate and then, in the hands of natural historians, became the model for the modern museum. But de la Mare's book has gone through three editions and at least five printings before this one, and its continuing appeal may owe less to the beguiling charm of a bygone mode of address than to the way the eccentric motion of its style enacts what it describes: embarking us on a journey teeming with the curious and exotic details of stories about strange lands and stranger travelers, and steering us uncannily to the center of our own most modern and familiar preoccupations.

What to call this sort of book was of some interest to de la Mare himself. Very much *not* a domestic "novel of manners," he writes, it's more a "Tale of Adventure" shot through with "romance." What's central to romance and the tale of adventure for de la Mare is distance, in the several senses of that word. Here's a small bouquet: "[I]t is *distance* that lends enchantment to the view," the distance of "the strange and the marvellous," "the fabulous and the apocryphal" (de la Mare's italics). "We pine for the curious, the bizarre. We return to find our peace in the familiar and the near." "[R]omance is invariably flavored with the extreme. It flowers in the mind not merely at an uncustomary but at a hazardous poise." And of physical solitude de la Mare writes, "What other theme in fiction is more deeply saturated with the romantic and the adventurous?" All of these are implicated in the basic premise of the desert-island story—most of all geographical distance, a place so remote from everyday experience as to be *terra incognita,* unknown land.

Less obvious, but equally central to what captures de la Mare's imagination in *Desert Islands*, is the feeling of the historically distant, the sense of the antique that permeates the outlandishness of this sort of experience, as well as the possibility that it may be ineluctably past. For "the *desert* island is now unfortunately by far the most infrequent in kind" (de la Mare's italics).

Although not chronologically ordered, *Desert Islands* sweeps us from classical antiquity to the twentieth century, through a vast archipelago of factual and fictional travels and authors both obscure and celebrated. But the book's balance point is the eighteenth century, an empirical age when romance came to connote "something indolent, seductive and untrue"; and much of the book leads up to, and charts the influence of, Daniel Defoe's *Robinson Crusoe* (1719). Part of this lead-up follows from the pleasure de la Mare takes in his wandering itinerary, which tracks not only books but also islands, and sometimes the solitary settlers who successively occupy the same island. His "ideal island" is the one of three, collectively called Juan Fernandez, that was first explored around 1570 by the Spanish navigator of that name, who landed "Indians," sheep, and cattle on it. A century later William Dampier, three-time circumnavigator of the world, recorded his return to Juan Fernandez in search of a Miskito Indian whom he accidentally had marooned there by his hasty departure four years earlier. Dampier's account of this man in *A New Voyage Round the World* contains a number of details that were to become paradigmatic of the desert-island denizen. De la Mare tells us that another castaway, Alexander Selcraig or Selkirk, was discovered on this same island in 1709 by Woodes Rogers, on whose *A Cruising Voyage Round the World* Defoe based the outlines of the novel he was to publish ten years later.

Enthralled as he is by the desert island, de la Mare is just as enthralled by the literary lore of the desert island. *Robinson Crusoe*, once conceived and delivered of Defoe's imagination, has gone on to become perhaps the most fecund of modern prototypes and to produce countless offspring, and de la Mare lets us know which of these he admires and which he doesn't. (*The Swiss Family Robinson* decisively falls into the latter camp.) But he also takes pains to remind us that Defoe's "prototype" is itself rooted in the past (as a friend of his remarks, "most good stories reach back to antiquity") and ultimately in Homer's pre-prototype *The Odyssey*. Much of the romance of the desert island lies for de la Mare in the vast literary distance this trope has traveled, always recognizable as such but always adaptable to its new conditions. De la Mare calls *Robinson Crusoe* a "romance," then corrects himself: not a romance "but the dressing-up of romance to make it look like matter-of-fact," adding that Defoe "was, in much, the first English novelist." By internalizing romance beneath the modern clothing of empirical truth, the novel, the great modern genre, both supplants and sustains the ancient narrative mode.

The quantifying calculations of modern science and commerce emerged during the same epoch as the novel, and we might expect all these to have tolled the death knell of the fantastic desert-island romance. De la Mare contrasts Defoe's imagined world with that of Sir John Mandeville, whose fourteenth-century *Travels* became a touchstone of enchanting mendacity. "In Mandeville there is as naive and greedy a delight in *things* as there is in *Crusoe*, but for their rarity, their strangeness, their preciousness. Their use, their age, and their marketableness seem not very much to have interested him." What enthralls us in Mandeville's *Travels* "is the remoteness of his romantic '*yles*.' They lie beyond verification. Their distance is incomputable." Defoe's Robinson, by contrast, is an empirical experimentalist, "incredibly methodical and statistical with those precise figures of his, his date-post . . . , his inventories, his bills of lading, his schedules of stores . . ." In *Gulliver's Travels*, Defoe's contemporary Jonathan Swift created an enduring adventure of cautious landfalls on unknown islands that seem to be deserted but actually are peopled by creatures far more fantastic than anything we hear of in Robinson's relatively realistic travels. But like many readers, de la Mare judges Swift's chapters in satire of the new science to be a decided falling off from the others. As he puts it, "The child in him died out in them." Figuring the stages of history as those of an individual's development, de la Mare locates the lore of the desert island in the childhood of humanity, but he also finds an unexpected parallel to its innocently fabulous discoveries in the lore of modern science, whose "discoveries are romantic in kind and effect while they remain novelties, and chiefly when they are concerned with the outskirts of knowledge . . . They are at least as seductive as the wildest extravaganzas of fiction."

The parallel between the old nautical and the new scientific discoveries made metaphorical sense to Robert Hooke, contemporary experimentalist and maker of scientific instruments, who anticipated many future discoveries—"*every considerable improvement of* Telescopes *or* Microscopes *producing new Worlds and* Terra-Incognita's *to our view*" (*Micrographia* [1665]). Perhaps the new scientific technologies are, like the novel, the old voyages of discovery "dressed up." De la Mare remarks—in 1930—that "[c]ivilized man, we are told, is on the point of vacating his nursery and will presently, poor soul of endless gallantries, set out to his preparatory school." But what if the childhood of humanity is not a single, determinate moment of origin but multiple and relative? De la Mare seems to support this view when he speculates that we can see once more, but now in the new world, the *Arabia Deserta* of the old with no more than "a glance at a map of the vast sterile State of Nevada—which drinks up its own rivers, and whose inhabitants now number less than two to the square mile." (What would he say today, seeing Las Vegas?) And two decades before *Robinson Crusoe* was published, the philosopher John Locke, discussing how the modern institution of private property had facilitated the cultivation of the primordial "state of nature," wrote: "Thus in the beginning all the World was *America*" (*Second Treatise of Government* [1690]).

So although it may be true that "this habitable world of ours consists of nothing *but* islands," "the *desert* island is now unfortunately by far the most infrequent in kind" (de la Mare's italics). Yet the ideas and emotions on which the desert island is grounded have a deep foundation in the experience of solitude, which modernity has given a new lease on life. A "complete solitude," de la Mare writes, "may be saturated with the romantic." But although he doesn't make this distinction, there's a difference between the ancient and medieval mode of "romance" and the "romantic" of late eighteenth-century romanticism, which self-consciously transvalued the romance mystique. Before modern times, the importance of community was so paramount that the idea of individual self-interest was inconceivable except as antisocial and sinful. Nowadays our sense of things is defined by the equal conflict between individual and society—but also by the utopian hope, most famously formulated toward the end of the eighteenth century by Adam Smith in *The Wealth of Nations* (1776), that even the most self-serving of individual motives redound to the benefit of the community.

De la Mare quotes the revelation had by his contemporary L. P. Jacks, which affirms not the capitalist utopia but its Christian counterpart: "Desolate Islands, more than I could ever explore, more than I could count or name, I found in the men and women who press upon me every day . . . And once came the rushing of a mighty wind; and the waves fled backward till the sea was no more. Then I saw that the islands were great mountains uplifted from everlasting foundations, their basis one beneath the ocean floor, their summits many above the sundering waters—most marvellous of all the works of God." Sir Thomas More's *The New Isle*

Called Utopia (1516) is a satire of late medieval England whose utopian ideal includes the communal ownership of property; part of the satire lies in More's clear vision that this ideal is also "utopian" in the word's other meaning, that is, "nowhere" to be found. More's island sits athwart a historical watershed: on the near side is community already on the defensive; on the far side is the defense of the individual, whose existential isolation (literally, made into an island—or as de la Mare puts it, having been "enisled") is seen increasingly as our natural right.

Two hundred years after *Utopia* and on the far side of that watershed, Defoe casts his aggressively acquisitive individual away from human community but into divine communion. As the converted Robinson puts it, "I gave humble and hearty Thanks that God had been pleas'd to discover to me, even that it was possible I might be more happy in this Solitary Condition, than I should have been in a Liberty of Society . . . That he could fully make up to me, the Deficiencies of my solitary State, and the want of Humane Society by his Presence . . ." Protestantism and its Lutheran priesthood of all believers helped ease the passage from the old dominance of communal welfare to the emergent authority of the individual by dispensing with ecclesiastical mediation and transforming faith into an intimate relationship between God and the solitary believer. Surprisingly, de la Mare dismisses the idea that the "heavenly thread" of religion does much to bind *Robinson Crusoe* into a meaningful whole. Yet even from a more secular standpoint, the meaning of isolation clearly has undergone a sea change.

"The English in particular," de la Mare observes, "are as a people naturally beguiled by the thought of the smallest strip or path of land that is surrounded by water . . . Again and again they have had to face the charge of insularity, but then was there ever a national shortcoming so inevitable?" England as a desert island: in 1651 the poet Andrew Marvell had used sublimely

allegorical language to tie that disastrous image to the
English civil wars and, ultimately, to the Fall:

> O thou, that dear and happy isle
> The garden of the world ere while,
> Thou paradise of foúr seas,
> Which heaven planted us to please,
> But, to exclude the world, did guard
> With wat'ry, if not flaming sword;
> What luckless apple did we taste,
> To make us mortal, and thee waste?
>
> ("Upon Appleton House," st. 41)

Defoe doesn't shun the suggestion of Christian allegory. When Robinson first surveys the island, so far from
being wasted, it "appear'd so fresh, so green, so flourishing, every thing being in a constant Verdure, or Flourish of *Spring*, that it looked like a planted Garden." But
de la Mare's intuition that insularity is England's "national shortcoming" suggests for Defoe's novel a less
pointedly political allegory (while sidestepping religion
altogether), which gains plausibility from the correspondence scholars have shown to exist between Robinson's
scrupulously recorded chronology of his adventures and
the signal dates of the English civil wars and their after-
math. Robinson must leave one island for another, we
might speculate, because English insularity has lost its
immemorial capacity to bind together the English island
community by isolating it from the outside world, and
instead divides the island against itself, isolating a self-in-
terested and absolutist elite from the people and foment-
ing civil war. Robinson's adventures on the desert island
offer in turn a utopian model for England's future, a
new and better foundation hacked out of the wilderness of Locke's "state of nature" by the solitary, industrious individual, *homo economicus*. As de la Mare reminds
us, before Robinson leaves his island he has become its
"Governor," an enlightened monarch who, unlike the actual Stuart monarchs, tolerates religious difference. So

Defoe's novel shows how England will adapt its absolutist insularity to the needs of modern community, through economic individualism and a just monarch's benign rule over a burgeoning British Empire.

This is one scenario of how the solitude of the desert island is revalued for the coming age. Another one recalls contemporary accounts of discoveries aided by newly invented scientific instruments. Consider Hooke's revelation that under the microscope the seemingly blank spaces dispersed around and threaded through our everyday lives become teeming *terrae incognitae*; or John Turberville Needham's remark that a "Drop of Water, the Diameter of which exceeds not a Line, may be a Sea ... affording Sustenance to millions of Animals ..." (John Turberville Needham, *An Account of Some New Microscopical Discoveries* ... [1745]). Like time and the question of origins, space and the question of solitude is relative. When we alter our normal perspective and see things from below, our sense of solitude becomes illusory—or for that matter from within: we commonly believe that what de la Mare calls "the inmost self of each one of us" is, as he writes, "a livelong recluse." But as he paraphrases Henry James, "inward communion" is "a solitude thronged with the phantoms of the universe of the mind." Elsewhere de la Mare observes that "islands, like human consciousness, are usually but the green or sandy tops of high hills or rocks hidden in the deeps below ..." Only from a single and superficial point of view is the human mind confined to the narrow compass of consciousness. Here Jacks's revelation that the multitude of desolate individuals share a deep foundation is internalized within each individual desolation. De la Mare is a child of both modernism and psychoanalysis, and he no doubt had heard about Freud's construal of Hamlet's "dread of something after death, / The undiscovered country, from whose bourn / No traveller returns ..." (*Hamlet* III.i.29–31). Hamlet soliloquizes about death and the afterlife, reminding us of the compelling island figure created by Shakespeare's contemporary John Donne (oddly absent from *Desert Islands*):

> No man is an island, entire of itself; every man is a piece of the continent, a part of the main ... any man's death diminishes me, because I am involved in mankind, and therefore never send to know for whom the bell tolls; it tolls for thee. (*Devotions upon Emergent Occasions*, no. 17 [1624])

The Freudian "undiscovered country" is not death but the unconscious, the vast and seemingly desert wilderness that, submerged from view, underlies and props up the tamed and cultivated island of the conscious mind. In the great period of the voyages of discovery, it was the islands themselves that needed taming, and by techniques adaptable to later Freudian expeditions: learning to translate an opaque and difficult language, overcoming the resistance of native inhabitants, domesticating the recursive logic of the savage mind to the linear pathways of civilized reason. So the tradition of the great voyages is extended by modern expeditions into the human interior.

*   *   *

I began by observing that *Desert Islands* shares some of the anomaly of its subject, and I'll end by pursuing that line of thought a bit further. Of all the features of *Robinson Crusoe* that fascinate de la Mare, it's on Defoe's style that he most often pauses: "His stories are like wood-cuts, now exquisitely clear and particularized, now blurred and dingy"; "It is indeed to Defoe's innate simplicity of spirit, combined as it is with so much worldly astuteness, that his appeal to 'the common reader' is mainly due"; "that 'drab,' surprising, go-as-you-please entrancing prose of his, 'everywhere beautiful, but plain and homely'"; "As for his craftsmanship, it appears—

when he chanced to turn to storytelling—to have depended, and how triumphantly, simply on a happy knack of improvisation, unfailing in invention, out of a memory brimming over with an inexhaustible variety of experience." In closely attending to Defoe's style, de la Mare doesn't seem particularly interested in distilling from it any explicit "meaning." His air is more that of someone on shipboard or seacoast engaged in watching the weather—its elemental contrariety and the complex, unpredictable, always-changeable patterns that coalesce and dissolve from moment to moment.

De la Mare's style, although it doesn't sound much like Defoe's, has some affinities with the terms he uses to describe it, especially the sense of "inexhaustible variety," unpredictability, and a richly idiosyncratic associativeness. The most striking expression of these qualities is not micro-stylistic but macro-structural. Like many books, *Desert Islands* consists of main text and subsidiary endnotes, but unlike most, de la Mare's notes are over three times as long as the text itself. The result is a self-consciously achieved imbalance, the more so because the labor done by the notes is less annotative than associative, keyed less to the local and needful clarification of the text than to indulgently enveloping it in a thick cloud of synesthesia. I confess that at first I found this structure rather irritating. The predictable unpredictability of the author's frequent, deliberate, sequentially-signaled digressions from the main line seemed like an intentional challenge to the reader's patience. Often enough the notes even curl in upon themselves to become associations within associations, threatening to mutate into an infinite regress of self-reflecting mirrors or a snake devouring its own tail. And sometimes de la Mare cheerfully acknowledges what he's doing, as in a note to "Selkirk" that weaves its way through contemporary accounts of this famous castaway; moves to a leisurely capsule biography of his later life; then to a book about other castaways, among them one whose beard grew so large that it interfered with his sleep and another's ingenious method of catching seagulls; to yet another castaway, whose adventure de la Mare narrates even as he admits it to be "somewhat on the outskirts of this particular theme." The note rambles on, eccentrically but divertingly, for two more pages . . .

What are we to make of this strange procedure? Reading de la Mare, I was reminded of a French publication, contemporary with Defoe, that was hailed as one of the most important intellectual works of the eighteenth century and whose innovative structure resembles that of *Desert Islands*, the skeptical thinker Pierre Bayle's massive, multi-volume biographical encyclopedia, *Dictionnaire historique et critique* (1697). The "Preface" to the English translation of 1734 cites an account that calls it "a Dictionary of a new and singular kind . . . In the text or body of the articles, Mr. Bayle gives a succinct, tho' very exact account of those persons whose lives he writes: but then he fully gratifies the Reader's curiosity, by the remarks subjoin'd to the text, which are a commentary on it . . . [S]ometimes the text seems to be written merely for the sake of the notes . . . Thus several articles which at first seem to promise little or nothing, are often illustrated with the most curious particulars." If de la Mare was influenced by Bayle's *Dictionnaire*, or by one of its imitators, it may be because its oscillating rhythms of movement down and up, its circuitous wanderings away from and back to the main, echo the ambiguity of the desert island: its destruction by modern "progress," but its persistence as the very condition of being enisled; the bit of land visibly isolated from the main, but invisibly linked to a common foundation below; individual solitude as the precondition for the plenitude of human community.

So the structure of *Desert Islands* recalls the relationship between desert islands and the mainland by which their isolation is defined. The book itself also aims to recapitulate, as an aesthetic and virtual experience, the actual adventures it's written about. This is hinted at in the author's preface, where de la Mare begins with a mock title page, itself a loving parody of eighteenth-century publishing practices:

> DESERT ISLANDS: being the VOYAGE of a HULK, called by courtesy a *Lecture*, that was launched under the Auspices of *The Royal Society of Literature* of *London* many years ago, namely, in 1920, was afterwards frequently in Dock again for Repair and then refitted for FARTHER ADVENTURINGS, and so at length became laden with an unconscionable Cargo of Odds and Ends and Flotsam and Jetsam, much of it borrow'd from other Vessels infinitely more Seaworthy than itself, . . . together with a rambling Discourse . . . which, being concocted in a most Unmethodical Fashion, is now presented to a World already groaning under an intolerable Burden of Printed Matter by its Humble Servant the Author, and dedicated to his son DICK, MDCCCCXXX.

A book is a ship, de la Mare suggests, and to read a travel narrative is vicariously to undertake a sea journey. The metaphor is no less thrilling—de la Mare would say "romantic"—for being conventional, perhaps the more so in an age like ours when sea travel has ceased to be the default mode of long-distance travel. And the authority of the sea journey as, more broadly, a figure for human experience persists undiminished. In the last note to *Desert Islands*, de la Mare quotes from a letter sent by Defoe to his son-in-law: "I am . . . near my journey's end, and am hastening to the place where ye weary are at rest, and where the wicked cease to trouble; be it that the passage is rough, and the day stormy . . ." And at the very end of the text, in the sentence from within which this note is signaled, de la Mare addresses his readers: "Indeed an hour will come, as it came to Defoe himself in Ropemaker's Alley, on April 26th, 1731, when, braving disaster, we shall be compelled, whether we will or not, to follow it into the unknown, and on the wings of the imagination fly away towards Ultima Thule [the mythical northernmost border of the world], skirting latitudes even remoter than that of 9 degrees 22 minutes north of the line."

Desert Islands leaves no doubt as to the one book Walter de la Mare would have chosen to take with him to his *terra incognita*, his ultimate desert island.

AUTHORS of the eighteenth century delighted in copious subtitles. These had one signal merit; they saved the reader further trouble. Thus:— 'DESERT ISLANDS: being the VOYAGE of a HULK, called by courtesy a *Lecture*, that was launched under the Auspices of *The Royal Society of Literature* of *London* many years ago, namely, in 1920, was afterwards frequently in Dock again for Repair and then refitted for FARTHER ADVENTURINGS, and so at length became laden with an unconscionable Cargo of Odds and Ends and Flotsam and Jetsam, much of it borrow'd from otherVessels infinitely more Seaworthy than itself, and the most of that concern'd with what are known as ISLANDS, some of them Real, some of them Allegorical, and the rest purely Fabulous; together with a rambling Discourse concerning a certain very Famous Man of Letters, viz. DANIEL DEFOE, and his Elective Affinity, ROBINSON CRUSOE: which, being concocted in a most Unmethodical Fashion, is now presented to a World already groaning under an intolerable Burden of Printed Matter by its Humble Servant the Author, and dedicated to his son DICK, MDCCCCXXX'. The fact of the matter is that the subject of a lecture is apt to prove too rich for summary treatment. When certain kinds of books come in, it is difficult to keep life out. And as soon as the first step is made in venturing a little further afield, a bounteous, an illimitable prospect beckons the explorer on, even though, as in this case, he may have nothing but the candle of curiosity and the will-o'-the-wisp of enquiring ignorance to light him on his way. He may not even have set out in the right direction. As Mr. E. M. Forster has intimated, there is no more sense in treating the fiction that has desert islands for theme as a branch of literature than there is in classifying the drama under the headings of plays that contain fat characters and plays that contain thin. The enterprise is at least the reverse of anything truly critical. Against that, let Mr. Ralph Hodgson's sovereign plea be my defence:

> Reason has moons, but moons not hers
> Lie mirror'd on her sea,
> Confounding her astronomers,
> But, O! delighting me.

Bright moons, too, on distant seas, and these familiar to a voyager before me whose tribute will be found towards the end of this volume: 'My haunting passion was the Island. I ransacked libraries for the literature of Islands, and the more desolate they were the better I was pleased'.

And last, however meagre and miscellaneous the spoil that has been so retrieved, and however numerous the blunders that have been made in retrieving it, I would conclude with the valediction which the anonymous translator of *Robinson Crusoe* into Italian addressed to *his* reader: 'Be kind to my mistakes, and live happy!'. W. D. L. M.

THE MERE cadence of the six syllables, a Tale of
Adventure, instantly conjures up in the mind a
jumbled and motley host of memories. Memories not
only personal but, as we may well suspect, racial; and
not only racial but primeval. Ages before history
learned its letters, there being no letters to learn; ages
before the children of men builded the city and the
tower called Babel and their language was confounded and they were scattered, the rudiments of this
kind of oral narrative must have begun to flourish.
Indeed the greater part of even the largest of dic-
tionaries, with every page in the most comprehensive
of atlases, consists of relics and records in the concisest
shorthand from bygone chapters in the tale whereof
we know neither the beginning nor the end—that of
Man's supreme venture into the world without, and
into the world within.

The mountains, the oceans, the stars bear witness to
it—at least in name; though many such names are
now but gibberish and may strive in vain to find
their once 'beloued tong' again. Whether, too, it has

I

been passed on from mouth to mouth or from hand to hand, not only has this order of fiction proved by far the most prolific, but it bids fair to continue to stuff our remotest descendants with rapture, envy, aspiration and nightmare, until humanity and the planet it occupies are no more.

Within its kind its range is almost illimitable. It ascends by steady gradations from the anecdote to the epic. It includes not only the penny plain and the twopence coloured, broadside and chapbook, but such masterpieces as the *Odyssey*, the *Golden Ass*, *Don Quixote*, *Simplicissimus* and the Scottish Ballads. Sweeney Todd and Sinbad the Sailor are as welcome in its vast hostelry as the Knights of the Round Table, Baron Munchausen and the hunters of the Snark; and some of the best of the 'flickers' or 'movies'—though their medium of expression is solely the play of light on a game of Let's Pretend, with what could not be too meagre a commentary in words—are still after the same pattern.

Its place in literature varies with its quality, its equivalent on the stage being melodrama, from *The Tragedy of Dr. Faustus* at one extreme to that of poor gay Mr. Punch and his dog Toby at the other. In its relation to poetry and *belles lettres* it is usually pretty much what earthenware is by comparison with porcelain, or the brass in an orchestra with the strings. In marrow and matter it appeals straight to whatever vestiges of the boy we have left in us rather than to what faint memorials we may still treasure of the child. Its chief concern is with the activities of the body; far less with the workings of the mind or the state

2

of the soul. Yet its order of morals is rigid if primitive. The bad man abounds in it, and less frequently the bad female also, but its hero invariably has 'his principles' to steer by, however crazy a helmsman he may be. Apart from this, the author's attention is fixed not on what in humanity is a little lower than the angels but on what is akin to the higher animals. And if he preach at all, it is usually by way of wholesome practice rather than of precept; while the virtues he instils are those of the ready hand, the nimble tongue and quick wits.

Hunger and thirst, danger and difficulty, the strange, the far-fetched, the outlandish, these are its chief incentives. And its reward, the adventure over, something not only of a material but of a solid order—a few sacks, say, of moidores, doubloons and precious stones; and, for makeweight, a ravishingly beautiful señorita from some castle in Spain, who was wooed perhaps in the first chapter, and thereafter only dreamed of until she is won in the last. All but all her joys, however, should await an untold epilogue. As positive cargo she is supererogatory.

Though not exactly hostile to them, the tale of adventure is for the most part indifferent to social or domestic interests. These are at best but its background and its foil, and even at that, it much prefers their primary colours to their finer shades. For in this blood-and-thunder type of fiction anything may happen at any moment. In the novel of manners, or of the ichor-and-Psyche type, very little (and to some tastes even that little may be too much), happens at all. In the one, character is of supreme importance; in the other *a* character, and that character need be

3

nothing more complicated than merely a man—raw *homo*, that is, with little admixture of *sapiens*. Such a tale, then, is apt to be rather coarse fare for the truly sophisticated.

Yet in its latest variant, the detective story, even philosophers have found a way of 'escape', and of one great divine at least it is recorded that he was kept up most of the small hours one night in 1883 in pursuit of a young person named Jim Hawkins. What wonder, indeed, if out of a continual twilight of abstractions and formulae (even though it may be suddenly irradiated at last with Sunrise), the metaphysically minded should pine at times for the grosser actualities; what wonder if many such tales have been the work of 'dreamers' who have been prevented or are by nature averse to seeking adventure in three dimensions; or of wanderers who having gone to and fro in the world have at length returned home yet still pine on for the wild and far.

The rapid narrowing in, alas, of our earthly area effected by modern invention suggests that there will soon be no wild and far for which to pine. A world measured by flying is a far smaller place than a world measured by walking; and out of sight was once out of hearing. Not so—and, for humane reasons, one must suppress a natural, Alas!—now. Changes of circumstance such as our new facilities provide—inveterate foes of those who prefer travel with travail—affect not only the fancy but the imagination, and it is *distance* that lends enchantment to the view.

Definite statistics are not available, but it seems probable not only that adventures in the usual

4

meaning of the term were more frequent in less crowded, secure, and gregarious ages than our own, but also that, *per* head of the population, they are at present on a richer scale than they are likely to be in the future. Once upon a time almost any journey by land or sea was at least an invitation to hazard, and a hazard strange, not familiar. Nowadays, though we are most of us more habitually in motion than our ancestors, the enfeebling slogan is 'safety first'. Otherwise we stay at home (more or less at ease), and dabble in physical extremes at second hand. Chiefly—dingy and dubious though most of such records are—in our newspapers. Our adventurings are less, that is, of the body than of the mind and imagination, though few of us even faintly realize the potential scope of the latter.

Still, even in the dullest of existences, this spicy flavour of adventuring cannot be entirely absent. It is the salt that keeps life sweet, it is the savour that preserves it from putrefaction; and we welcome every fleeting taste of it. Contrast is much; novelty is more; the unforeseen, if it refrain from the tragic, is seldom without its charm; and a gay heart is hospitable even when its giddiest up or its dismallest down verges on an ordeal. A crooked sixpence on a crooked stile, a noise in the night, a new hat, a kiss under the mistletoe, a forty-to-one chance, to fall asleep in the wrong train, to break one's leg, to lose one's heart—or one's head, to drink two bottles of wine where one would serve, to be a worm—and turn: all such little experiences may be tinged with the adventurous. And a tinge is enough.

The most disconcerting of little *mis*adventures, too, may wear the prettiest colours in retrospect; for the wounds of vanity leave amusing scars. And to have made a preternatural fool of one's self for half an hour is apt to wear better in memory than months and months of undiluted self-respect.

While there is still any life left in our bones we most of us at least desire to live vividly and variously, if not dangerously. It is only the tepid who idolize the happy medium; only the too-safe who never risk anything; only the over-complicated who pine after what is nowadays called—and apparently with no intention of irony—the simple life. And though the very derivation of the word proves that 'adventures' come not for the seeking but are the gift of Fortune, it is none the less true that they are the reward of the adventurous. The open eye and heart and mind[1] may enjoy them daily—a sunshine morning, a moonlight night, snow at daybreak, a baby in the cradle, honey for tea; to cite only the less evidently intellectual. Merely to be alive, indeed, is adventure enough in a world like this, so erratic and disjointed; so lovely and so odd and mysterious and profound. It is, at any rate, a pity to remain in it half dead.

Yet another ingredient either in essence or in tincture is seldom absent from the tale of adventure—the romantic[2]. And whatever else this battered term may signify, romance is invariably flavoured with the extreme. It flowers in the mind when life is being lived not merely at an uncustomary but at a hazardous poise. It must come of itself, yet is so much sought after that we talk of the romance of Commerce and of Big Business, though for the most part such talk is only flattery. One hears less of the romance of slow failure, the romance of growing old, the romance of disease and death.

The sudden attainment of wealth, or of power, or of fame may be romantic; an abrupt unforeseen fall from high estate[1] is hardly less so. Rare beauty, human or natural or supernatural, is romantic. So too may be a unique ugliness. The romantic is also not far distant from the tragic on the one side, and on the other from the sentimental. Lay it on too thick and it is as insipid as a wedding-cake consisting solely of sugar-icing. It is perhaps most effective when it is most unexpected; then a mere relish, a mere glint of it may redeem a situation which otherwise would be commonplace. And even wit may have that glint. Charles II knew it: I fear, gentlemen, I am an unconscionable time a-dying; and Wilde: Alas, I am dying beyond my means.

The romantic is a thing of moments rather than of hours. Repetition or monotony dulls the appropriate nerve. A novelty, then, may or may not be romantic, but singularity almost always is. In part for this reason, perhaps, a piece of handicraft with all its defects is preferable to anything flawless turned out by a machine. What other charm, except indeed of the homely order, has the home-made? We dull life by a mechanical repetition and imitation. We dull it still more if we submit it to mere system and if we ourselves become machines. In the game of follow-my-leader little depends on the led.

So with science: its discoveries are romantic in

7

kind and effect while they remain novelties, and chiefly when they are concerned with the outskirts of knowledge. There romance may glitter like the dawn-lit crags of El Dorado, even though the man of science (until recently at any rate) has been a rather chilly friend to those who indulge in it. When the ignorant novice reads that a certain kind of oak tree has lately been discovered which is more sensitive to gradations of colour than the human eye; that an ant knows her queen is near though cold steel a half-inch thick dissevers them one from the other; that Sirius has a companion sun whose mass, as compared with steel, is what that of steel is compared with oxygen—when such crumbs of fact as these come his way, he gapes for joy and wonderment. He loves them not for their truth's sake but for themselves. They are at least as seductive as the wildest extravaganzas of fiction. Since facts are but facts, however, it is we of course who must supply the charm, and for this reason alone a little learning—just as much as one can treasure—may be no less fascinating than it is dangerous.

We boast, on the other hand, of the stupefaction of our grandfathers if they could be roused from their graveyard slumbers to marvel at our automobiles and our gramophones, our submarines and aeroplanes, our wireless, our poison gases. They might— for an hour or two. And then perhaps they would begin to marvel at our smoke and our smells, our nerves and our newspapers. For singularity soon wears off, and mere novelty soon stales. And after that sad mutation things must wait awhile—and not

8

always in vain—for the most beguiling change of all, since it is Time itself that sheds on all things human, even on the velocipede, the antimacassar, the bustle and the Piccadilly weeper, the last and loveliest iridescence—that of romance.

For an object which is not of a perishing nature becomes first old, then old-fashioned, then antique, then antiquated, then archaic, then ancient; and at last may be drenched with a romanticalness of which its original owner had not the faintest inkling—Noah's gangway, Absalom's hair, Cleopatra's looking-glass, Tutankhamen's slippers, Caesar's sword. Our newest of novelties, our very last things out, even our youngest poets, are all on their way to this home of rest. We pine for the curious, the bizarre. We return to find our peace in the familiar and the near. For which reason —as Edward Thomas, faithful lover of all things old and English, realized—such simple ancient familiar things as a plough, a ship, or a farm-wagon continue to shed, for the eye that can see and dream together, a romance which is shared by the ruins of Babylon, the songs of the Sirens, and the roses of Damascus.

It may be observed, however, that what to a secure onlooker is a pleasingly romantic situation may be grim matter-of-fact to those actually engaged in it. To be besieged with Helen in Troy; to be congealed amid the icy wastes of the Arctic, or lost in the Sahara; to be a royal fugitive in an oak tree, a Colonel Lawrence in Mecca, a Charles Doughty in the sandy wilds of Arabia, a Mallory on the ultimate peak of Everest; all these are probably more *romantic* situations to contemplate than to share. And one of their chief conditions is that of the precarious and fleeting. The sword hangs suspended by a thread. That harlequin, Luck, is as capricious as genius. That siren, Fortune, sings sweetest among rocks.

Perhaps the chief charm of the *Thousand and One*, the *Arabian Nights*, for example—one of the very few books in the world, I suppose, of little account in the country of its origin, and a classic abroad—is, first, the peculiar density of its romance[1], and, next, the extraordinary penalties bestowed on the characters who indulge in it. To have one's thumbs lopped off as a punishment for an innocent attachment to garlic; to be flayed alive for ogling a princess; to submit to such indignities as did Sinbad the Sailor— ordeals like these so related belong rather to the romantic than to the classic order of events and show a glint on their imaginative surface like the colours on a stagnant pool.

So too with life simplified and essentialized rather than distorted. Barren must be the mind incapable of being enchanted by the limpid and unadorned romance enshrined in the *Old Testament*[2]. Are not the first chapters of *Genesis*, with their history of the Creation and their tale of the Garden, entirely apart from their spiritual truth and their imaginative sufficiency, one of the most romantic stories in the world? Are not the histories of Jacob, of Joseph, of Absalom, of Daniel, of Naaman, of Jonah, and even of Job— whatever other inexhaustible riches of spirit or symbol or 'meaning' are theirs—coloured through and through with this strange dye?

Strangely enough, too, gregarious by instinct

though we humans are, and though two in a garden may make a paradise of the everywhere: a complete solitude, also, may be saturated with the romantic. Is not this great globe itself a celestial solitary?

> Hope, fear, false joy and trouble—
> These the four winds which daily toss this Bubble.
> His breath's a vapour and his life a span,
> 'Tis glorious misery to be born a man.

That bubble[1] floats on in the severing ether, voyaging, as I have read somewhere, towards a remote (and somewhat inscrutable) goal in the void of space called *Mu* in Leo[2]. And as with the world, so with the conscious beings that inhabit it—possibly the only beings of their specific nature, as our modern astronomers surmise, in the complete stellar and physical universe. Almost impassably cut off as we now are from the natural trust and fellowship of unhumanized beast and bird[3], so too in some degree we are severed even from our nearest and dearest. By means of those frail tentacles, our senses, we explore the outward semblance of our fellow-creatures; but flesh is flesh and bone is bone, and only by insight and by divination can we pierce inward to the citadel of the mind and soul. We can only translate their touch, their gestures, the words they use, the changing looks on their faces into terms of our own consciousness and spirit. We believe them to be in all essential things like ourselves—whatever their arresting and delightful differences. We trust them not to be mere deceiving automata. Nevertheless, the inmost self of each one of us is a livelong recluse.

Yes: in the sea of life enisled,
    With echoing straits between us thrown,
Dotting the shoreless watery wild,
    We mortal millions live *alone*.
The islands feel the enclasping flow,
And then their endless bounds they know.

But when the moon their hollows lights,
    And they are swept by balms of spring,
And in their glens, on starry nights,
    The nightingales divinely sing;
And lovely notes, from shore to shore,
Across the sounds and channels pour;

O then a longing like despair
    Is to their farthest caverns sent!
For surely once, they feel, we were
    Parts of a single continent. . . .

The vivid and positive realization of this may come
seldom, but, when it does, it is sharp and appalling.
The moment falls, unforeseen, inexplicable and, as if
at the insidious wave of an enchanter's wand, the
faces, the voices of the believed-in and beloved seem
to be nothing but the creation of our own fantasy,
and we are 'enisled'. Even the 'echoes' then, like the
languageless scream of sea-bird and the drumming of
wave on rock, are nothing but a mockery. We may
work or play away most of our lives in evading this
realization, but in the end we shall become our own
Showman's boy and know that as mortals we are
alone.

And though, before that end come, and in spite
of the ramifications of butcher, baker, postman and
tax-collector, the kind of solitude one may pine for
is to be found even in the England of our own day,
and that of the astronomer, the bookworm, the miser[1],
the lover and the king are not beyond imagining;

of the extreme spiritual solitudes familiar to many of our fellow-creatures we can be but vaguely aware. What spectres share the small hours with a criminal[1] hemmed in at every turn by the physical and moral forces of law and order—an animal rejected of its kind? The solitude of the lunatic, of the devil-haunted, the habitually drugged[2]? One savours a taste of this world's romance indeed with the realization that the cold relics on the dissecting-tables and in the brine-tanks of our hospitals, of which there appears to be an unfailing supply, are the refuse of men and women abandoned by life to so desolate a loneliness that there is no one on earth who will spare the time or the few shillings necessary to secure them a *friendly* burial.

We may now and again, too, encounter in our walks abroad a fellow-creature touched with a certain cast of strangeness and aloofness. We scan the fleshly house, but the windows are darkened. He or she was born, we may assume, to at least a concerned mother, into some imitation of a home, and lived for a while in childhood and youth within call of humanity. But by slow and infinite degrees, whether because of eccentricities of mind and character, pride, grief, aversion, fear, weakness, poverty, or riches, that human being has gradually become more and more withdrawn and insulated, and lives on, enringed ever more and more inaccessibly with barriers that divide the living one within from the natural advances, the active fellowship, the compassion, even the mere interest of mankind.

There are some, like Katherine Mansfield's char-woman, who have no place quiet or solitary enough to cry in; there are some to whom the insect-like hosts of London seem nothing but the bodiless and hostile spectres of a nightmare; and but a moment's divining thought of them assures us that the whole world's fiction and autobiography can tell us only a fraction of what mortal life at such extremes may come to mean.

And some there are of a mind so self-secure it needs but little company; and some of a heart all-welcoming, all-hospitable, who, though never less alone than when alone, shed on the world around them a peace and loving-kindness of a source as fresh and sweet as it is inexhaustible.

But apart from the life of the actual, of life at first hand, there are few experiences which we can so easily share and enjoy, by proxy, as that of *physical* solitude. What other theme in fiction is more deeply saturated with the romantic and the adventurous? Stories of this kind abound; and particularly in English fiction. What in general are their conditions?

First, the victim and the hero of such a fate must fight—not, as we all do, for life—but for a bare existence. And unlike many of his fellow-creatures in real life he must not fight in vain. His one problem, his one craving and desire (however irrational it may be), must be merely to continue to keep alive. He must, then, have courage and enterprise. No mere dreamer[1], thinker or philosopher need apply.

Next, since he is to be—and for some time to remain—alone, his place of exile should be remote from the thronging haunts and highways of man-

kind and dangerous of access though not quite inaccessible. A naked and waterless waste from which
no escape is possible would admit of but the briefest
period of physical torture and a morbid activity of
the mind. His resort then must offer *some* hospitality
to its guest, though it should be well this side of the
luxurious, since he must spend in it a quick and
lively existence. And though the odds against his
survival must not be overwhelming, they should at
least appear to be long. He must indeed survive to
tell us his tale; for of the solitude of the grave[1],
whether in St. Innocent's churchyard or beneath
the sands of Egypt, we can retrieve no direct tidings, or at best—tidings dubious, meagre and un-
satisfying.

Our solitary, too—if his record is to be moving—
should be more or less continually aware of his isolation. So much the better if from some point of
vantage[2] amid his wild and barbarous scenery he can
keep watch on the horizon whence at length rescue
will come. Finally, he may effect his own rescue.
But to see him merely walk out of his trap is an eventuality not quite romantic enough. A profoundly sundering yet traversable medium must sever him, then,
from his fellow-creatures.

The sands of the Sahara or of the Gobi desert would
keep such a secret, or, failing these, some green and
peaceful oasis in a region encircled by an unintermit-
tent cyclone, or by a ring of subterranean fire. Jules
Verne, for example, may not have completely explored
the monster-haunted deeps in the centre of the earth[3];
and the practicability of voyaging into space[4] seems

15

to be once more engaging the speculations not of mere visionaries only but even of the matter-of-fact.

Short of the subterranean, the submarine, and the wild vacancies of space, however, the conditions of an ideal retreat from the tumult and artificialities of man are fulfilled—solitude, danger, strangeness, the unknown, the discoverable, the eventual means of escape—if our hermitage is an island. An island volcanic or coralline[1], an island that out of the mists of daybreak, or in the cheating lights of evening, lifts itself from the snows of its surges, serene, strange, aloof in its forlorn beauty, dumb clock of countless ages, the haven of a few birds and roving brutes, the kindly nursery of seal and sea lion, and green with palm and tamarisk.

An island let it be, say, three or four hundred to a thousand miles or so from the nearest habitations of humanity and well out of the usual sea-trade routes, preferably uncharted, fairly commodious[2], say thirteen miles by four, of a climate whose extremes are not of a pitiless severity, an island which Nature's bounty has endowed with shade, fresh water, shelter and food fit for human consumption. And there—our recluse.

Every seaman, every wanderer on the deep, has hearkened to the decoy of that ideal island; and where is the landsman with soul so dead—even though his eye has been lifted over no greater expanse of salt water than can be scanned from the steps of a bathing-machine—who in his homesick moments has never caught its enchanting echo? The English in particular are as a people naturally beguiled by the thought of the smallest strip or patch of land that is surrounded by water. How could it be otherwise, since theirs is that notorious little three-cornered island[1] of 'a natural bravery . . . with rocks unscalable and roaring waters', against whose western coasts for ever beats the prodigious Atlantic? The seas are in their blood. They have been scoffed at as a nation of shopkeepers; 'merchant adventurers[2]' has a pleasanter sound. They have been eyed askance as a horde of money-hunting land-grabbers; freeborn crusading colonists is a pleasanter way of putting it. Again and again they have had to face the charge of insularity, but then was there ever a national shortcoming so inevitable? What wonder that, rather greedily maybe and not always with too nice a gesture, they have sucked 'of the abundance of the seas, and of treasures hid in the sand'?

Man's longed-for havens indeed are for the most part curiously simple in structure. But though the sweet, spoon-fed, simple *dolce far niente* of the South Seas may for a while allure his weary or indolent body, his true happiness must consort with desires of the mind. It is not the gemlike gates of Jerusalem but what they are the symbols of that will bring him peace in the blissful plains of Paradise, where there will be no more sea and therefore no more islands. Meanwhile he may cheat himself with the pretty illusion that if only he could secure a modest freehold of *terra firma* surrounded by water he would be at peace—not entirely perhaps with the self which it was impracticable to leave behind him, but at any rate with the world at large.

Mere insularity will not however suffice. A glance at a map of the world is usually misleading or rather, seldom illuminating; but a moment's brooding over it will reveal, first, that it is but a cabalistic picture in the flat[1], and that the great globe is actually an enormous solid, a prodigious mass of uninviting matter[2], of which man knows very little apart from its skin; and next, that the seas and oceans are but puddles of salt water of various sizes occupying the hollows of its surface, many of them, the North Sea and the English Channel, for example, disillusioningly shallow. We next perceive that this habitable world of ours consists of nothing *but* islands —the whole of America (since man's ingenious ditch[3] at Panama can hardly be taken into count) being one, Europe with Asia another; and Australia, a dumpy red, irregularly shell-shaped configuration in the right-hand lower corner, a third.

But an island worthy of romantic respect[4] is not one of this magnitude. Even the 235,000 square miles of vast and barren Baffin Island with its two great inland lakes, though it may be as rich as Croesus in coal and gold, scarcely 'invites the soul'. One pines for something a little more in proportion to one's own few inches, and it is only when we begin to examine more attentively what appear on our atlas to be specks as minute as the vagrant footprints of some tiny insect that has strayed into the cartographer's ink and then sallied out into the pale blue of the oceans, that we catch a glimpse of our actual quarry.

For these specks represent in fact a multitude of

18

such islands, and they make a braver and more enticing show on the map, say—all to itself—of the Malay Archipelago in which that entrancing skeleton of a sea-serpent called Java and Sumatra sprawls its dusky length along from west to south. There hitherto indiscernible microscopicalities now become apparent—Flat, Spratly, Matty and Yowl, for example; also the Moresses, the Moscos, Mandioli, Moa, Mai and all the Mes—not to mention Money for make-weight, and seed-pearls *ad infinitum*.

Nor does one need to be a globe-trotter or even much of a traveller to indulge this hobby. Childhood, a mill-pond, a raft and a willow are enough to begin with; and shall I ever forget a certain daybreak on the edge of the Atlantic when, after only a week of the open sea, my hungry eyes alighted on three bare, lovely, lone and everlasting objects which man calls islands, and which as if out of a dream had silently revealed themselves from beneath the veils of dawn against the blue of sky and water: the Bull, the Cow, and the Calf—a mere Cockney's treasures, maybe, but still for that instant his own?

Even, too, what on the map resembles nothing more impressive than England's door-mat, the Isle of Wight[1], may, whether in sun or drizzle, show very dear to the eyes of an Englishman on his way home. Indeed life has few welcomes more precise, pungent, and heart-disturbing than the first glimpse of lighthouse, light-ship or beacon or winking light-buoy rocked in the cradle of the deep. Its rapid stare at you may have little speculation in it. It is not affectionate, it may even have a tinge of the ironic, yet it may stir as many memories in one's mind as the prod of a stick in an ant-heap in an English wood stirs ants. And some of these memories may be of longer continuance than even the mere number of one's birthdays would imply.

Assuredly, at any rate, of islands, and of little ones, there is no lack. Precisely *how* numerous they are, what their sum total is, as they lie scattered over the enormous wastes of the world's waters, I have not as yet been able to ascertain. Three hundred, it is said, may be counted, when clear weather stretches between sea and heaven, from the highest hummock of St. Columba's Iona alone. But then Celtic islands, unlike the common kind, may, like the Irishman's pigs, easily be counted twice. And how be sure of one's eyes in a world where so much is the creation not of men of science but of fantasy? The earlier map-makers at least attempted to be informative on this point. The Catalan map of 1375, for example, shows a prolonged semicircular cluster of islands, in shape more or less engagingly rectangular, representing no fewer than '7,548' of them in all in the *Mar de les Indes* and in the Ocean Sea washing the coasts of the empire of 'Holubeim, i.e. the Great Can', and the realms of *lo gran Senhor de* GOG *I* MA-GOG. Spice Islands¹ every one, and 'naked savages' then their sole inhabitants.

That 'cosmographical dilettante' Martin Behaim (who in the green of his youth was sentenced to a week's imprisonment for dancing at a Jew's wedding in Lent), like Fra Mauro and Martellus Germanus before him, delighted in islands. In his own honour he boldly renamed Annobom *Insula Martini*, and was hospitality itself to such little oceanic paradises as the Island of the Seven Cities and the Island of St. Brandan—the pious abbot's haven at last, in A.D. 565, after his five years of voyaging over seas perpetually dark. Behaim's 'apple' or globe of the great world of 1492, now at Nuremberg, is a feast for the eye. It is adorned with no fewer than a hundred and eleven miniatures —coloured red, gold, black, blue, green, umber and silver—depicting flags, banners, coats of arms, kings enthroned, saints and proselytizing missionaries, naked savages seated on pillows in tents of red and green, wild elephants roving near, and, a little aloof, tiled towers and campaniles; ships, sea-serpents, mermaids, camels, parrots, ostriches, serpents, and various other devices, though, alas, no Eden.

But little space in Behaim's day could be spared for *Engelant*[1] and *wildt Scotlant*, though York, huntingdon, cambridge, edmundeburgh—and lambeth—are specified. The Orkneys are referred to but not shown. Of the western Hebrides he names *irgan*, *bea* and *dseds*, and he remembers *Tillf* or Thule. He gives us also Taprobana, of the Greeks, alias Serendib of the *Nights*, alias Seilan or Ceylon; and Pentan (Bintang[2]), whose coasts with a very shallow sea, says Marco Polo, are 'wild and uncultivated but the woods abound with sweet scented trees'.

Then again, the British Museum has lately acquired a probably unique copy of Giovanni Contarini's Map of the World of 1506, the first printed map, apparently, to show the naked coast (with *Terra S. Crucis*, i.e. Brazil, in the N.E. corner) of South

America. Neighbouring its shores, islands are shown, which Master Christopher Columbus', 'viceroy of Spain and Admiral of the Ocean', discovered at the instance of the 'most serene king Ferdinand' and his Queen Isabella. And not far from Martin Behaim's Seilan is inserted this record: 'Before Taprobana there are very many islands, which are said to be 1,778 in number'.

It is that 'said to be' which is apt to prove deceptive when objects so actual as islands are the quarry. And the *desert* island is now unfortunately by far the most infrequent in kind. Man, none the less, has been going to and fro in the world and down to the sea in ships for a good many centuries, and during these voyagings hosts of poor sailors must have found themselves the sole survivors of shipwreck on shores that, apart from fish and bird and insect, never showed faintest sign of life or heed or human company. It is remarkable, then, how scanty trustworthy narratives which tell of their experiences appear to be.

Even more remarkable, there is one island more or less precisely after our ideal pattern[2] that has in recorded fact proved a sanctuary to no less than three such adventurers. That island is Más-á-tierra. It is one of a group of three called Juan Fernandez, the second being Más-á-fuera, i.e. 'Further-out'. This lies a hundred miles to westward; it has nine ravines on the eastern face of its rocky *massif*, and to each ravine its water-course. The third, only a mile or so away, is an islet called Santa Clara or Goat Island. Craggy and wooded (twelve and a half miles long by three and two-thirds across at its widest), Más-á-tierra lies under the Southern Cross, one hundred and ten leagues from Valparaiso on the main. Its highest hill, El Yunque, rears itself 3005 feet above the sea. And about the year 1570 it was chanced upon by the Spanish navigator—Juan Fernandez[1]— who gave the group his name.

Más-á-tierra was then virgin soil. Fernandez landed 'Indians' on it, brought in sheep and cattle from the mainland, built thatched and timbered houses and traded in sea-lion oil and salted fish. But his enterprise failed. He abandoned the island, and bestowed it as a gift on a friend of the same name as himself, who bequeathed it to the Jesuits. Spaniards possessed it for a while for the sake of its fish and timber and sandal-wood. Then they too deserted it, and after further vicissitudes it became towards the end of the seventeenth century a wasps' nest of buccaneers.

On March 22nd, 1684, Captain William Dampier, the great English sailor, while voyaging round the world, landed on it for the second time. John Fernando, he called it. He came to seek a Mosquito Indian, one of a minute nation of Amerindians, civil, good-natured and monogamous, only a hundred men strong. A prudent people too, for when its men-folk enjoyed a carousal, the women used to hide their weapons. This Indian while engaged in hunting goats had been marooned[2] on the island four years previously when Dampier's ship had been chased from its anchorage by Spaniards.

'Long-visaged, hard-favoured, lank-haired', his sole defence against his solitude had been a gun, a knife, and a small horn of powder. By notching his knife he had made a saw with which he sawed into pieces the barrel of his gun. Out of these he smithied harpoons, lances, fish-hooks and another long knife. He built himself a wooden hut and lined it with goat-skins. He fished with tackle of sealskin and hunted John Fernando's goats, which had long since managed to survive the Jesuits' dogs. When Spaniards landed and chased him, such were his wiles and his cunning that they began to suspect he was an apparition. When his English clothes were worn out he girded a hairy goatskin about his loins.

Having sighted Dampier's ship the day before it cast anchor, this hospitable soul killed three of his goats for his rescuers' entertainment and cooked them and served them up (English fashion) with cabbage from the 'cabbage-tree'. His English name was Will—for the Mosquito Indians were men so poor in this world's goods, they told Dampier, that they had no names of their own; and the first man to leap ashore to greet him was his fellow-countryman, Robin.

'Running to his brother Moskito man', says Dampier, 'he, Robin, threw himself flat on his face at his feet, who helping him up, and embracing him, fell flat with his face on the ground at Robin's feet, and was by him taken up also....And when their Ceremonies of Civility were over, we also drew near, each of us embracing him we had found there, who was overjoyed to see so many of his old friends come hither, as he thought, purposely to fetch him.' 'Of such consequence is a Man to himself!'

These English seamen were not, we may remind ourselves, plenipotentiaries at a Peace Conference or candidates for the American Presidency. Of such we expect all the charms and graces. They were buccaneers. They pillaged, they burned, they massacred. Yet on apt occasions these were their manners; and it is 'manners makyth man', as John Silver knew well; as knew King Charles I, also, when after rising from his bed on the cold morning of January 30th, 1649, he decided to put on a second and warmer shirt, with its silk knots of blue and red, in case he should be seen to shiver on the scaffold.

Twenty-five years after Will's and Robin's touching reunion, on the last day of January 1709, Captain Woodes Rogers, then commander-in-chief of two privateers of Bristol, and himself in the *Duke* (a ship of 320 tons, 30 guns and 117 men), sighted Juan Fernandez. For master of the *Duke* he had Dampier himself, who meanwhile had been marooned on the island of Nicobar, whence he escaped in a cockleshell canoe whose gunwale was only three inches above the water-line, and had also been wrecked on Ascension. Rogers had come to Juan Fernandez to water. The next evening lights were seen on shore and surmised to be those of French ships lying at anchor.

As a matter of fact, they were the watch fires of a sailor named Alexander Selcraig, or Selkirk, who on the following morning was brought off in the ship's pinnace amid a cargo of shell-fish. He was clothed in goatskins, and 'looking wilder than the first owners of them'. It is our first glimpse of one who was des-

25

tined to become the prince and prototype of all castaways.

Like Hans Andersen and so many folk-tale heroes, he was the son—and the seventh son—of a cobbler. He was born at Largo, a sea-village in Fife. There to-day stands his effigy in stone, gazing—like Martin Behaim's at Nuremberg and Drake's at Plymouth— (and a little ironically, one might suppose) on the haunts of his youth. When he was nineteen he was cited for misbehaviour in kirk and ran away to sea. Six years afterwards he came home again, but quarrelled with his brothers, once more decamped, and in the spring of 1703 shipped with Captain William Dampier as sailing master of the galley, the *Cinque Ports*, Dampier himself being in command of the *St. George*. Having arrived, in a leaky ship, at Juan Fernandez, after a bitter altercation with his commander, and at his own suggestion—of which he speedily repented—Selkirk was marooned on Másá-tierra in September 1704.

He landed there a man much richer in this world's goods than the Mosquito Indian. He had a sea chest, clothes, bedding, a firelock, a pound of gunpowder, a bag of bullets, flint and steel, some tobacco, a hatchet, a knife, a kettle, a Bible, mathematical instruments and some books of devotion. Yet in spite of these luxuries, after four years and four months' solitude, Selkirk told Rogers his story in a Scots English so broken and rusty for want of use as to be hardly intelligible. 'We could scarce understand him . . . he seemed to speak his words by halves.'

So too Marco Polo when, with his father and uncle,

he returned from the splendours of Kublai Khan to Venice in 1295. It is recorded that when these three famous travellers reached home in their shabby Tartar clothes after four and twenty years' absence they had not only almost lost the use of their native tongue, but that their relatives failed to recognize them. When, however, on ripping up the seams of their clouts they disclosed a secret store of precious stones, all doubts were set at rest. For precious stones, like fennel, have a secret and singular 'propertie to mundifie our sight and take away the filme or web that overruleth and dimmeth our eyes'.

For eight long months Selkirk had lived in melancholy and horror, 'scarce able to refrain from doing himself violence'. Day after day he had sat in watch, his face towards the sea, until his eyes and the light failed him and he could watch no more. By night he had lain shivering with terror at the howlings of sea-monsters on the shore, and the first show of dawn lighting up his great prison-house had roused him only to a sharper consciousness of his forlorn and miserable state. He spent his time for weeks together roaming aimlessly about his island, staring, listening, weeping, talking to himself.

As time went on, however, Selkirk's spirits began to revive, as human spirits, please Heaven, are apt to revive even in the most adverse of circumstances. He vanquished his blues, he set to work, kept tally of his days, and, like Orlando, cut his name in the trees. He fed plentifully on turtle until he could no more stomach it except in jellies. He built himself two huts, thatched them with grass and lined them with goatskins; the one for a kitchen, the other wherein to sleep, to read, to sing Scots psalms and to pray. Thus he became, he confessed, a better Christian than he had ever been before, or was likely to be again.

For warmth, cheer, and candle he burned the fragrant allspice wood, but had squandered nearly all his gunpowder before he got fire by rubbing two sticks together. He had no grain, physic, salt, ink, paper, or even rum. He fed on crawfish, goats' flesh, broiled or boiled[1], turnips[2]—sown by Dampier—and a small black plum, difficult of access on the island's rocky heights. Of living things, apart from goats, he had the company only of seals, which in November came ashore to 'whelp and engender', their bleating and howling so loud that the noise of them could be heard inland a mile from the shore. Another creature strange to Selkirk was the sea lion, the hair of whose whiskers is 'stiff enough to make tooth-pickers'. Of birds there was only a sort of blackbird with a red breast, and the many-coloured humming-bird, 'no bigger than a large humble bee'.

So life went on. When his ammunition failed him, he came to run, barefoot, with such celerity that he had chased down and killed, he said, no less than 500 goats. After ear-marking and laming their young kids, he had set free as many more—beasts which Lord Anson was thus able to identify over thirty years afterwards. When his clothes fell off his back, Selkirk took to himself hairy breeches, and, unravelling the worsted of his worn-out stockings, hemmed himself shirts out of his scanty stock of linen, by means of a shred of goat sinew threaded through

28

a nail. When his knife was worn to the back, he made substitutes out of hoop-iron, beaten thin and ground on the rocks.

Twice he narrowly escaped death, the first time from a fall of a hundred feet—he lay unconscious for three days and nights, a period which he afterwards computed by the appearance of the moon; and the second time from voyaging Spaniards, who, sighting his fire at sea, landed and pursued him. He hid himself in a tree-top and listened to them talking beneath. But rats were his worst enemy; they gnawed his calloused feet and his clothes, until he had bred up cats to teach them manners. These would 'lie about him in hundreds'. Thus best we picture him, praying aloud, singing and dancing with his kids and cats in the flames and smoke of his allspice wood, and the whole world's moon taunting and enchanting him in her seasons.

His feet restored to shoes, and his tongue to its original English, Alexander Selkirk sailed away as mate of the *Duke*. She was crammed with booty in the shape of wine and brandy taken from a Spanish prize; and a mutiny broke out which her commander ingeniously suppressed by making one ringleader flog the other. Selkirk came home safe but weary to England in October 1711, and after the publication of Captain Woodes Rogers' book, *A Cruising Voyage Round the World*, in the following year, seems to have enjoyed, or at any rate to have endured, a passing notoriety. He was interviewed by Prue's wayward and enchanting husband Richard Steele, and was made the subject of a paper in the *Englishman*, from which most that we know about him is derived.

Better still, but less certainly, Selkirk[1] is said to have actually met in Bristol at the house of a Mrs. Damaris Daniel (seductive name) yet another and a more notorious journalist, a man—as his enemies described him when about twenty years previously he had been 'wanted', and at £50 reward—'a man middle-sized and spare...of a brown complexion, and dark-brown-coloured hair, but wears a wig; a hooked nose, a sharp chin, grey eyes, and a large mole near his mouth'. This man, though in the well-known portrait his chin is almost femininely rounded and the mole appears to be missing, was Daniel Defoe[2]. And rather more than two centuries ago— on April 25th, 1719—Defoe being then about sixty years of age—forty-eight years older, that is, than a boy of twelve!—Samuel Johnson ten, the first George five years on the throne, and the South Sea Bubble on the eve of bursting, appeared *The Life and Strange Surprizing Adventures of Robinson Crusoe[3], of York, Mariner . . . Written by Himself.*

It is of course only the *bad* debts of authors and artists to other men's experiences and other men's books that affect their reputation and their honesty, debts not paid back: Shakespeare's, for example, to the many noble and gifted authors of his plays—including John Milton, as a somewhat low-spirited 'second-hand bookseller' once sadly admitted to me. Even Crusoe was alleged to be the 'illegitimate brat' either of Arbuthnot or of Defoe's 'patron', Harley, Lord Oxford.

But apart from such little extravagances as these, literary origins are not of very much importance; though it may be curious and enlightening to observe how each generation in turn borrows from those that have gone before. Of these strands is woven that strange tapestry called tradition. Just over a century before Steele met Selkirk, Shakespeare himself, for instance, and apart from what he borrowed from Montaigne and the Patagonians, had caught a good deal more than an enkindling spark for his Ariel from Jourdain's *A Discovery of the Bermudas, otherwise called the Ile of Divels*, and from other accounts of the voyage and wreck of the *Sea-Venture*. The fact is of trivial importance except in so far as it helps one to realize what a marvel of creativeness his Ariel was.

The vital question is not whence comes the literary seed, but what life, beauty and virtue have flowered and fruited on the tree that has sprung out of it. As with *The Ancient Mariner* so in a lesser degree with *Robinson Crusoe*, we can drink of their original wellsprings. In Coleridge's case Professor J. L. Lowes has given us the magic hazel-twig; in the other Selkirk. It is indeed one of the charms of Defoe's book that we can compare its fiction with at least a fair number of the facts on which it was founded. In that scrap of looking-glass we can see reflected his vivid and limited genius actually at work, and surprise in the act his faculties of selection, invention and realization.

With a few trifling but interesting exceptions, Defoe, after waiting for about eight years, borrowed most of the realistic particulars which the ne'er-do-weel of Largo had to lend—a debt which he has repaid to the world at large, and apparently *ad infinitum*, at an incomputable interest. Who indeed could estimate what humanity owes to the writers of such books as this, or *Pickwick*, or *Huckleberry Finn*, or *Alice in Wonderland*, and, in their own degree, *The Diary of a Nobody* and *Vice Versâ*—all of them tales which were chiefly the outcome of sheer high spirits? Art for art's sake Defoe's first novel was not. 'The Editor,' he wrote, 'is of opinion that the improvement of it, as well to the diversion, as to the instruction of the reader, will be the same; and as such, he thinks, without farther compliment to the world, he does them a great service in the publication.' Since these last nine words were nothing but the bare truth it is immaterial perhaps from whose well they were drawn up. The diversion afforded by the *Adventures* is certain, but how far the complete career of Crusoe may 'justify . . . the wisdom of providence' is a more debatable question.

Apart from such intentions as these and the mere zest that carried him on, Defoe's aim in writing it was nothing worse—and nothing better—than money. Money is money's worth[1]. He hoped by this means to provide a dowry for the second of his three lovely daughters, Hannah. Fortunate Hannah[2]; her dowry, ample though it would seem for the purpose, never succeeded in securing her a husband, but she thus became the foster-mother not only of *Moll Flanders*, *Roxana*, and *Captain Singleton*, but also of the naturalistic novel.

Astonishment at her father's performance is not lessened by the knowledge that during the year in which he was writing *Robinson Crusoe*, and apart from his contributions to no fewer than four newspapers, this 'animated writing machine living down a scandalous past', this 'the most discredited and mercenary journalist of his day', was responsible for no less than seven other publications¹, including *The Anatomy of Exchange Alley; or a System of Stock Jobbing* ('proving that Scandalous Trade, as it is now carried on, to be knavish in its private Practice, and Treason in its Public'); an account of *The King of Pirates*—Captain Avery, known as the Mock King of Madagascar, and a little treatise of 64 pages entitled *The Dumb Philosopher: or, Great Britain's Wonder, viz. Dickory Cronke*².

Like other renowned books, including *Paradise Lost*, 'the whole circle of the trade' examined and rejected the manuscript of *Robinson Crusoe* before at last it found its happy sponsor in William Taylor 'at the Ship'. He is said to have cleared a thousand pounds by his enterprise—five times as large a sum as Swift received for *Gulliver's Travels*. The venture was an instantaneous and complete success. As Byron said of Gray's *Elegy*, 'it pleases instantly and eternally', and, like 'the most unblushing volume of lies that was ever offered to the world', Sir John Mandeville's³ *Travels*, it took the public by storm. To such a degree that the printers could scarcely keep pace with their orders. Four editions of it followed one upon another between April and August. And in the same summer this indefatigable man of Stoke Newington was ready with the *Farther Adventures*⁴.

They shared the fate of most sequels. For this, Mrs. Crusoe was chiefly responsible. She should have died hereafter, not just when in his Bedfordshire farm her husband was beginning to recover from the 'ecstasies of vapours' that had incited him to be up and away. As for his meddling nephew, he positively persecutes him to be gone. A graceless son, Crusoe then proves himself a heedless father. He abandons his 'two young children', leaving them in the care, forsooth, of his widow-woman, and they have apparently slipped out of his fickle memory when he turns again home.

But all this and much more could easily be forgiven him if only his Second Part had approached his first. Alas, it is a book by no comparison equal to the original, and, lesser disaster, it lost its publisher £200. Unabashed, Defoe followed it up a year later (five years, that is, before *Gulliver's Travels* was published), not only with his 'unreadable' *Serious Reflections*, enshrining *A Vision of the Angelic World*, but also with three immense romances (not mere pamphlets of less than a hundred pages like those of the year before) which are certainly not so. These were *Duncan Campbell* (3 April); *Memoirs of a Cavalier* (21 May); and *Captain Singleton*[1] (4 June).

In his prefaces to the three several parts of *Robinson Crusoe* Defoe sounds what is now a familiar decoy. 'The Editor,' he says, in the first preface, 'believes the thing to be a just history of fact; neither is there any appearance of fiction in it'.* 'There is a man alive, and well known too,' runs the preface of the *Serious Reflections*, 'the actions of whose life are the just subject of these volumes.' And in the preface to the *Farther Adventures*

* And then he adds, and one sees a smile creep in at the back of his grey eye, 'However that may be, for all such things are disputed'.

Defoe answers the critics who had bitterly attacked the original. 'All the endeavours of envious people to reproach it' (not merely with errors in geography, inconsistency and contradictions, but) 'with being a Romance have proved abortive, and as impotent as malicious.' But in all three cases, we must mournfully remind ourselves, Defoe was addressing the great public—an exercise in which the tongue tends to stray into the cheek.

The *Adventures*, it is true, and as Defoe asserted, abound with 'religious and useful inferences', but it would be far easier to discover in Bunyan's *Pilgrim's Progress* nothing but 'an earthly story' than to follow a continuous heavenly thread in *Robinson Crusoe*. Roughly it may be said that in the one a poor castaway, named Christian, wins his way out of this world into a heavenly paradise; and that in the other a poor castaway, named Crusoe, wins his way out of an earthly paradise back into this wicked world; and both of them by their resolution, resource, and trust in Providence. Defoe's text and moral is the fifth commandment: ' " Now ", said I aloud,' says Crusoe on his island¹, ' " my dear father's words are come to pass " ' (namely, 'If that boy...goes abroad he will be the miserablest wretch that was ever born'), ' " God's judgment has overtaken me and I have none to help or hear me ".' But when at last Crusoe returns home, his self-congratulations over the prodigious fortune he has acquired are more conspicuous than any mention of his deceased parents.

Defoe's was an age of journalism and prose; the novel (apart from the *novella*) was not yet even a novelty. Romance meant something indolent, seductive and untrue. His readers hungered to be informed and edified, they liked to feel 'they were being done good to', while they relished the accompanying spices; and Defoe, apart from his other gifts and graces, had enough of the spirited tradesman in his composition to attempt to meet their demands.

The enduring influence of most great writers and of all poets springs out of the livelong conflict within them between the world of their imagination and the great world without. It is rather their unlikeness than their resemblance to their fellows that distinguishes them; the rareness of the qualities they reveal, often at strife with those common to all. They may be popular, either during their lives or after they are dead, but not necessarily for the best reasons. For popularity is often little more than the smile that comes into the face of a generation seated before its favourite author with palm outstretched, asking not a bluntly truthful delineation of its fortune or accomplishments, but for a dose of artful flattery. And flattery takes many disguises.

There is, however, another greatness which is not dependent on any extreme of originality but consists in the attraction afforded by the ideas, characteristics and sentiments of the vast majority of mankind made lucid and articulate. Great writers of this order, because, though fashions may change, the crowd that follows them changes but little, inherit a continually renewed following both from the many and the few. Their writing is usually of the earth earthy, their ideals are substantive and rational, their subject-matter is of the texture of daily and common life. And of all such writers none with so solid and acute an understanding, surely, ever crept so low and kept so close to the normal intelligence and experience of mankind as Defoe.

Nowadays it would be agreed, perhaps, that some power of imagination is as essential to a true sanity as the faculty of reason; and that it flourishes of course on what is called the imaginative. It might be agreed, too, and more unanimously, that any specific moral in a piece of fiction, and certainly in a tale of adventure, is the better if it be not too openly talked about by the author. And, Jane Taylor, Isaac Watts and Mrs. Turner notwithstanding, and though all children delight in seeing the wicked confounded, the young detest a story-book that is merely a lesson-book in disguise and groan to see poetry made a drudge-of-all-work. The adult eighteenth century, however, revelled in 'morals'; and Defoe wrote for his time. It was a malicious libel, he maintained, to dismiss his Robinson's adventures as romance.

And rightly. The spell of his enchanting master-piece is not, of course, mere romance, but the dressing-up of romance to make it look like matter-of-fact. Defoe's passion as a writer of fiction was this craving to mimic life itself, and, in his later books, preferably its wrong and seamy side—a literary craving that is not inactive in our own enlightened day. The comment is hackneyed enough but worth repeating, if only as a reminder, first, that Defoe largely originated the method, though most of the old broadsides and chapbooks were of the same complexion; next, that he was, in much, the first English novelist; and last, that the craft and art of fiction are far from consisting in this alone. Still, in this close lively likeness to actuality Defoe hardly falls short of Pepys and Boswell; and all seems so easy and so natural that one is aware neither of the difficulty nor the skill.

It may shock us to realize that the denizens of Selkirk's Juan Fernandez now adorn their correspondence with Chilean postage stamps specially surcharged for their use, and doubtless listen in to jazz music broadcast from San Francisco. But Crusoe's 'little kingdom' has had better luck. It is beyond change and chance and lives on in memory among the vividest events of our childhood. Utterly remote in its latitude of 9 degrees 22 minutes north of a line even less tangible than any known to the cartographer, utterly uninhabited, enshrining and embosoming in its greenery (as does Easter Island[1] its ancient and amazing images) the rotting relics of its Governor's industry during the twenty-eight years, two months and nineteen days of his unlimited monarchy, it has survived even the depredations of Progress. In that little kingdom solitude is still to be found—a solitude broken only by the occasional incursions of the cannibal—a visitor, all geniality and innocence itself by comparison with the noisy and mannerless crooks that infest the productions of the modern printing-press.

The island of Utopia[2] is the mere device of a wise and delightful mind; the New Atlantis the museum of a sententious intellect; Oceana is sunken deep as

Lyonesse beneath the waves. Gulliver's Lilliput[1], Brobdingnag, Laputa, interest us far less for their own romantic sake than for the sake of their outlandish and exemplary inhabitants. Crusoe and his green oasis in the ocean's blue is another story. We believe in it. We have been there—we ourselves. So perfectly realizable is its story, that we should be little surprised if on arriving to-morrow in Robinson Kreutznaer's birthplace (to give him for once his real name)—in, that is, the ancient and beautiful city of York, with its Roman ruins, medieval walls, its beautiful minster and fourteenth-century glass— we should scarcely be surprised, I say (and Defoe's idiom is catching), to find neatly reposing in their glass case in the Town Hall the very reliques and souvenirs which our friend tells us he carried off from his island for sweet remembrance' sake: his hairy hat, his umbrella, and maybe—stuffed, glass-eyed, a little mothed and dusty—one of his later parrots.

None the less, it was Defoe's little cherub alone that saved him. For he himself was guilty of every treachery to his Robinson. In his infatuation for the naturalistic he did his utmost to destroy for us both Crusoe and his island. In the 'second part' of his adventures Crusoe is transformed into a mere globe-trotter, caravanning from Nanking to Tobolsk, and with buccaneering phlegm scoffing at the yellow man, shooting down the black, and burning Chan-Chi-Thaungua on his way. In spite of what he calls his inexpressible grief at the death of 'poor honest Friday', he immediately thinks of returning to his island in search of a facsimile, and would as likely as not have called him Monday Morning. Presently indeed we find him with a sigh of petulance and surfeit dismissing even his island itself from all remembrance. 'I have done with my island,' he cries, 'and all manner of discourse about it; and whoever reads my memorandums will do well to turn his thoughts entirely from it.' Turn his thoughts to what?—to 'the follies of an old man'. And that old man our arduous Robinson!

This wanton attempt[1] of an author to ruin his finest piece of handiwork is, so far as I know, unparalleled in English literature. But like the ever-rolling stream of Time itself, Defoe's one difficulty in fiction, for various reasons, was to leave off. This is hardly a sufficient excuse for his thus going on, but how otherwise can we explain and forgive his having peopled those sacred solitudes with Spaniards, mutineers, black women, coffee-coloured piccaninnies, blacksmiths and carpenters, and even saddling them with marriage laws?

This last extravagance Professor Saintsbury thinks may have been due to Defoe's having chanced on a romance by Henry Neville that appeared in 1668, entitled *The Isle of Pines*. It is a brief tale of only 31 quarto pages. The Pines, discovered on this island by a Dutch ship astray in the Southern Ocean, are not, as might be assumed, trees, but humans[2]. They are the descendants of a certain George Pine who many years before had been cast away upon its shores with four other survivors, his master's daughter, two white maid-servants, and a young negress. 'To prevent', in Professor Saintsbury's words, 'unfairness and ill feeling' George had wedded the complete quartet. When the Dutchmen arrive, George's grandson William is the governor of the island, and the patriarch¹ expires leaving behind him a population of 1,789 souls, a rather depressing manifestation of man's rivalry with the rabbit.

Not so Crusoe. When, in his middle fifties, 'a perfect stranger to all the world', but with 'about £5000 *sterling* in money', not to mention an 'estate in the Brasils', he returned to England, he himself promptly married a wife, 'not either to my disadvantage or my dissatisfaction'; and with no such qualms as afflicted Lemuel Gulliver. But he refrained from any such matrimonial adventures on his island. Those of his subjects, however, caused him many anxious moments; especially when, despairing of fathoming God's Providence, he asks himself why from among the blackamoors available his two best sailors specifically chose the two worst wives, and why by far the best wife fell to the lot of that master wicker-worker but otherwise nefarious villain, Will Atkins.

To that extent, and to that extent only, *Robinson Crusoe* is a problem novel². Otherwise his island remains for us an Eden uncomplicated by the wiles and distractions of an Eve.

The old Serpent, it is true, in the person of the cannibal's god, Benamuckee³, erects his horns one fine morning above the nearer hill. Simply and patiently Crusoe endeavoured 'to clear up this fraud' to his man Friday, explaining that Benamuckee, with his old medicine-man called Oowokakee, was 'nought but a cheat and a devil'.

But, says Friday, in the theological discussion that follows, '"but if God much *strong*, much might as the devil, why God no kill the devil, so make him no more do wicked?"'

At which Crusoe confesses to himself that though now an old man he is still but a young doctor and ill enough qualified for a casuist. And though he presently continues to expound the consequences of man's first disobedience, the most memorable words are Friday's.

'"Well, well," says he, mighty affectionately, "that well; so you, I, devil, all wicked, all preserve, repent, God pardon all."'

Crusoe himself may seem to the orthodox a little too easy-going in his views. He was amused and gratified to find himself at last Governor of a realm of three subjects, of whom Friday was a Protestant, Friday's father a pagan, and the Spaniard rescued from the cannibals a good Catholic. Whether or not, whatever mischief Satan might find to do on that island, he sought in vain for idle hands.

Macaulay, who could not understand 'the mania of some people' about Defoe, grudgingly admitted that he had a 'knack' and that he had written one excellent novel, 'Robinson Crusoe'. It had been his delight when he was a small boy of five. In later life he attributed its success a little scornfully to 'the union of luck with ability'. But what happier union could there be? It would be folly indeed to admit impediments to it. How many of the world's masterpieces have been its offspring?

The reappearance of Selkirk into the civilized

world was certainly for Defoe a stroke of luck, but then, Selkirk for full seven years before Defoe made use of him had been 'a common prey to the birds of literature'. It was sheer ability that not only recognized the literary value of this nugget, but prevented Defoe from being too clever in his tale—though clever in all conscience he could be. It is not so much in spite of its limitations as to a large extent because of them that it remains one of the most famous books in the world. It taxes no ordinary intelligence. There is nothing complicated, delicate, abstruse, subtle to master. It can be opened and read with ease and delight at any moment, and anywhere. Its thought is little but an emanation of Crusoe's seven senses and of his five wits. Its sentiments are universal.

If we ask ourselves how, say, Samuel Richardson, Henry James or George Meredith would have improved upon his theme we remain no less grateful to Defoe. For though, unlike Prospero's island in *The Tempest*[1], Crusoe's asks little of the imagination, it asks of that little its all. The moods, the emotions it exacts from us are those of our common workaday selves. We are autocrats there—monarchs of all we survey, from its vines and goats[2] to its stars and its ocean; yet autocrats, except perhaps when we stand by and see the mutineers whipped and pickled, innocent of tyranny, and burdened, for emblems of royalty, with nothing more uneasy than a conical skin hat and a rather cumbersome umbrella. We are merely that poor forked radish, a Man—with a thickish vigorous active headpiece, legs, hands, a Bible, a

43

hatchet and a gun—face to face with grisly circumstance. And with how masterly a character, apart from that streak of filial ingratitude, with what a stubborn will-to-stay-alive has Defoe endowed his shipwrecked sailor. Or does it require perhaps less anxious efforts to keep our balance at a moral altitude somewhere below that of the angels and above that of the brutes that perish when we are alone than when we are in the company of our fellows?

Neither dangers from the unseen, nor difficulties staring him in the face, nor disaster, nor terror, nor even his own follies and mistakes, daunt or dismay Crusoe for more than five minutes together. With unwearying cheerfulness and good sense and with infinite 'application' this recluse toils his solitary years away. A dreadful despair at times may chequer his 'melancholy relation of a scene of silent life', but realizing that 'a state of idleness is the very dregs' of mortal existence, that the diligent live well and comfortably, and the slothful hard and beggarly, he labours on¹, as he says, in a 'passionate' contentment, his heart welling with gratitude. He is 'a happy prisoner', because he is 'master of his soul's liberty'. Like the Prince whom Crusoe afterwards hobnobbed with in Siberia, he knew that 'the height of human wisdom is to bring our tempers down to our circumstances, and to make a calm within, under the weight of the greatest storm without'. Defoe himself delighted in this particular metaphor—he had applied it, and introduces it twice into his verse. And the joy of his *Adventures* is that Crusoe himself richly practises what he seldom preaches.

How could one possibly resent such a sentiment when it is made manifest in the extravagant toil of this sun-baked derelict over his preposterous pots, his periagua, which he took months and months to burn and chop into shape and then found to be immovable, over his goats and his wicker ware, his powder magazine, his stockade, his corral, his vineyard, and the education of his man Friday? Half drowned on the rocky shore in that appalling tempest, besieged with the awful unknown, famished, half naked, with nothing but a knife, a tobacco-pipe, and a little tobacco in a box, what does he do—and the very next morning after his shipwreck? Up with the sun, as much a monopoly now as his own breeches, he instantly sets to work for all the world as if he intended, when he should come to die at threescore years and ten, that his funeral should be no less costly than Enoch Arden's.

Crusoe's industry indeed is at the same time absurd and entrancing. It saved his life and sanity, it is the sovran charm of his book. He broods at times, he talks to himself[1], he prays, he makes his peace with Providence—'Religion joined in with this prudential'. None the less his busy-ness is almost invariably centred upon events and things. And that business is all the more beguiling because it is work of the hands rather than of the brain.

Is there any book in the language indeed where mere things, goods and chattels, are at once so commonplace and so engrossing? We gloat over those first burnt-up potsherds of Crusoe's as if they were priceless porcelain. He at last succeeds in making a table;

and we congratulate this now 'complete natural mechanic' as though he were a Benvenuto Cellini, or a Grinling Gibbons. He is incredibly methodical and statistical with those precise figures of his, his date-post (*minus* a twenty-four hours somehow lost under the influence of rum and tobacco), his inventories, his bills of lading, his schedules of stores, and his list of *pros* and *cons* in respect to his 'sad situation'. Last and not least, in those detailed summaries of the cannibals he slaughters, more precise by far than most butchers' bills.

With his exquisite prudence and caution, he hoards up his useless treasure-trove from the unnamed 120-ton ship that wrecked him, just 'in case':

> I smiled to myself at the sight of this money[1]. 'O drug!' said I aloud, 'what art thou good for? Thou art not worth to me, no, not the taking off of the ground; one of those knives is worth all this heap. I have no manner of use for thee; even remain where thou art, and go to the bottom as a creature whose life it's not worth saving.' However, upon second thoughts, I took it away; and wrapping all this in a piece of canvas, I began to think of making another raft.

So, too, when he plunders the second wreck. He finds the 'linen white handkerchiefs' ('about a dozen and a half' of them) 'exceeding refreshing to wipe my face in a hot day'—so refreshing that in reading of it one almost mimics the gesture! But as for the money, about a pound of solid gold, ''twas to me as the dirt under my feet'. He would have given it all for some shoes and stockings. *But*—'Well, however, I lugged this money home to my cave, and laid it up'. That *Upon second thoughts*, that *Well, however*, what a power they wield over the fancy[2].

46

But Crusoe had learned to be diligent in the school which his maker himself attended for a complete half-century. For Defoe had spent his days, good, bad and indifferent, in a furious cloud of industry, his sixth and last decade being his busiest. The son of a butcher, but destined for the Presbyterian ministry, he had practised as a hose-factor (and not, he insisted, as a hosier), as the secretary of a brick-works, a soldier, and a merchant adventurer. He is said to have made and as characteristically to have lost several fortunes. In 1692, many years before he became a professional author, he went bankrupt for £17,000— and lived to redeem something of that unsatisfactory situation.

Apart then from his pen, and whether openly or by stealth, he was a man of endless activities. So much so that in his popular appearances in the pillory, garlanded with flowers and huzzaed by his devotees, he may have come nearer to that peace wherein emotions are remembered in tranquillity than at any other moment in the course of his fevered life. And so went the see-saw to the very end; for at last, poor soul, 'he died of a lethargy', in distress and under a cloud.

'None but an author', says Cowper, 'knows an author's cares'. Nevertheless, few of Defoe's fellow-craftsmen have been over-kind to him. He was 'an unprincipled hack', says Macaulay. 'A grave, sententious, dogmatical rogue', says Swift. During his life, and for a good many years after it, he was considered by general agreement a medley of 'knave and patriot'. Even Leslie Stephen, after the fair and square assertion that Defoe as a writer had 'the most

marvellous power ever known of giving verisimilitude to his fictions', ungraciously paraphrases himself by adding that he had, that is, 'the most amazing
talent on record for telling lies'.

But none of Defoe's detractors, contemporary or
posthumous, has ever charged him with indolence.
His published works number over 250. He contributed 5000 printed pages in about nine years to his
triweekly *Review*. In open citizenship he was no less
industrious and in much far-sighted[1]. If the London
shoeblacks of his day owed him a grudge, we ourselves owe him in some part our National Savings
Banks, our high roads, our Idiot Asylums, our Friendly Societies, our London University and our Police.
Finally, his first publication, of 1687, was concerned
with liberty of conscience; his last, of 1731, with a
scheme for the prevention of street robberies and the
routing of those 'Sons of Hell, called Incendiaries'.

That his gift for romance should have survived
this industry, almost as disconcerting a spectacle as
that of a queen bee laying eggs, is the most remarkable fact of all. It wore down and impoverished much
that a quiet private life may leave untarnished, but
it failed to quench his youth and spirit, his sublime
naivety, and his zest for the attentions of the busy
fractious world of men. How astonishing too was
his power to forget himself. Day by day, the whole
world blissfully foundering beneath him, this dark,
spare, hawk-nosed champion of the common people,
this vigorous, volatile, quick-headed, 'unabashable'
gentleman close on sixty shut himself up in his
handsome large white house in Church Street[2], Stoke

Newington, and casting his inmost being away upon an island ostensibly 'near the mouth of the Great River of Oroonoque', but actually in the midst of the vast Ocean of Nowhere, reincarnated himself in his fantastic affinity, Robinson Crusoe.

'I can affirm,' says Crusoe in his *Serious Reflections*, and surely it is not only his own full manly voice we hear but Defoe's also, 'I can affirm that I enjoy much more solitude in the middle of the greatest collection of mankind in the world, I mean, at London, while I am writing this, than ever I could say I enjoyed in eight and twenty years' confinement to a desolate island.'

So also in reading his story—in that 'drab', surprising, go-as-you-please entrancing prose of his, 'everywhere beautiful, but plain and homely'—we too become a kind of second self. We are cut off completely from the actuality—the chairs, the tables, the walls and the world around us. We see with Crusoe's eyes, hear with his ears, feel in the heat of tropic sunlight the cool air 'whistling under our shirt'. Shut up as it were in one of those matter-of-fact dreams in which we are spectators of our own actions and with no possibility of interruption from within or without, we read on and on and on— hardly conscious either of the book in our hands or of the eyes in our heads. It is as if one had chanced on the story of one's own life, but a life how marvellously renewed, and of how guileless a career. For 'Thou art the man', Crusoe cries on his reader. We can but listen then like a three years' child; the mariner hath his will.

Is there too any other character in English fiction that is at the same time not only so occupiable as Crusoe but so engaging an object to the inward eye? Picture and pantomine have lent their aid perhaps, but he himself left nothing to chance. Even after twelve years' residence on the island, as he stalks the sea-strand between the washing tide and the blue salt shallow pools it has left behind it, 'I frequently', he says, 'stood still to look at myself'. 'Be pleased', he adds, 'to take a sketch of my figure, as follows:'

I had a great high shapeless cap, made of a goat's skin, with a flap hanging down behind. . . . I had a short jacket of goat-skin, the skirts coming down to about the middle of my thighs; and a pair of open-kneed breeches of the same. The breeches were made of the skin of an old he-goat, whose hair hung down such a length on either side, that, like pantaloons, it reached to the middle of my legs. Stockings and shoes I had none, but had made me a pair of somethings, I scarce know what to call them, like buskins, to flap over my legs, and lace on either side like spatter-dashes. . . . I had on a broad belt of goat's skin dried, which I drew together with two thongs of the same, instead of buckles; and in a kind of a frog on either side of this, instead of a sword and a dagger, hung a little saw and a hatchet, one on one side, one on the other. I had another belt, not so broad, and fastened in the same manner, which hung over my shoulder; and at the end of it, under my left arm, hung two pouches, both made of goat's skin too; in one of which hung my powder, in the other my shot. At my back I carried my basket, on my shoulder my gun, and over my head a great clumsy ugly goat-skin umbrella, but which, after all, was the most necessary thing I had about me, next to my gun.

His beard, though he had both 'scissors and razors sufficient', from being a quarter of a yard long, he had cut pretty short, but had trimmed the hair that grew on his upper lip into a large pair of Mahometan whiskers or mustachios. 'I will not say they were long enough to hang my hat upon them, but they were of a length and shape monstrous enough, and such as in England would have passed for frightful.' We hesitate; but seeing must be believing.

And why whiskers at all[1]? Chiefly, of course, to amuse Defoe. His endless pleasure in his own inventions, indeed, is one of the open secrets of his fiction. 'To have seen me and my little family', says Crusoe, 'sitting down to dinner would have made a stoic smile'—but it had made Defoe laugh out first. Even to *think* of his admirable hermit is to be cheerful and to take heart of grace. He watered his small stock of ink 'till it was so pale it scarce left any appearance of black upon the paper'—a piece of universal experience which is almost an epitome of man's life on earth! He endeavoured to breed pigeons up tame, and did so, but 'when they grew older they flew all away'. What is it that suffuses a hundred such passages as these with the shimmer on shot silk? Humour, of course, but that mixed with *good* humour, tolerance, childlikeness—a host of things. Unlike Swift in *Gulliver* or the *Tale*, Defoe in *Crusoe* is never witty or acridly sardonic, and, his Tracts perhaps having cured him of it, he seldom indulges in irony. There is a schoolboy humour, of Swift's own brand, in *Gulliver*, e.g. in the account of the fire in the Queen's palace in Lilliput. There is a racy variety peculiar to Bunyan in *The Pilgrim's Progress*. But Defoe's humour, though it is often little else than a kind of shrewd, or coarse, or ingenuous good sense, is as pervasive as it is indefinable, and fails him only when he becomes a little too jocose and self-conscious and cosmopolitan.

His was a mind too busy and restless for a profound insight, for an absorbed joy, gravity, or melancholy. And it was limited in other respects in sensi-
bility. Beauty, of earth or of heaven, is seldom his
desire or dream, and only *Duncan Campbell* shows
evidence that he found much delight in colour. His
stories are like wood-cuts, now exquisitely clear and
particularized, now blurred and dingy. He leaves, as
far as I can remember, no recorded music on the ear;
flowers, stars, sunsets for their own sake are rare with
him; and his trees are referred to chiefly for the shade
they afford.

Intent on his foreground, he seldom raises his eyes
to dream awhile, with longing or hope or remembrance, on distant horizons[1]. This is to say little more
maybe than that he was a man of his own place and
time, when Nature was not as yet in fashion; the
marvel actually being that this true-born Englishman, this citizen of the world, should have spent
even in fancy a single Sabbath so far out of town as
the Caribbean Seas.

Nevertheless in his descriptions of weather and scenery Defoe draws so near nature that in his company
we cannot but be at times a little homesick. Though
'his fondness for the industry of man limited his
sympathies' he is capable of 'transports' too, but
these less of the soul than of the eye. Of lustrous
silks and velvets, of gold and rich merchandise and
such works of art as in *Captain Singleton* 'put our
artificer to his trumps' he never fails to speak with
real emotion, with an undisguised rapture of avarice.
He pounces with joy on the graduated charges of a

midwife. His adventurers, like the Queen of Sheba, bestow lavish gifts wherever they voyage, and record with punctilio both the gross quantity of the goods they acquire and their sterling value. And though Roxana grows almost ecstatic over her charms of face and shape and her unpainted skin, this is little more than a leering confidentiality across the counter. It is in fact the absence of certain aesthetic qualities in Defoe that is one of the secrets of his peculiar power.

As for his craftsmanship, it appears—when he chanced to turn to story-telling—to have depended, and how triumphantly, simply on a happy knack of improvisation, unfailing in invention, out of a memory brimming over with an inexhaustible variety of experience. This variety enabled him to race off complete treatises on themes as diverse as trade, travel, marriage, apparitions, servants and the devil. Nothing in his stories appears to have been far-sought however far-fetched. We never seem to catch him pen on lip. That the first draft of one of *his* first pages of MS. ever consisted of nothing but words scratched out is inconceivable. What need for art when mere instinct can produce such a little nugget of verisimilitude—whatever its origin—as *The True Relation of the Apparition of one Mrs. Veal*[1], its style a kind of copious breathless gossiping?

And so with his characters. An actuality as ordinary as his could be peopled only with commonplace intelligences perhaps—the one being a reflex of the other. Whether or not, the best and the worst of them, and little more than a moral hairbreadth divides them, never shock us with our own inferiority, though they may with our lack of enterprise and re-source. Apart, let us say, from their criminal tendencies, they are just such human beings as we ourselves must day by day appear to be to the outside world that knows not even so much of us as our names. Their good and evil are as primitive as the good and evil with which a common jury is concerned.

'Defoe's creed', says Mr. Masefield, 'was earnest and solemn, the temper of his mind was earnest and solemn'. It was also troubled about many things and in effect there is little that is profoundly earnest and solemn in the repentance into which he drives all such of his wicked characters as escape the gallows or Virginia. Their remorse, like Crusoe's, springs usually out of soreness after punishment, not, like Christian's, from a broken and contrite heart. And has any author, except perhaps Guy de Maupassant in *Bel Ami*, left prosperous a more despicable Worldly Wiseman than the sententious Quaker in *Captain Singleton?*

Yet much of this is due, one feels, to Defoe's perfunctoriness, for it is easy enough to be indolent and industrious at the same time. He knew mankind more profoundly than he had either the patience or inclination, or than it seemed always worth while, to show. Betty, indeed, before she becomes Mrs. Flanders—and would that Defoe's ends were as good as his beginnings—might easily have inspired Thackeray. There is a French vivacity in the earlier chapters of her history. And one of her many husbands reminds us unmistakably of the art of Mr. George Moore. 'Let the naturalists explain these things, and the reason and manner of them: all

I can say to them is to describe the fact,' exclaims Crusoe, almost petulantly, after that touching cry from the heart, 'O that it had been but one—but one soul saved!' And this sly pretence of artlessness sounds like a direct challenge to Henry James. But even the best things in Defoe's fiction seem to have drifted into his mind like dewy mists of the morning and as naturally as apples fall at the autumnal equinox. There is no more direct (and far less indirect) evidence in his stories, plots and paraphernalia of sheer painstakingness than in *Twelfth Night* or *Hamlet*. None the less, if it were nothing but a natural inclination without any forethought that made Singleton and Crusoe men so ordinary in their extraordinary experiences, it sprang from so sharp and crystalline an intuition that it almost amounts to pure genius. Defoe descends with limpid ease to the level of the boy latent in all men and active in his heroes, and so within this narrow range comes near to being the most imaginative author the world has ever seen. But how many untraversable leagues away from the author, no less simple in language, of 'How sweet I roamed from field to field'.

Even in his passages of real human feeling, his moderation and presence of mind are more memorable than most men's rhapsodies:

... I was now landed, and safe on shore, and began to look up and thank God that my life was saved in a case wherein there was some minutes before scarce any room to hope.

I walked about on the shore, lifting up my hands, and my whole being, as I may say, wrapt up in the contemplation of my deliverance, making a thousand gestures and motions which I cannot describe, reflecting upon all my comrades that were drowned, and that there should not be one soul saved but myself . . .

And after this he adds with that particularity which only heedless life itself can equal:

For, as for them, I never saw them afterwards, or any sign of them, except three of their hats, one cap, and two shoes that were not fellows.

So again, on the 16th of May, by Crusoe's 'poor wooden calendar'—the day of the wreck of the Spanish galleon:

. . . I cannot explain, by any possible energy of words what a strange longing or hankering of desires I felt in my soul upon this sight, breaking out sometimes thus: 'Oh that there had been but one or two, nay, or but one soul, saved out of this ship, to have escaped to me, that I might but have had one companion, one fellow-creature, to have spoken to me, and to have conversed with!' In all the time of my solitary life, I never felt so earnest, so strong a desire after the society of my fellow-creatures, or so deep a regret at the want of it.
But it was not to be. . . .

All that he actually ever saw of that galleon's crew was the corpse of the ship boy cast up upon the strand, in a seaman's waistcoat, a pair of open-kneed linen drawers, and a blue linen shirt; and nothing in his pocket but two pieces of eight and a tobacco-pipe. And—Defoe cannot resist it—'the last was to me of ten times more value than the first'.

Though of all that he wrote, his verse is perhaps the least likely to bring poetry to mind, there are passages in Defoe's best work that recall not only the clarified and essentialized experience of actuality but even the *sounds* out of which poetry is made[1]—and that not of the Pope or Gay or Prior kind. But Defoe himself fell short of making it. Such

56

vestiges, for example, as, 'It was one of the nights in the rainy season of March'; 'He told me one day that if our God could hear us beyond the sun ...'; 'I saw the sea come after me as high as a great hill, and as furious as an enemy'; or 'That great thoroughfare of the brain, the memory, in this night's time'. In that wistful thought of Crusoe's too, that perhaps long after he has sailed away the parrots will still be calling him over the lonely island and there will be none to heed or answer. What Defoe sees, he sees with a peculiar sharpness and simplicity, with senses awake and aware; and in his naked references to actual objects he may even recall no less a poet than Dante himself¹. The titles, too, of some of his books have a peculiar solemn sonorousness:

A *Trumpet, blown in the North,* and sounded in the ears of John Erskine, called by the Men of the World, DUKE OF MAR. By a ministering Friend of the People called Quakers.

Or, again:

The *Secrets* of the *Invisible World Disclos'd* or, An *Universal History* of *Apparitions, Sacred and Profane,* under all *Denominations;* whether *Angelical, Diabolical,* or *Human Souls Departed....*

The words alone might convert the heretic in these matters, and it was Defoe's second attempt. His first, which in some respects is even more impressive, ran:

An *Essay* on the *History* and *Reality of Apparitions.* Being an Account of What they are, and What they are not; Whence they Come, and Whence they Come not; As also how we may distinguish the Apparitions of Good and Evil Spirits, and how we ought to behave to them....

Such fragments as these glance into the imagination and are gone. Occasionally they linger. Take that passage in the *Journal of the Plague Year:*

57

In the first place, a blazing star or comet appeared for several months before the plague, as there did the year after another, a little before the fire.... The old man remarked that these two comets passing directly over the city, and that so very near the houses, that it was plain they imported something peculiar to the city alone. The comet before the pestilence was of a faint, dull, languid colour, and its motion very heavy, solemn, and slow; but the comet before the fire was bright and sparkling, or, as others said, flaming, and its motion swift and furious, and that accordingly, one foretold a heavy judgment, slow but severe, terrible, and frightful, as was the plague. But the other foretold a stroke, sudden, swift, and fiery, as the conflagration; nay, so particular some people were, that as they looked upon that comet preceding the fire, they fancied that they not only saw it pass swiftly and fiercely, and could perceive the motion with their eye, but even they heard it; that it made a rushing mighty noise, fierce and terrible, though at a distance, and but just perceivable.

How curiously effective is the sinister mildness of that *something peculiar* and the deliberate whittling away of the *just perceivable*. Defoe characteristically lays the burden of this fantasticalness on the backs of the old women 'and the phlegmatic hypochondriac part of the other sex who I could almost call old women too'. Yet his saddler's narrative enslaves the mind and shuts off all retreat. The doubts and forebodings of the opening chapter, the cumulative innuendoes, the facts and figures[1] that take on in their nakedness as sinister a bearing as the far-off waft of a pirate's 'ancient' itself, the thronging, mocking, terror-stricken crowds, the quacks and seers and occultists, the hush broken ever and again by a piercing cry, and then at last the deserted grass-grown streets, the barred doors, the watchman with his bell, and the gathering shifting mist of death settling thickly upon all. An icy muffled-up shape stoops at our shoulder while we read.

Here to the full is Defoe's compassion for the outcast, the unfortunate, the suddenly abased, the simple and the misled; even though it is seen only in glimpses and is often elsewhere concealed or stifled by the haste and worldliness of the practical man, by that cold and weary indifference which horrified the creator, and destroyer, of Little Nell. And here, also, are seen Defoe's absorption in every aspect of human malady, his delight in the marvellous, his love of detail, his passion for deception, his trade instincts, his social inclinations, and his sense of citizenship.

In his *Crusoe* youth itself swept back into a mind jaded and harassed by years of journalism and politics, and Defoe drank deep of romance at an age when most of us have completely finished with it. When joy and grace appear in his work they are from this well-spring. In his sincere but tedious *Family Instructor*, not very far removed in its ideals from *The Complete Tradesman*, with its telling touches of characterization and natty dialogue, the fragment that remains in memory is the opening talk between the little boy and his father. It is indeed to Defoe's innate simplicity of spirit, combined as it is with so much worldly astuteness, that his appeal to the 'common reader' is mainly due.

According as Crusoe's fortunes set, we are dejected, exalted, horrified, unutterably grateful. We watch his grain in its first green blade, tremble at the footprint, garner his raisins, milk his goats, and all but cry aloud to him in warning when he is in danger. We revel in a reiterated, 'I told you so!'. We sit with heart drawn tight watching fate's insidious perfidies—the ravaged grapes, the prolific cats, the noble hapless venture out to sea, the immovable roll of sheet lead, which we modestly and vaguely surmise Robinson *might* have thought to hack into strips, the sea-caked barrel of powder.

On our own unworthy heads fall the blissful and sometimes even superfluous benefactions of that 'Superior Power' which not even the most impious of Defoe's adventurers ever really questioned—the complete magazine of muskets, the few grains of barley spared by the rats, the sleep of the mutineers; the Cavalier's saddle stuffed with gold, or Jack's hollow tree in the lonely field beyond *The Blind Beggars* at Bethnal Green.

How still and clear[1] that island of Crusoe's is, how near and small. An ample sky must arch it over though we seldom lift our eyes to it. At echo of gun a crying host of birds flies up; then quiet descends again. The sea stretches around us in its concave immensity, and it is with a shocked astonishment that we realize the continent of America is in sight from the hill-top. No, not the continent; only the islands about the mouth of the Oroonoque. But we thought we were alone[2].

We hearken on and on to winds that toss the leaves in woods of Crusoe's planting and to the crash of breaker; we watch those lights of night and daybreak, tremble at the vast roar of his tropical rains, and start[3] as though transfixed at the voice[4] of the friendly ghost that sups with him, and calls out

60

upon him from the horny bill of his parrot'—'Robin, Robin, Robin Crusoe, poor Robin Crusoe! Where are you? Where have you been?'

What wonder such a book as this has been not only translated into every civilized, and into most barbarous languages, but has been brazenly imitated[2] on and on, and bids fair to remain a literary incentive until time is no more. Within a year of its publication it was put into French[3], and in less than a century into Arabic. In Germany alone 'some fifty' *Robinsonaden* appeared in the nineteenth century.

Foremost among these imitators appear the authors, father and son, the one a pastor, the other a professor of Philosophy—Johann Rudolf Wyss—of that hotch-potch, *Robinson Suisse*, a title translated, oddly enough[4], into *The Swiss Family Robinson*. The book was 'home-made', a large part of it having been 'written down from recollections of the original and instructive conversations' of Wyss père. It was begun in 1800 and published in 1841, eleven years after the professor's death. It found its way from its original German by way of French into English, and its English continues to show perceptible signs of these vicissitudes.

No admirer of Crusoe should (or ever perhaps did) miss this very practical romance, but it has its limitations. As cocoa is to champagne, so are the adventures of Mr. Robinson to our Crusoe's—as nutritious, it may be, but less exhilarating. There is a wreck[5] and a rescue, but that of a complete domestic circle. Elephants, ostriches, crocodiles, the wild ass and the boa constrictor are substituted for cannibals and mutineers. But while Crusoe owes not merely his rum but his daily bread to his own exertions and his mother wit, the indefatigable Robinsons are tenants of a tropical garden long since laid under intensive cultivation by Dame Nature.

'"A ham!" cried one and all; "a ham! and ready dressed!"'—that, too, is 'tropical', but in another sense. And even though the ham, viewed for this brief instant not in the wilds but in coif and breadcrumbs in a caterer's window, was accompanied by such 'a pretty side-dish' as Mrs. Robinson's omelette of turtles' eggs, a dainty which to the uninitiated might suggest the mixture of glue and gutta-percha which her husband made into bird-lime, the feast remains a little dubious—at least on a desert island.

Crusoe was a rolling-stone flung by Providence into the wilderness. Mr. Robinson—bosom friend, surely, of Miss Tupper and Mr. Barlow—is a man of culture, infinite in resource and in sententiousness. His wilds are merely a daylong pulpit and afford him an inexhaustible supply of texts. He never stirs from his tree-top or his grotto but talc, india-rubber, pineapples and turpentine assail him on the one hand, and sago, manioc, cinnamon and the tea-plant wave him greetings on the other. And concealed in his waistcoat pocket he carries an advance copy of the first edition of the *Encyclopaedia Britannica*.

His sentiments are mealy-mouthed enough but little serve him when he slaughters the monkeys, and, base creature, blows up the wreck. Such a vivacious family as his too, in spite of its being an example of an institution out of odour with a certain school of thought just now, is a valuable unit of society and may be a boon to its members, though occasionally a tax upon its acquaintance. But on a desert island it hardly makes for romance. Crusoe lives from hand to mouth, a grisly anatomy—such as even Holbein never excelled—peering up at him from out of the shadow of the nearest rock. Mr. and Mrs. Robinson and their little circle, tented in by a Robinsonian heaven, enjoy a prolonged picnic.

But whatever the shortcomings of the book, it has been the perennial joy of numberless nurseries. It is full of that complacent and pacifying kind of instruction which glides into and out of the mind like water off a duck's back. It is as densely packed with what appear to be facts as there should be plums in duff. It can be read on and on with an eye bordering on vacancy; and can be shut up without remorse. Half a dozen pages every night before sleeping will make it last for months. One laughs with —and sometimes at—its author, which soothes one's vanity. And, like all sound tales of adventure, it mildly bubbles with what is almost as necessary to life as it is to fiction—the expectation of the unexpected.

A similar decoy entices on the reader at least half-way through *The Life and Singular Adventures of Peter Wilkins among the Flying Nations in the South Seas*. Its full title varies in its several editions, and it preceded *The Family* by nearly a century.

The author of this work, Robert Paltock, who concealed himself under the initials R.S., was an attorney, and for what of his theme he did not owe to Crusoe and Gulliver he was indebted to John Wilkins, Bishop of Chester, and brother-in-law of Oliver Cromwell. The bishop died in 1672, and besides being the author of *The Discovery of a New World...in the Moon* wrote also *Mathematical Magic* and *Mercury*—'showing how a man may with privacy and speed communicate his thoughts to a friend at any distance'. He also busied his ingenious wits with the problem of perpetual motion. Many authors have followed in *his* wake also, Poe, Jules Verne and Mr. H. G. Wells; and like that of the desert island this moon-theme is by no means yet exhausted.

Only a fragment of the *Discovery*, however, is concerned with the moon, and this chiefly in respect to the difficulties of getting there—how to overcome the forces of gravitation; to convey a sufficiency of luggage, there being no inns on the way nor castles in the air; and how to secure sleep and food, 'apart from the music of the spheres'.

Francis Bacon[1], who began his *New Atlantis* about the year in which Wilkins was born, also touches on this subject: 'We imitate also flights of birds: we have some degrees of flying in the air'. But Bishop Wilkins went a good deal beyond this: 'Yet do I seriously affirm it possible to make a flying chariot[2], in which a man shall sit, and give such a motion unto it as shall convey him through the air.... It is not the bigness of anything in this kind that can hinder its motion, if the motive faculty be answerable thereunto.'

Mr. Robinson went further yet. '"It is *false*", he

64

tells Fritz, "that a man himself can fly; it is *probable*, that, by the aid of a machine of his own invention, he may be enabled to mount and sustain himself in the air; and it is also *absolutely true* that this has been effected by man, though without his having yet found a certain means of guiding these factitious wings; a defect which, in a great measure, renders his discovery useless."' Though too emphatic this was bold, for his own *Encyclopaedia*—as late, I think, as the year 1900—assured its readers that flying machines heavier than air had been proved impracticable.

Robert Paltock preferred wings *au naturel*, and with these he endowed his flying-men—wings ribbed and bat-like, which when at rest so completely envelop the body as to resemble the delicate silk of a neatly folded umbrella, the entire surface then being 'as smooth as a dye'. His *glumms* and *gawreys* are denizens of a country called, in a style made familiar in the War, Nosmnbdsgrsutt, and are the subjects of a monarch—suggestive of the Ancient Order of Buffaloes—who is left ruler of a consolidated Sass Doorpt Swangeanti—syllables so beguiling that they conjure up into memory not merely Brobdingnag and Erewhon, but the haunts of the slithy tove and the fastnesses of the Snark.

Peter Wilkins is good only in parts; these being chiefly in the middle, and there, excellent. His matrimonial affairs with Patty, 'one of our maids', while he is still in his teens and at an academy, have even less bearing on his subsequent adventures than had Crusoe's home life on his. 'Mr. G.', too, his stepfather, who defrauds him of his inheritance, is a little superfluous. Peter leaves this wretch to its enjoyment and never even attempts to win it back.

And he dies a pauper. For when, borne along over the ocean by the breezes on a wooden structure suspended by cords held by six naked *glumms*, he is deposited in the wake of the *Hector*, he is encumbered with nothing more substantial in the way of a fortune than his remarkable memories. He is a 'man quite forgotten and pennyless'. And since he expires before the *Hector* reaches port, the friend on board who had acted as his amanuensis, bearing in mind that he had defrayed Wilkins' funeral expenses, thought he had 'the greatest right to the manuscript'. Poor Peter's heirs, then, if he had any, made not a single guinea even out of that. Defoe would have been more circumspect.

As with Crusoe, so with Wilkins, we have to wait awhile for the island. But when a sudden tempest of wind sweeps his ship away from the sailors left on shore, and only himself and a John Adams on board, and when presently John Adams also is disposed of, all is well. His wreck immovably jammed between the crags of an adamantine island, Peter suffers a sea-change into yet another happy castaway, and is the better company for owing so much to Defoe.

'O! who can have a notion how a man could feel such sorrow as I have for want of a little oil!' 'After my first transport I found myself grow serious.' 'My boat had, during my sleep, wafted through the cavern and I now found myself in a prodigious lake of water.' 'So thinks I, (and said so too, for I always spoke out) here is sauce for something when I want it.' No nodding acquaintance even of Crusoe's could fail to recognize whose voice is ventriloquized in such passages as these. While fragments like: 'By this time I was a tolerable mechanic' and 'My kingdom, (as I called it)' are pilferings almost word for word.

Any such sentence as 'After my new love had been with me a fortnight'', however, is assuredly not so. Peter's 'new love' is the beautiful winged Youwarkee, and though she hardly merits Leigh Hunt's rapturous 'A lovely woman set in front of an ethereal shell and wafted about like a Venus', she is a charming addition to Peter's island. Gentle, loving, serene, sagacious, her solitude with him is hardly disturbed by the arrival as the quiet years go by of a numerous family; and her week-end riflings of the wreck are an exciting series of interludes.

The lingo of the book is not perhaps particularly happy, such a word as *glumm* being far more suggestive of a lump of lead or a variety of butterscotch than of a human Ariel. *Gawrey*—the female of the species—is no better, though *Mouch*, a church—obviously ultra-sectarian, *yacom*, a man child, *arco*, the first murderer, and *hoximo*, the grave, come a little nearer home.

The moment Youwarkee's winged relatives (apart from her children) begin to multiply *Peter Wilkins* begins to flatten, fade and die. When solitude vanishes, the charm of the island goes with it, though, if man be naturally so gregarious an animal as he is supposed to be, it is a little difficult to see why.

As a corrective to *The Swiss Family Robinson*, Captain

Marryat wrote (for children) his *Masterman Ready*. He had been, he confesses, incensed by Mr. Robinson's seamanship[1], and by his innocent enrichment of an island in the neighbourhood of Van Diemen's Land with plants, birds and quadrupeds found only in the interior of Africa or the torrid zone. That is all to the good. Even the most docile of Mr. Robinson's admirers must be relieved to hear that much of that gentleman's facile informativeness is wholly false.

But, alas, *Masterman Ready*—though the fight with the savages is rich reading—is not comparable with *Mr. Midshipman Easy*, or a patch on *Robinson Crusoe*. Marryat restored the stockade, but he kept the family—Mamma, Papa, William, Tommy, Caroline, and Albert, the last still in his months. His island—lovely and peaceful spot—suggests a definite memory; Crusoe's, whatever its origin, is a region of pure fantasy. Mr. Seagrave, too, though 'a very nice gentleman', is a little amateurish and depressing, and Juno is but a passable substitute for Friday. This small boy Tommy was of course intended to be a horrid warning to all other self-willed and mischievous little boys, and must be endured. But why, why did Captain Marryat drag in the infant Albert? The mere name, too, Selina Seagrave, though Selina herself, so far as I can remember, never realizes how ominous a part of it she shares with her husband, suggests, and rightly, 'an amiable woman', but she is in poor health. And I venture to be perfectly certain that ladies in poor health and infants in arms should refrain from being marooned.

No story indeed after Defoe's pattern[2] has shaken

68

its supremacy[1], even though in *Treasure Island*[2] and in Mr. Masefield's *Lost Endeavour*[3] and in William Morris's[4] prose romances there are joys in abundance to which Crusoe was a stranger. And *Enoch Arden*[5] is no exception. I recall also a female Crusoe, Robina by name. Can it be nearly half a century ago that she gaily and gallantly trod the pages of *The Girl's Own Paper?* Almanacs are stubborn things. To the small boy who shared her adventures, and the pictures of them, she was an enchanting companion in her goatskins, cap and gun—but possibly she consisted of little more than the funny-bone of her great original, and I dare not go back[6] to make sure.

None the less Robinson Crusoe himself is not the end of the matter. Throughout Defoe's fiction there are vague hints and whispers of the mysterious and the marvellous, dreams and wraiths and phantasms. The highwayman's 'clairaudience' does not surprise us when he hears 'very plain' Moll's heart-broken far-away cry, 'Oh, Jemmie, come back, come back!' Nor does Roxana's glimpse of the second-sight, just before, like Lorenzo, the murdered jeweller rides out to his doom. Nor the oft-repeated 'veridical' dream; nor even the line of piracy on Singleton's tell-tale palm. And so too with Robinson Crusoe. 'When I was in my island kingdom I had abundance of strange notions of my seeing apparitions. . . . The story of my fright, with something on my bed, was word for word a history of what happened.' 'How strange, and chequered a Work of Providence is the life of man!' And never so strange as when the abnormal visits perfectly ordinary people. It is then

69

that the preternatural steals in on us with its most persuasive air.

All this suggests that if Defoe had really faced, as he might have tried to face, the problem set in *Crusoe* his solution could not have been in that book's precise terms. All praise and thanks that it is what it is, a triumph in its kind; and yet one may pine for what, given a more creative imagination and a different Crusoe, the book might have been if the attempt had been made to reveal what a prolonged unbroken solitude[1], an absolute exile from his fellow-creatures, and an incessant commerce with silence and the unknown, would mean at last to the spirit of man. A steadily debasing brutish stupidity? Hallucinations, extravagances, insanities, enravishment, strange guests?

Selkirk after but four years' silence[2] was scarcely articulate. Crusoe after his eight and twenty years addresses the three strangers whom he finds trussed-up on the beach with the urbanity of a prince, the courtesy of an Oriental, and in faultless Spanish:

'"All help is from heaven, sir," said I. "But you can put a stranger in the way how to help you, for you seem to be in some great distress...." The poor man, with tears running down his face, and trembling, looking like one astonished, returned, "Am I talking to God, or man? Is it a real man, or an angel?"'

Crusoe smiles the question aside, '"If God had sent an angel to relieve you he would have come better clothed...."' It was a reply exquisitely polite to all concerned; but how much real heed or heart

70

or hard thinking went into it? Answer to that can come none.

But there are islands of many kinds[1]; solitudes of sundry degrees[2]; and their all depends on the castaway. And for myself, like Sancho Panza, 'I know no more what belongs to them . . . than a blind buzzard'. As for the brief spells of solitude a jog-trot life affords, Johnson's counsel to Boswell seems to be sound: 'If you are idle be not solitary, if you are solitary be not idle'. And he borrowed that from the last page of the only book that ever decoyed him out of his bed an hour earlier than was his wont.

The ancient Egyptians, I have read, believed that immortality is not the universal lot; that some poor wayfarers evade or escape it, and achieve in their dust the endless solitude of the tomb:

> . . . And when thy heart is resting
> Beneath the church-aisle stone,
> I shall have time for mourning,
> And thou for being alone.

But an endless sleep, unstirred, unillumined by any phantom of dream, is unimaginable, since even in the conceiving of it the self within hovers over the envied ashes[3]—envied, because the spirit may be compelled to endure a weariness beyond the body's power to allay.

Flaubert's St. Anthony[4] lived on in years beyond a hundred, in a twilight between the real and the visionary, and had strange company enough. Crusoe came back[5], rejoicing, to civilization again, and the 'allegory' of his 'shifty and casuistical' creator who as he himself confessed had 'bowed himself in the house of Rimmon' pierces not very far either into heart or soul. O then that there had been many such simple souls as his saved that we might share the record of *their* strange and surprising adventures!

Nevertheless for those not exclusively intent on life's subtleties Defoe's book never fails to reward even the most casual of visits. Like honest bread and cheese it will satisfy a natural hunger when richer and rarer kickshaws may fail to titillate or cheer. His derelict sailor is as original as his name, and he left his theme unexhausted and inexhaustible. 'He is read', says one of his most sympathetic critics, 'by schoolboys and kitchenmaids, by sailors.' Not an exacting circle, at least on the positive side. And yet surely one's mind and taste must have become a little surfeited or belletristic or too, too fastidious, if —when the occasion offers—one cannot be content to shut out even the greatest awhile and all the Muses, and hobnob with Jack in *The Blind Beggars* at Bethnal Green, or with Crusoe and Singleton dare the high seas, bound for Friday, or the sources of the Nile.

And does not a voice out of 'the little nowhere of the mind' astonish every one of us at times with its insistent—'Robin, Robin, Robin Crusoe, poor Robin Crusoe! Where are you? Where have you been?' Indeed an hour will come, as it came to Defoe himself in Ropemaker's Alley[1], on April 26th, 1731, when, braving disaster, we shall be compelled, whether we will or not, to follow it into the unknown, and on the wings of the imagination flee away to-wards Ultima Thule, skirting latitudes even remoter than that of 9 degrees 22 minutes north of the line.

And About Them

Page 6 [1]—The open eye and heart and mind:

¶ One such adventure, even, and that apparently a pure gift of Fortune, may be the nucleus of a complete career. Witness Richard Hakluyt's 'epistle dedicatorie' of his *Principal Navigations:*

Right Honorable, I do remember that being a youth, and one of her Majesties scholars at Westminster that fruitfull nurserie, it was my happe to visit the chamber of M. Richard Hakluyt my cosin, a Gentleman of the Middle Temple, well knowen unto you, at a time when I found lying open upon his boord certaine bookes of Cosmographie, with an universall Mappe: he seeing me somewhat curious in the view thereof, began to instruct my ignorance, by shewing me the division of the earth into three parts after the olde account, and then according to the latter, & better distribution, into more: he pointed with his wand to all the knowen Seas, Gulfs, Bayes, Straights, Capes, Rivers, Empires, Kingdomes, Dukedomes, and Territories of ech part, with declaration also of their speciall commodities, & particular wants, which by the benefit of traffike, & entercourse of merchants, are plentifully supplied. From the Mappe he brought me to the Bible, and turning to the 107 Psalme, directed mee to the 23 & 24 verses, where I read, that they which go downe to the sea in ships, and occupy by the great waters, they see the works of the Lord, and his woonders in the deepe, &c. Which words of the Prophet together with my cousins discourse (things of high and rare delight to my yong nature) tooke in me so deepe an impression, that I constantly resolved, if ever I were preferred to the University, where better time, and more convenient place might be ministred for these studies, I would by Gods assistance prosecute that knowledge and kinde of literature, the doores whereof (after a sort) were so happily opened before me.

'Things of high and rare delight to my yong nature'— has the poise of the kestrel, the serenity of a portrait by Vermeer.

Page 6[2]*—The romantic:*

¶ The *word* has had a comparatively brief history; and this Mr. Logan Pearsall Smith has lately explored. It is descriptive of a state of mind, since in nature and in life there is nothing romantic unless thinking or feeling makes it so. Objects *per se* know it not; it is an aspect conferred on them by the watcher behind the eye. The kind of experience thus acquired is distrusted or deplored by the classicist or the realist or the materialist, either because he cannot share it, or because, while perceiving it, he believes it to be a deceit of the mind or a lie in the soul.

To define mystery as that which is not as yet revealed and made plain, and magic as a method of effecting a feat which only eludes the observer for the time being, is sound enough in theory, but rather sterile in practice. And though to see truly (as truly at least as man can) needs no spectacles, and, even if they do straddle one's nose, there should at least be no cheating colour in the glass, yet even the intellect may have its flaws; and how for certain keep the heart and imagination out of one's eyes?

To the Greeks and Romans romance was alien, though certainly not to the Egyptians or the Hebrews. None the less, as the *Anthology* would alone prove, the Greek mind was not innocent of its illusions. Apart from the ancients, at least eight centuries have now gone by wherein, in varying intensity, romance has held its sway in human consciousness. To ignore the romantic in the age of Elizabeth is to deny its glitter to gold.

Even the literary realism or naturalism of our own day may become sicklied over in retrospect with the romantic when it is shared by the yet unborn. The dead dogs and offal in Swift's *Shower* are now museum pieces, and the dead dogs and offal of our own day will follow in their wake. For mere distance in time is apt to tinge with romance the prosaic and the severe alike.

This prolonged conflict of desire and ideal between the classic and the romantic, though it may lull at times and change its field and even its ensigns, shows no signs of abating. Of late, indeed, the fray has been passionately renewed. But though, as Mr. Laurie Magnus quotes from Walter Pater, 'to discriminate schools of art, of literature, is, of course, part of the obvious business of literary criticism, the legitimate contention is, not of one age or school of literary art against another, but of all successive schools alike, against the stupidity which is dead to the substance, and the vulgarity which is dead to form'.

There are eyes and ears, it is true, that remain romance-blind and romance-deaf; but the test at least is an easy one. Open *English and Scottish Popular Ballads* at random, and if merely the first stanza of the ballad that shows itself sounds no decoy, then romance is spreading its nets in vain:

> Fair Marjorie sat i her bower-door,
>   Sewin her silken seam,
> When by then cam her false true-love,
>   Gard a' his bridles ring. . . .

> In summer time, when leaves grew green,
>   and birds were singing on every tree,
> King Edward would a hunting ride,
>   some pastime for to see. . . .

> Both gentlemen, or yoemen bould,
>   Or whatsoever you are,
> To have a stately story tould,
>   Attention now prepare. . . .

Nor can you ever be quite certain, even when browsing on the severely practical pages of a journal or a volume devoted to scientific discovery, that at any moment you may not stumble on such a fragment of romance as might suffice the born story-teller for the writing of a book. This, for example, from the *Journal of the Voyage of H.M.S. Beagle*:

75

One day we accompanied a party of the Spaniards in their whale-boat to a salina, or lake [on James Island] from which salt is procured. After landing, we had a very rough walk over a rugged field of recent lava, which has almost surrounded a tuff-crater, at the bottom of which the salt-lake lies. The water is only three or four inches deep, and rests on a layer of beautifully crystallized, white salt. The lake is quite circular, and is fringed with a border of bright green succulent plants; the almost precipitous walls of the crater are clothed with wood, so that the scene was altogether both picturesque and curious. A few years since, the sailors belonging to a sealing-vessel murdered their captain in this quiet spot; and we saw his skull lying among the bushes.

But while specimens of the romantic are easy to find, it is more difficult to define the term than to be certain for one's own personal purposes of the finer shades and degrees of what it means. The most trivial tests may be the clearest. It might perhaps be generally agreed, for instance, that as regards the four orders connected with horse-racing—owner, trainer, jockey, stable-boy—the romantic 'appeal' is precisely in the reverse order, unless stable-boy and jockey run a dead heat. A barber in this respect excels a hairdresser, a poacher a M.F.H., a cat's-meat-man a butcher, a chimney-sweep (though only just) a lamplighter, an inn-keeper any hotel proprietor, a marquis a duke, a baronet a baron, and any chamber-maid almost any head-waiter, however profuse the gratuities he extorts.

Palace, castle, manor-house, mansion, grange, villa, parsonage, farm-house, cottage, hovel, cave—which of these in the eye of fancy is the most romantic habitation? Thief, robber, highwayman, footpad, pirate, buccaneer, housebreaker, burglar, smuggler, bushranger, brigand—which is the most romantic calling? Prejudice apart, tastes differ. The dark Adonis in some eyes may be excelled by the fair, more rarely the Helen blonde by the Helen brunette. And of what complexion was Apollo? Of all meals supper is most hospitable to the romantic, while, in spite of the lure of the *alfresco*, a picnic *may* prove to be the least. Of all garbs a nun's and a widow's; but not so with man, with whom that of bridegroom and of widower contend for last place. And why is it that one's future promises to be less productive of romance than, even in the most prosaic of existences, a survey of one's past would seem to warrant?

Page 7¹—A . . . fall from high estate:
¶ In *Gifts of Fortune* Mr. H. M. Tomlinson describes a rajah he saw in Ceylon. He was sitting in a railway station.

He was an old man, but as stout as my English fellow-traveller. He wore a yellow sarong, and yellow is the royal colour. But his tunic was the old scarlet affair, with yellow facings, of an English infantry-man. Instead of the hat of a Mohammedan, he wore a white regimental helmet. He had a blue sash. On his breast were displayed a number of ornate decorations, brass regimental badges, and medals won by other people in the past for the most diverse things—for swimming at Plymouth and running at Stamford Bridge. And central on his breast, hanging by a cord, was a conspicuous red reflector from the rear lamp of a bicycle.

He too wears the livery of romance—turned inside out.

Page 10¹—Romance:
¶ 'Like the cuckoo she buildeth her nest most often in the sallows. In the spring time she cometh abroad and or ere the Dog-days arise she is gone and hidden.'

Page 10²—The romance enshrined in the Old Testament :
¶ It is not too precise a word to use in this connection even if it be given the best that it can mean. Never there by set intention or for its own sake, it is an emanation; and the difficulty is to choose from such abundance passages that most nobly, simply, starkly or tragically enshrine it:

And three of the thirty chief went down, and came to David in the harvest time unto the cave of Adullam: and the troop of the Philis-tines pitched in the valley of Rephaim. And David was then in an hold, and the garrison of the Philistines was then in Beth-lehem. And David longed, and said, Oh that one would give me drink of the water of the well of Beth-lehem, which is by the gate! And the three mighty men brake through the host of the Philistines, and drew water out of the well of Beth-lehem, that was by the gate, and took it, and brought it to David: nevertheless he would not drink thereof, but poured it out unto the Lord. And he said, Be it far from me, O Lord, that I should do this: is not this the blood of the men that went in jeopardy of their lives? Therefore he would not drink it. These things did these three mighty men. *2 Sam. xxiii. 13.*

And Gideon said unto God, If thou wilt save Israel by mine hand, as thou hast said, Behold, I will put a fleece of wool in the floor; and if the dew be on the fleece only, and it be dry upon all the earth beside, then shall I know that thou wilt save Israel by mine hand, as thou hast said.

And it was so: for he rose up early on the morrow, and thrust the fleece together, and wringed the dew out of the fleece, a bowl full of water.

And Gideon said unto God, Let not thine anger be hot against me, and I will speak but this once: let me prove, I pray thee, but this once with the fleece; let it now be dry only upon the fleece, and upon all the ground let there be dew.

And God did so that night: for it was dry upon the fleece only, and there was dew on all the ground.   *Judges vi. 36.*

Then went Abimelech to Thebez, and encamped against Thebez, and took it. But there was a strong tower within the city, and thither fled all the men and women, and all they of the city, and shut it to them, and gat them up to the top of the tower. And Abimelech came unto the tower, and fought against it, and went hard unto the door of the tower to burn it with fire.

And a certain woman cast a piece of a millstone upon Abimelech's head, and all to brake his scull. Then he called hastily unto the young man his armourbearer, and said unto him, Draw thy sword, and slay me, that men say not of me, A woman slew him. And his young man thrust him through, and he died.   *Judges ix. 50.*

And it came to pass after this, that Absalom the son of David had a fair sister, whose name was Tamar; and Amnon the son of David loved her. And Amnon was so vexed, that he fell sick for his sister Tamar; for she was a virgin; and Amnon thought it hard for him to do any thing to her.

But Amnon had a friend, whose name was Jonadab, the son of Shimeah David's brother: and Jonadab was a very subtil man. And he said unto him, Why art thou, being the king's son, lean from day to day? wilt thou not tell me? And Amnon said unto him, I love Tamar, my brother Absalom's sister.

And Jonadab said unto him, Lay thee down on thy bed, and make thyself sick: and when thy father cometh to see thee, say unto him, I pray thee, let my sister Tamar come, and give me meat, and dress the meat in my sight, that I may see it, and eat it at her hand.

So Amnon lay down, and made himself sick: and when the king was come to see him, Amnon said unto the king, I pray thee, let Tamar my sister come, and make me a couple of cakes in my sight, that I may eat at her hand. Then David sent home to Tamar, saying, Go now to thy brother Amnon's house, and dress him meat.

So Tamar went to her brother Amnon's house; and he was laid down. And she took flour, and kneaded it, and made cakes in his sight, and did bake the cakes. And she took a pan, and poured them out before him; but he refused to eat. And Amnon said, Have out all men from me. And they went out every man from him.

And Amnon said unto Tamar, Bring the meat into the chamber, that I may eat of thine hand. And Tamar took the cakes which she had made, and brought them into the chamber to Amnon her brother. And when she had brought them unto him to eat, he took hold of her, and said unto her, Come lie with me, my sister. And she answered him, Nay, my brother, do not force me; for no such thing ought to be done in Israel: do not thou this folly. And I, whither shall I cause my shame to go? and as for thee, thou shalt be as one of the fools in Israel. Now therefore, I pray thee, speak unto the king; for he will not withhold me from thee.

Howbeit he would not hearken unto her voice: but, being stronger than she, forced her, and lay with her. Then Amnon hated her exceedingly; so that the hatred wherewith he hated her was greater than the love wherewith he had loved her. And Amnon said unto her, Arise, be gone. And she said unto him, There is no cause: this evil in sending me away is greater than the other that thou didst unto me. But he would not hearken unto her.

Then he called his servant that ministered unto him, and said, Put now this woman out from me, and bolt the door after her. And she had a garment of divers colours upon her: for with such robes were the king's daughters that were virgins apparelled. Then his servant brought her out, and bolted the door after her.

And Tamar put ashes on her head, and rent her garment of divers colours that was on her, and laid her hand on her head and went on crying.   *2 Sam. xiii.*

There Tamar's own brief tragic story ends, though not that crying. But time goes on; nothing is stayed; Absalom treacherously revenges himself upon Amnon; Joab thrusts his three darts through the heart of Absalom hanging helpless by his hair 'between the heaven and the

79

earth' in 'the thick boughs of a great oak'; and David at last in the solitude of the chamber over the gate laments his son, and Bath-sheba's—weeping and mourning. Not one overt word of horror or of warning or of admonishment, only the bare clear record; but beyond it the poising of scales so delicate and so sure that the secrets of every heart are revealed and the judgement never in doubt.

Page 11¹—¶ That bubble:

> A narrow roome our glory vaine unties,
> A little circle doth our pride containe.
> Earth like an Ile amid the water lies. . . .

Page 11²—Mu in Leo:

¶ 'We will swoop outward into the starry meadows beyond Orion, where for Pansies and Violets, and Heartsease, are the nets of the triplicate and triple-tinted suns.'

> He knows he hath a home, but scarce knows where:
> He says it is so far
> That he hath quite forgot how to go there. . . .

Page 11³—¶ The . . . fellowship of unhumanized beast and bird:

. . . In Charles Island [says Darwin in his *Voyage*] which had then (1835) been colonized about six years, I saw a boy sitting by a well with a switch in his hand, with which he killed the doves and finches as they came to drink. He had already procured a little heap of them for his dinner; and he said that he had constantly been in the habit of waiting by this well for the same purpose. It would appear that the birds of this archipelago, not having as yet learnt that man is a more dangerous animal than the tortoise or the Amblyrhynchus, disregard him, in the same manner as in England shy birds, such as magpies, disregard the cows and horses grazing in our fields. . . . In the Falklands, the sportsman may sometimes kill more of the upland geese in one day than he can carry home; whereas in Tierra del Fuego, it is nearly as difficult to kill one, as it is in England to shoot the common wild goose.

In the time of Pernety [a priest who accompanied Bougainville on his voyage round the world in 1766-9, and afterwards became a disciple of Swedenborg], all the birds there appear to have been much tamer than at present; he states that [that little 'dusky-coloured bird'] the *Opetiorhynchus Patagonicus* would almost perch on his finger; and that with a wand he killed ten in half an hour. At that period the birds must have been about as tame as they now are at the Galápagos. . . .

From these several facts [and Darwin mentions many], we may, I think conclude, first, that the wildness of birds with regard to man, is a particular instinct directed against *him*, and not dependent on any general degree of caution arising from other sources of danger; secondly, that it is not acquired by individual birds in a short time, even when much persecuted; but that in the course of successive generations it becomes hereditary. . . . We may infer from these facts, what havoc the introduction of any new beast of prey must cause in a country, before the instincts of the indigenous inhabitants have become adapted to the stranger's craft or power.

As for the 'new beast of prey', it is usually man. Dr. William Beebe, in his account of an expedition to the Galápagos Islands in 1923, from which he returned with, among much else, 160 bird skins, 150 reptiles, 200 fishes and 3,000 insects, bears similar testimony.

This particular little group of 'about sixty islands and islets' has been sporadically written about since 1592, yet though, Dr. Beebe tells us, the smaller ones ('mere specks on the largest charts') were scenes of infinite variety, even earlier expeditions which had spent a whole year in their neighbourhood had failed to penetrate to the central craters of the larger. In consequence, 'ever since the time of the first voyagers to the archipelago', 'the extreme tameness of all birds except the migratory species has been remarked, and most human observers have celebrated this fearlessness by knocking as many as possible on the head'.

And always with what most of them would regard as defensible intentions—in high spirits, for sport, for dead zoos, as a small boy described a natural-history museum, and for food. Some in order 'to deck a woman' and at the same time put money in the purse. With this end in view that most courageous of minute fighters, the mole, helps. It takes only 300 moles to make a fashionable coat. To this end mink, badger, opossum, martin, ermine, fox, sable eagerly surrender their pretty skins by scores of thousands *per annum*, and the gentle intelligent seal by the hundred thousand. The seal, if fortunate, does not always even wait to be born for this purpose, since,

81

like that of the lambs of Astrakhan, its foetal skin is so much daintier to feminine sight and touch. Nor does it always wait to die, since it is easier, in its wild Northern frozen wastes, to skin it alive and be helped by its wrigglings than to wait for it to be dead when it cannot help at all.

> There's mercy in every place,
> And mercy, encouraging thought!
> Gives even affliction a grace
> And reconciles man to his lot.

Page 12¹—The miser:

❡ As, for example, William Jennings, who was not only a miser, but the friend of a miser more famous than himself, John Elwes of Meggott. He on his part inherited a fortune from an uncle, Sir Harvey Elwes, who was also a famous miser, while his mother, 'though she was left nearly one hundred thousand pounds by her husband—a brewer—is said to have starved herself to death'.

He was born in the year 1701, and his father died when he was on the point of completing a most sumptuous and magnificent country-seat, which, for the grandeur of its hall, and the massive elegance of its marble chimney-pieces, as well as the beauty and extent of its stables and other offices, is totally unrivalled in that part of the country, and is excelled in few others. The staircase, however, and one entire wing of the house, which was to have been principally devoted to a vast and superb ballroom, were left totally incomplete; and notwithstanding the son, when he attained his majority, found himself possessed, in real and personal estate, of not less than 200,000*l*, he never added another stroke to the unfinished structure, which remained in precisely the same state in which it was left on the decease of its more worthy projector.

In this extensive palace, for it scarcely deserves a meaner appellation, Mr. Jennings resided, when in the country, to the latest hour of his life—yet not in the finished and furnished apartments, but merely in the basement floor alone, which, by being not less than ten or fifteen feet below the surface of the court, and illuminated by small and heavy windows, admitted but very seldom the reviving rays of the sun in any direction. Here, on a level with most of the offices of this superb pile of building, in the midst of his servants, was his breakfast-room, his dining-room, and his bed-chamber, the entire furniture of which was of his own procuring, and consequently very mean, and its whole value, perhaps, did not exceed twenty pounds; nor were the rooms above (excepting those in the wing already described), although completely finished and magnificently furnished by his father, ever opened but once during the whole period of his possessing them, which extended to nearly a century.

He had, nevertheless, more family pride than Mr. Elwes, and maintained a table in some degree superior. In this dark and miserable compartment of the house his dinner was always served up, even when he was alone (and he was seldom otherwise), in the family plate: nor, if any portion remained after the wants of his diminutive household had been satisfied, would he suffer it to be again introduced to assist in the dinner of the ensuing day. The poor, however, were never benefited by this profusion of diet; for it was his express order, and an order uniformly adhered to, that the surplus should be distributed among his dogs. He was never known, throughout the whole period of his life, to exhibit one single charitable action: and so cold and unsocial was his animal constitution, that a male friend was scarcely ever invited to sleep beneath his roof, and there is no instance of a female of any description having been indebted to him for the hospitality of a single night.

In these respects he was a character infinitely more despicable than his neighbour, who at all times evinced the utmost degree of politeness and gallantry to the fair sex; and who, if he withheld his hand from the needy, withheld it in an equal degree from himself. In his mode of increasing his property, Mr. Jennings was also a more contemptible miser. Elwes, when in London, occasionally frequented the gaming-table, but it was to participate with his associates in the various chances of the dice. [He once played two days and a night without intermission, and the room being small, the party, one of whom was the Duke of Northumberland, were nearly up to the knees in cards.] Jennings, too, frequented the gaming-table, and was, in reality, at one period of his life, an habitual attendant at Brookes's or White's: but it was not to partake in the multiplied fortunes of gambling, but to accommodate the unlucky with money for the evening, and to draw an enormous profit from the general loss. It is asserted that for every thousand pounds he thus advanced, he received the next morning a thousand guineas. To enable him to persevere steadily in this profitable concern, he ventured to purchase a house in Grosvenor Square, where, indeed, he occasionally resided to the day of his death, and long after the infirmities of age compelled him to relinquish his dishonourable traffic.

On quitting either his town or country-house, he was accustomed to draw up, with his own hand, an inventory of articles left behind, even to the minutest and most insignificant; and to examine them with the most rigid scrutiny on his return, to satisfy himself that he had not been wronged of his property. The arrangement of this catalogue, when he was quitting the country, was attended with no small degree of labour; for, according to the fashion of our forefathers, almost all the chimney-pieces throughout the house had been left to him furnished with an infinite variety of pieces of china, small as well as large. Every little dog and duck, however, every tea-cup, ewer, and other toy, was duly noticed, and expected to be found, on his return, not only uninjured, but accurately occupying its immediate post.

Page 13¹—A criminal:

¶ On Friday, December 2nd, 1831, three men, John Bishop, James May and Thomas Williams, were 'placed at the bar of the Old Bailey to take their trial upon the charge of murder preferred against them'. The court was crowded to excess at eight o'clock in the morning. The jury retired twelve hours afterwards and returned into court after half an hour's absence.

The most death-like silence now prevailed throughout the court, interrupted only by a slight buzz on the re-introduction of the prisoners.

Every eye was fixed upon them; but though their appearance and manner had undergone a considerable change since their being first placed at the bar, they did not seem conscious of the additional interest which their presence at this moment excited.

Bishop advanced to the bar with a heavy step, and with a slight bend of the body; his arms hung closely down, and it seemed a kind of relief to him, when he took his place, to rest his hand on the board before him. His appearance, when he got in front, was that of a man who had been for some time labouring under the most intense mental agony, which had brought on a kind of lethargic stupor. His eyes were sunk and glassy; his nose drawn and pinched; the jaw fallen, and the mouth open; but occasionally the mouth closed, the lips became compressed, and the shoulders and chest raised, as if he were struggling to repress some violent emotion. After a few efforts of this kind, he became apparently calm, and frequently glanced his eyes towards the bench and the jury-box; but this was done without once raising his head. His face had that pallid appearance which so often accompanies and betokens great mental suffering.

Williams came forward with a short quick step; and his whole manner was the reverse of that of his companion in guilt. His face had undergone very little change; but in his eyes and in his manner there was a feverish anxiety, which was not to be observed during the trial. When he came in front, and laid his hand on the bar, the rapid movement of his fingers on the board—the frequent shifting of the hand, sometimes letting it hang down for an instant by his side, then replacing it on the board, and then resting his side against the front of the dock, showed the perturbed state of his feelings. Once or twice he gave a glance round the bench and the bar, but after that he seldom took his eye from the jury-box.

May came forward with a more firm gait than either of his fellow-prisoners; but his look was that of a man who thought that all chance of life was lost. He seemed desponding; but there appeared that in his despondency which gave an air of—we could not call it daring, or even confidence—we should rather say, a physical power of endurance, which imparted to his whole manner a more firm bearing than that of the other prisoners. He was very pale, but his eye had not relaxed from that firmness which was observable in his glance throughout the whole of the trial.

Ordinary physiognomists, who (without having seen the prisoners) had read the accounts of their examinations at the police-office—of their habits and mode of living, and the horrible atrocities with which there is now no doubt they were familiar—would have been greatly disappointed in the appearance of all of them as they stood at the bar. There was nothing in the aspect or manner of any of them which betokened a predisposition to anything like the outrage on humanity of which they stood convicted. There was something of heaviness in the aspect of Bishop, but altogether his countenance was mild. Williams had that kind of expression with which men associate the idea of sharpness and cunning, and something of mischief, but nothing of the villain. May, who was the best-looking of the three, had a countenance which most persons would consider open and manly. There was an air of firmness and determination about him; but neither in him nor his companions was there the slightest physiognomical trait of a murderer, according to the common notions on the subject.

The sentence on May, who was a 'tall, light-haired and rather good-looking man, about thirty years of age, and who was the natural son of a barrister', was afterwards commuted to transportation for life. When he was told that its 'execution . . . had been respited during His Majesty's most gracious pleasure . . . the poor wretch fell to the earth as if struck by lightning. . . . All persons present thought he could not possibly survive—it was believed that the warrant for mercy had proved his death blow'. May himself asserted that he was innocent of any share in the murders which the other two prisoners had confessed to—murders committed with a view to obtaining 'subjects' for dissection in the hospitals, at eight to ten guineas apiece. But he admitted that after taking up the trade of a body-snatcher and lodging for that purpose in one of the houses in Clement's Lane, Strand, the back of which looked into the burying-ground in Portugal Street, he had been 'very successful', that he had made no secret of his profession and 'considered it meritorious'. His 'very successful' was no exaggeration. In this brief career he had disposed of between five hundred and a thousand bodies.

Every detail is appalling, but not more appalling than the fact that less than a century ago (Burke was executed on the 28th January, 1830) May's trade, though nocturnal, was notorious; and while the stealing of a dead man's shroud was a felony punishable with transportation, to rob his coffin of his body was only a misdemeanour. So hungry were the anatomists that watch-towers and spring guns in the graveyards were not proof against their tools. When dawned the last morning of 'these wretched and atrocious criminals', Taylor and Bishop, the old Bailey, from one end of it to the other, was a dense mass of spectators. A crowd that at one o'clock in the dark of the small hours numbered many thousands had swollen to a mob of thirty thousand at eight. At sight of the hangman's procession 'a general cry of "Hats Off!" took place, and in an instant the immense multitude were all uncovered'. But it is not stated whether this was an act of courtesy or only in order to ensure young and old of either sex as good a view as possible. 'The appearance of Bishop was the signal for the most tremendous groans, yells and hootings from all parts of the crowd. . . . Williams next ascended the scaffold, on reaching which he bowed to the crowd, who returned his salutation with the most dreadful yells and groans. . . . The moment the drop fell, the crowd, which had been yelling all the time, set up a shout of exultation that was prolonged for several minutes'.

It is difficult to share *that* solitude. Or John Amy Bird's. 'Our readers will be astonished,' runs Camden Pelham's account of him, 'when they learn that this wretched malefactor at the time of his execution had attained the age of fourteen years only.' Only eight thousand persons were present at 11.30 a.m. on August 1, 1831, when he came on to the scaffold. He 'gazed steadily around him; but his eye did not quail, nor was his cheek blanched. After the rope was adjusted round his neck, he exclaimed in a firm and loud tone of voice, "Lord, have mercy upon us! Pray, good Lord, have mercy upon us! Lord, have mercy upon us! All the people before me, take warning by me!"'.

So rapid at this time was the progress of humanity in the humane that 'in 1810 a bill actually passed the House of Commons to take away the punishment of death from the offence of privately stealing in a shop to the value of 5s.'. On the second reading of this Bill in the House of Lords, however, Lord Ellenborough, then Chief Justice, moved its rejection. 'My Lords,' he said, 'if we suffer this bill to pass, we shall not know whether we are on our heads or our feet.' And he spoke 'to an approving Senate, and in the name of an unanimous Bench'!

And here, for companion piece to the vision of John Amy Bird on Newgate gibbet, and one that may take a little of the taste of iron out of one's mouth, is the picture of *this* serene immortal creature, though one of no less deep a dye, from Montaigne's *Diary* of 1580-1; he was in Rome:

On Palm-Sunday, at vespers, I saw in a church a boy sitting on a chair by the side of the altar, dressed in a large new gown of blue taffeta, bareheaded, with a crown of olive-branches, holding in his hand a lighted white wax torch. He was a boy of fifteen or thereabouts, who, by the Pope's order, had been liberated from the prison on that day: he had killed another boy.

Malefactors of fourteen are not publicly hanged nowadays. Yet there are things we take for granted that may seem equally atrocious a century hence. Body-snatching, too, appears to be a trade of the past. Indeed, since the supply of home-born subjects for dissection is inadequate, we import from France.

87

Page 13²—Drugged:

⁊ 'Some people', says De Quincey, 'have mentioned, in my hearing, that they have been drunk on green tea; and a medical student in London, for whose knowledge in the profession I have reason to feel great respect, assured me, the other day, that a patient, in recovering from an illness, had got drunk on a beef-steak'. And no less a poet than Dryden is said to have eaten raw meat for the sake of the splendid dreams it evokes. Even mere physical fatigue or want of food may have an influence like that of alcohol on the mind; so may a heady moment of success, a stroke of good luck or an overdose of vanity. And whatever the means may be, even the mildest degree of intoxication is slightly isolating to the owner of the head so affected.

A scarcely perceptible rift between the past and the present begins to appear, a slight haze spreads over the face of actuality; and the wine that makes glad the heart of man, loosens his tongue, whets his courage and may improve his company, will in due course clean cut him off for its while from his fellows and hem him in with varying kinds and degrees of solitude. What curious veils descend over the self that then so intently looks out of the eyes. One small dose of heroin will induce, I am told, a mood of 'supreme superiority'; one (or, rather, the first,) of morphia a sensuous melting mood, all forgiveness and damask roses; while, yet, a common dose of 'medinal' once cast me into a dream the horror and agony of which no words could possibly relate.

But this is a far cry from De Quincey's three-weekly *'glass of laudanum negus, warm, and without sugar'*, which, waking or sleeping, unquestionably isolated *him*, and by its Circean spells induced the bizarre dreams he tells of. The effects, he says, were these:

1. As the creative state of the eye increased, a sympathy seemed to arise between the waking and the dreaming states of the brain in one point—that whatsoever I happened to call up and to trace by a voluntary act upon the darkness was very apt to transfer itself to my dreams; so that I feared to exercise this faculty; for, as Midas turned

88

all things to gold, that yet baffled his hopes and defrauded his human desires, so whatsoever things capable of being visually represented I did but think of in the darkness, immediately shaped themselves into phantoms of the eye; and, by a process apparently no less inevitable, when thus once traced in faint and visionary colours, like writings in sympathetic ink, they were drawn out by the fierce chemistry of my dreams, into insufferable splendour that fretted my heart.

2. For this, and all other changes in my dreams, were accompanied by deep-seated anxiety and gloomy melancholy, such as are wholly incommunicable by words. I seemed every night to descend, not metaphorically, but literally to descend, into chasms and sunless abysses, depths below depths, from which it seemed hopeless that I could ever reascend. Nor did I, by waking, feel that I *had* reascended. This I do not dwell upon; because the state of gloom which attended these gorgeous spectacles, amounting at last to utter darkness, as of some suicidal despondency, cannot be approached by words.

3. The sense of space, and in the end, the sense of time, were both powerfully affected. Buildings, landscapes, &c., were exhibited in proportions so vast as the bodily eye is not fitted to receive. Space swelled, and was amplified to an extent of unutterable infinity. This, however, did not disturb me so much as the vast expansion of time; I sometimes seemed to have lived for 70 or 100 years in one night; nay, sometimes had feelings representative . . . of a duration far beyond the limits of any human experience.

4. The minutest incidents of childhood, or forgotten scenes of later years, were often revived; I could not be said to recollect them; for if I had been told of them when waking, I should not have been able to acknowledge them as parts of my past experience. But placed as they were before me, in dreams like intuitions, and clothed in all their evanescent circumstances and accompanying feelings, I *recognized* them instantaneously. I was once told by a near relative of mine, that having in her childhood fallen into a river, and being on the very verge of death but for the critical assistance which reached her, she saw in a moment her whole life, in its minutest incidents, arrayed before her simultaneously as in a mirror; and she had a faculty developed as suddenly for comprehending the whole and every part. This, from some opium experience of mine, I can believe; I have, indeed, seen the same thing asserted twice in modern books, and accompanied by a remark which I am convinced is true; *viz.* that the dread book of account, which the Scriptures speak of, is, in fact, the mind itself of each individual. Of this, at least, I feel assured, that there is no such thing as *forgetting* possible to the mind; a thousand accidents may, and will interpose a veil between our present consciousness and the secret inscriptions on the mind; accidents of the same sort will also rend away this veil; but alike,

whether veiled or unveiled, the inscription remains for ever; just as the stars seem to withdraw before the common light of day, whereas, in fact, we all know that it is the light which is drawn over them as a veil. . . .

The text quoted is that of the earlier edition of the *Confessions*. In the later, with a few other and unimportant corrections, it is interesting to observe that De Quincey takes out the words in the first paragraph, 'so that I feared to exercise this faculty'. In a long footnote, too, he relates that the near relative to whom he refers in the last paragraph was a child of nine when she fell into the river, and that at ninety-nine she would still recount every moment of that tiny infinitude of time as vividly as ever.

Is it Circe herself that gives De Quincey's prose, so lucid, leisurely and urbane, its faintly menacing tone, and—though less here than usual—the effect of being supercharged with some self that is never precisely articulate? And was he aware of Coleridge's shadow at his shoulder when he wrote the words, 'chasms and sunless abysses'?—a decoy that as instantly brings *Kubla Khan* to mind as it does the enchanted ravine of *The Domain of Arnheim* and *The City in the Sea*, which came after. When literary origins thus take the form of an invocation, the enquiry becomes less dusty. Was it, too, because Poe also had fed on honey-dew that abnormal solitude was for him so frequent a theme?

'The realities of the world affected me as visions,' says Egaeus, in *Berenice*, 'and as visions only, while wild ideas of the land of dreams became, in turn, not the material of my every-day existence, but in very deed that existence utterly and solely in itself'.

And was it his absorption in such wild ideas as these in that strange mind of his, otherwise abnormally wide awake, that accounts for the fact that 'he liked the night better than the day' and that 'his love of the darkness amounted to a passion'?

Hashish is a drug less familiar in its effects than opium. Like opium, it induces an extravagant sense of isolation —which, strangely enough, even to those who have no experience of it, may be to a very great extent communicable in words. The following record of his experiences under its influence has been given to me by my friend, Mr. J. Redwood Anderson. Whether or not hashish —a word to which we are indebted for our English *assassin*—ever has a comparable effect on a mind less intent and imaginative than that of the author of *Babel* and *Vortex*, I cannot say.

A Note on Cannabis Indica: The form of Cannabis Indica that I used in my experiments, or adventures, was the ordinary Extract. This was made up into pills of one grain and of half a grain. My first experiment was a complete failure. I began with a dose of half a grain and at the end of an hour, during which nothing happened, I took another half-grain. This, too, was without result. A few days later I tried again. I began with one grain, and took one half-grain each successive half-hour until an effect was produced. I took altogether three and a half grains before I experienced anything unusual.

That first successful experiment was one of the most terrible experiences that I can remember. The first effect—and this remained true of every subsequent occasion—was the alteration in time-values. Time was so immensely lengthened out that it practically ceased to exist. The nearest analogue to what I felt is found perhaps in the slow-motion picture; only the slowing-down was a hundred times as great. But this slowing-down applied only to physical events: my own movements, for instance, and those of other people; it did not apply to the processes of thought. These, on the contrary, appeared to be very greatly accelerated. When it is remembered that my actual movements, as witnessed by another, were *above* the normal speed in execution—*feverishly* performed—it will be grasped to what extent the actual speed of thinking was accelerated. I thought with a rapidity comparable to that of dreaming, but with an acuteness and logical sequence very rarely experienced in dreams.

Cannabis is credited with producing a double personality: the only doubling that I ever experienced was a doubling of my own identical activities. I seemed to be conscious in two registers simultaneously—a purely mental register and a physical one—and much of the distress of these experiences, and nearly all the difficulty in describing them while still under the action of the drug, was due to the very great discrepancy in time between the two registers. It was as if the mind was intensely active in its own domain—extra-cerebrally—and met a very heavy resistance when it came to translate its thought into audible words, or its acts of will into physical actions. As an example I may take the experience of writing under the drug. The whole sentence came quickly and clearly into my mind—much as it would under favourable normal conditions—but by the time I had written the first word (and remember I wrote actually quickly) the whole sentence had slipped away into a past as remote as ancient Assyria, and a thousand subsequent thoughts had followed it. It cost me a severe effort to recall what the second word of the original sentence had been in order to write it down in its turn, and when it, too, was written, I found once more that the original sentence had dived back into a still remoter past. It has occurred to me that the dissociation might have been between that part of the brain which is connected with thinking and that part which directly controls movement.

Another typical example is the following: I desired to get up and open the door. This desire formulated itself in my mind in a perfectly ordinary manner. About fifty years later, as it seemed, I found myself in the middle of the room and had considerable difficulty in recalling why I was there and what I had set out to do. Again a long period of *otherness*, and I found my hand on the knob of the door: vaguely remembering how, long ago, I had made up my mind to open the door—and so on. The *actual* getting up, crossing the room and opening the door was accomplished in under the normal time for these actions; but I felt all through a great weight in my limbs and found all movement difficult and irksome. This splitting of consciousness and duplicating of the 'planes' of experience was, in some degree, characteristic of all my subsequent experiments.

On this first occasion very little else struck me; I saw no 'visions' and experienced nothing unusual in the working of the senses. After aeons of time (some four hours by the clock) I began to come round —and at this point the horror sets in. With a dreadful shock I found that my heart had stopped beating! I felt one beat and waited in terror for the next: *it never came!* Consequently, *I was dead!* I had taken an over-dose of the drug and this was the result. I will not attempt to describe my sensations. With intermissions, during which the original effects of the drug mercifully returned, this state lasted for a hundred years—it had a recurrent, timeless feeling about it, analogous to that experienced under Nitrous Oxygen, which was inexpressibly awful.

At last, however—when I felt the next heart-beat—this state passed (it was, as a matter of outward fact, of but an instant's duration) and was succeeded by a much more prolonged and scarcely less awful condition. I was alive right enough; but—I was mad! I had for ever cut myself off from the clean, sweet, ordinary things of life, from the world and the folk around me. I would have given anything to undo the past. My remorse cannot well be described. Never since the beginning of time had there been such a fool as I! But this, too, passed in time and I came to myself—not all at once, but at increasingly frequent intervals and for increasingly long periods—rather tired, a little dazed, very sick with myself, but otherwise none the worse. By the following day I was quite normal, and the only marked effect of my recent adventure was the determination never to touch the damned stuff again. And this, too, passed! . . .

The specific types of experience under Cannabis fell, in my case, under these two heads—intellectual and sensuous. Most noticeable of the sensuous kind was the seeing of sound and the hearing of colour. I ought to say that these 'faculties' are in some degree normal to me and that the drug only intensified them. I have listened to Tchaikowsky's Fifth Symphony over the wireless, when in a perfectly awake condition, and seen against the screen of my closed eyes the whole thing deploy itself in form and colour, every theme and every instrument translating itself into some definite shape or series of shapes and into definite colours, sharp or confused, fine-outlined or massive. Under Cannabis this was so greatly intensified that I ceased to be conscious of hearing anything at all. My most vivid recollection of this was hearing a friend play Debussy's 'La Lune descend sur le Temple qui fut'. I heard nothing after the first few bars, but I lived for many years in a strange dream-land (modelled in part on memories of Egypt) in which the moon, for ever setting, never actually set—and all this in steady three-dimensional form and brilliant colouring. Even if I only imagined a Fugue of Bach's I saw every entry of the subject as a recurrence of the same pattern, the inverted subject showing as an inverted pattern. The patterns and colours, moreover, were always appropriate to, or symbolic of, the music. Conversely, a red book on a green cloth sounded like a keen piercing note against a softer background of sound, while a sunset appeared as an indescribably beautiful 'poème symphonique'.

Another common feature of these conditions was the vertical elongation of natural objects—this same elongation is seen well in Aubrey Beardsley's work, and has once or twice been produced in my own case by opium in place of Cannabis. With this went a curious heightening of the sense of beauty, due largely to a lowering of the critical faculty: a perfectly ordinary poplar (if there is such a thing?) looked like one of the trees of Paradise, and a woman of merely 'homely' countenance a person of unearthly loveliness.

A third minor sensuous effect was a stimulation of the sense of the ridiculous—or perhaps this should be classed in part at least under the 'intellectual' effects. Things mildly humorous in themselves, or even quite devoid of humour, or sense, seen with the cold light of reason, were sufficient to intoxicate me with Homeric mirth. No one who has not laughed either under the effect of Cannabis or in his dreams can know what real laughter is. This laughter was the most exhausting of all my experiences while under the action of the drug, and the only one which gave the show away to an observer.

93

But more interesting than any of the above were the 'intellectual' experiences. Three instances must suffice; but I am convinced now, as I was at the time, that an analysis of these and of similar experiences might be made of very great value in the study of the mind's action.

The first instance is as follows. When I was a boy, between the ages of seven or eight and of eleven, I had a series of very curious dreams. I say a series, for, though the same dream never occurred twice, the same scenes and people did occur in all. Some features of these dreams were very strange, and to this day I can think of no 'orthodox' explanation of them. In these dreams I was not a boy, but a grown man; I spoke and thought a language which was neither English, French nor German, the only languages I knew, but some tongue I have never been able to identify—though I have a strong suspicion that I have identified its script, utterly unknown to me at any time. In the dreams I knew not one word of English. Further, I had no knowledge of any person, place or event with which I was actually acquainted in 'real' life. I had different parents and different friends—all, like myself, of dark complexion and dressed in un-European clothes. The locus of the dreams was always the same region, but by no means the same part of that region. It was a country of very high, sharp, and almost snowless mountains, of terribly desolate, stony valleys, of elevated and wind-swept plateaux. Somewhere in the midst of these mountains was a city, towards which I was frequently journeying on foot, but which I never remembered to have reached. The landscape was absolutely consistent, and as fixed and material as the landscape of the Lake District: it had none of the blurred edges or suddenly shifting outlines so common to dream landscapes.

At the time of my experiments with Cannabis (twenty-six to twenty-eight years of age) these dreams had faded into mere nothings; but, on one occasion, when I was under the influence of the drug, the whole series came back to me with intense vividness—*with many other recollected incidents belonging to the same life but not belonging to any of the dreams.* I did not recall these things as things I had dreamed, but as places and persons whom I had known—I remembered having been the dream-person, not having dreamed about him. It was then that the peculiar script of the dream-language came clearly again before me and that I *recognized* it. It is a genuine human script and no mere dream-invention; but it is a script and a language of which neither I nor anyone with whom I have ever spoken has the faintest knowledge. When I saw it again under the drug it had become to me also a foreign and unknown tongue, though in the dream-series it had been my mother tongue. If I believed in reincarnation, and at times I am more than tempted to, I could hazard an explanation;

94

as it is I cannot even guess at it—not even with the help of Freud and his kind.

The second instance of the intellectual operation of Cannabis is still more remarkable, and it was a fairly normal thing, not, like the first instance, a unique occurrence. It consisted in a great heightening of the imaginative faculty—or rather of a new kind of abstract imagination. You know how you can 'see' that two and two make four? Well, under the drug, I could 'see' in the same way the truth of certain propositions about the mathematical Infinite which, while demonstrable by symbols to the reason, are beyond the 'seeing' of the imagination. Take, for instance, (a) the series of the positive integers—1, 2, 3, 4, 5 . . . *ad inf.*; now take (b) the series of the powers, say, of 2—2 to the 1st, 2nd, 3rd, 4th, 5th . . . *ad inf.* It is clear that series (b) is contained in series (a) as part of itself, and yet that it has as many terms (*viz.* an infinite number) as the series which contains it. That is, the part is equal to the whole. Now under Cannabis, this sort of proposition required no demonstration, it was as intuitively evident as 2 plus 2 equals 4. I only wish I had been familiar with the Theory of Relativity in those days; I might have 'seen' it also!

The third, and last, instance was unique in that it admitted of external corroboration by an observer not under the influence of the drug. It was, in fact, suggested to me by a young doctor as a definite test of a certain theory that we had together talked about. That theory was to the effect that man contained in his subconscious a species of clock by means of which he could, in certain cases, wake himself at a specified time, etc., etc., and further (on my part) that under Cannabis it might be possible to bring this subconscious mechanism into the light. The test took this form. My friend was to tell me the *exact* time by his watch, then to request me to let him know when an exact number of minutes and seconds had elapsed, in the meanwhile engaging me in conversation so that I could not make any conscious calculation of the passage of time. We were in the garden of the house I then occupied, and no sooner had he told me the time by his watch than I saw, surrounding that part of the horizon not cut off by the house, what looked like an enormous tape-measure, save that, instead of being marked in feet and inches, it was graduated in seconds, minutes, hours, days and years. Along this scale moved a pointer. When my friend gave me the time (say, 10 min. 30 secs. after 3 o'clock) I noticed that the pointer pointed to that time on the scale. I was to let him know when (say) 5 min. 37 secs. had elapsed. I found that I had only to glance now and then at the pointer and to say 'Now!' when it reached 16 min. 7 secs. after 3 o'clock. We tried this experiment many times, a dozen times or more, and I was right in every instance. I had not to keep my mind on the pointer; that, in fact, would have been next to impossible under the drug; but just to give an occasional look to the moving finger as it progressed along the scale. This 'scale' was objective, in the sense that it did not move as I moved. Whatever it was, it was not an optical illusion. As I walked in one direction along the garden path, the part of the scale along which the pointer was travelling was before me; when I walked in the opposite direction, it was *behind* me. The scale and pointer appeared, in fact, to be as 'real' as the trees and the house. I do not know what extent of time was indicated on the scale, but it covered many years; the pointer indicated the exact present—to its left was the past, and to its right the future, while itself moved steadily and inexorably on.

It only remains for me to add that Cannabis Indica never induced a habit in me. Shortly after the experiment last described I gave up its use—not gradually but at one stroke. For many years, however, the effects remained in my system, and, now and then, at more and more infrequent intervals, I found time lengthening itself out; but these effects were short-lived in themselves and at last ceased altogether to recur. It is perhaps pertinent to note that two effects usually ascribed to Cannabis (at least in the form of Hashish) played no part in my experience: I saw no 'visions', nor did I suffer any intensification of the animal appetites—on the contrary, my usual aloofness was but more aloof.

As a last note: these experiments were made before the restrictions of the Dangerous Drugs Act affected the sale and purchase of Cannabis Indica, and so my transactions were not illegal, though of somewhat dubious lawfulness, . . .
J. R. A.

Time, place, sound, colour, mental lucidity, even sense of humour—we build up out of the norms of consciousness our reassuring little house of life; and a glass of laudanum negus or a few grains of hemp—or of strychnine —thins it away and transmutes it as if it were no more than the fabric of a dream. We know with fair assurance where safety lies; but the positive facts of the situation are another matter.

Page 14¹—No mere dreamer, thinker or philosopher need apply: ¶ Since, if the dreamer were a Newton, a Socrates or a Blake, he would be wasted on the island. And the thinker? Well, such is the intellect's indifference to environment, the island might be wasted on *him*. As for the philosopher, the author of *The Psychology of Philosophers* comes to five general conclusions about him, namely, that as a type he is a man of strong impulses and with pronounced inhibitions, that he is apt to show unsuitableness for ordinary life, that he tends to poetical expression and is 'predisposed to neuroses'. It sounds a little severe yet is not unendearing. And it is not so much his unsuitableness for ordinary life, as his inhibitions and neuroses that might hinder a career on the high seas or in the company of the turtle and the seal.

Page 15¹—The solitude of the grave:
¶ One day about noon, in the summer of 1824, George Borrow found himself at the bottom of Oxford Street, where it forms a right angle with a road 'that used to lead to Tottenham Court'. It appeared that something uncommon was expected. People were standing in groups on the pavement; the upstair windows were thronged with faces; and not a few of the shops were closed. This scene of excitement and expectation reminded him of Gentleman Harry and Tyburn Tree and of the big stone gaol at Newgate. 'Oh, oh, thought I, an execution!' But no:

Just then I heard various voices cry 'There it comes!' and all heads were turned up Oxford Street, down which a hearse . . . black, with its tall ostrich plumes . . . was slowly coming; nearer and nearer it drew; presently it was just opposite the place where I was standing, when, turning to the left, it proceeded slowly along Tottenham Road; immediately behind the hearse were three or four mourning coaches, full of people, some of which, from the partial glimpse which I caught of them, appeared to be foreigners; behind these came a very long train of splendid carriages, all of which, without one exception, were empty.

'Whose body is in that hearse?' said I to a dapper-looking individual, seemingly a shopkeeper, who stood beside me on the pavement, looking at the procession.

'The mortal relics of Lord Byron,' said the dapper-looking individual, mouthing his words and smirking—'the illustrious poet, which have been just brought from Greece, and are being conveyed to the family vault in ——shire.'

'An illustrious poet, was he?' said I.

'Beyond all criticism,' said the dapper man; 'all we of the rising generation are under incalculable obligation to Byron; I myself, in particular, have reason to say so; in all my correspondence my style is formed on the Byronic model.' . . .

97

I thought of Milton abandoned to poverty and blindness; of witty and ingenious Butler consigned to the tender mercies of bailiffs; and starving Otway: they had lived, neglected and despised, and, when they died, a few poor mourners only had followed them to the grave; but this Byron had been made a half-god of when living and now that he was dead . . . the very sun seemed to come out on purpose to grace his funeral. . . .

'Good poet, sir,' said the dapper-looking man, 'good poet, but unhappy'. . . .

Methought I saw

Life swiftly treading over endless space:
And, at her foot-print, but a bygone pace,
The ocean-past, which, with increasing wave,
Swallowed her steps like a pursuing grave.

Sad were my thoughts that anchored silently
On the dead waters of that passionless sea,
Unstirred by any touch of living breath:
Silence hung over it, and drowsy Death. . . .
And there were spring-faced cherubs that did sleep
Like water-lilies on that motionless deep,
How beautiful! with bright unruffled hair
On sleek unfretted brows, and eyes that were
Buried in marble tombs, a pale eclipse!
And smile-bedimpled cheeks, and pleasant lips,
Meekly apart, as if the soul intense
Spake out in dreams of its own innocence:
And so they lay in loveliness, and kept
The birthnight of their peace, that Life e'en wept
With very envy of their happy fronts;
For there were neighbour brows scarred by the brunts
Of strife and sorrowing—where Care had set
His crooked autograph, and marred the jet
Of glossy locks, with hollow eyes forlorn,
And lips that curled in bitterness and scorn—
Wretched—as they had breathed of this world's pain,
And so bequeathed it to the world again
Through the beholder's heart in heavy sighs.

So lay they garmented in torpid light,
Under the pall of a transparent night,
Like solemn apparitions lulled sublime
To everlasting rest—and with them Time
Slept, as he sleeps upon the silent face
Of a dark dial in a sunless place.

Thomas Hood.

Page 15²—¶ Some point of vantage
which will afford him, that is, a watch-tower or look-out.
But it should not become his building-site, since, as Poe says:

> Grandeur in any of its moods, but especially in that of extent,
> startles, excites—and then fatigues, depresses. For the occasional
> scene nothing could be better—for the constant view nothing worse.
> . . . In looking from the summit of a mountain we cannot help
> feeling *abroad* in the world. The heart-sick avoid distant prospects as
> a pestilence.

Besides, when the eye sees all, what office has the imagination? And 'heart-sick'—how true that is. Let the castaway take warning then.

Page 15³—In the centre of the earth:
¶ It is curious that of this so-called solid earth we know little but the mere skin. All that delights us in green things growing, from the grass of the field to the cedar of Lebanon, is only that skin deep. The kindly soil itself is but a scurf. And the deepest mine that man has sunk in search even of gold is but a three-thousandth part of the journey to the centre of the earth. Adventures, then, one might naturally assume, are *likely* to await any traveller thither.

At Concepción, on the island of Quiriquina, on February 20, 1835, occurred a violent earthquake, followed by a tidal wave at Talcahuano—a wave with a smooth outline visible from the shore while it was still three or four miles out at sea. Its prodigious breakers carried a cannon about four tons in weight fifteen feet inland. 'The space from under which volcanic matter . . . was actually erupted', wrote Charles Darwin, who witnessed it, 'is 720 miles in one line, and 400 miles in another line at right angles to the first: hence, in all probability, a subterranean lake of lava is here stretched out, of nearly double the area of the Black Sea'. A rather formidable obstacle! The earthquake 'came on suddenly, and lasted two minutes, but the time appeared much longer. . . . The motion made me almost giddy: it was . . . like that felt by a person skating over thin ice. . . . The earth, the very emblem of solidity . . . moved beneath our feet like a thin crust over a fluid;

—one second of time created in the mind a strange idea of insecurity, which hours of reflection would not have produced.'

Page 15⁴—Voyaging into space:

⁋ Here at least there is ample scope. Indeed as recently even as June 1845 'the most brilliant discovery . . . of which astronomy can boast'—that of the planet Neptune —was made independently, almost simultaneously, and by pure mathematical deduction by a Cambridge undergraduate named Adams and by a young Frenchman, Leverrier, a discovery which was telescopically and once more independently verified within a week by Challis in Cambridge and Galle in Berlin. *Minor* planets since then have rapidly multiplied—in human consciousness. And though many, meanwhile, have vanished, over a thousand of them had been recorded by 1923. They may prove exceedingly useful, since the positive need for the general migration of humanity may some day become extreme; and Mr. J. B. S. Haldane has recently not only explained why, but suggested when and how and whither.

Could there at first sight be anything more inviting to the really obstinate recluse than—not perhaps dull, leaden, crape-ringed Saturn, but, say, the reddish *Ceres Ferdinandea* tracked down on New Year's night, 1801; or strangely luminous *Vesta*, an orb that in a fortnight might be comfortably and completely circumambulated by any human on his two legs at the rate of about seventeen miles a day; and where his only difficulty, owing to its feeble force of gravitation, would be to keep to his feet? For the less active voyager there is an ampler choice. Many of the *minimi* are less than ten miles in diameter. What fantastic minute company might be his!

Alone, there, with the huge dappled disc of Terra Mater looming high over his head, but no notion inside it of how to return thither, he is unlikely to escape the occasional qualms of nostalgia: 'Now would I give a thousand furlongs of air for an acre of barren ground; long heath, brown furze, anything!'

Page 16¹—An island volcanic or coralline:
¶ But, for a man of taste, not 'continental'. Apart from
the slow enormities of the coral insect, and the sudden or
gradual heavings and shiftings of the floors of the oceans,
both the sea and the weather have multiplied the earth's
islands. It has been opined, indeed, that once it had none:

' . . . the proverb,' says Sir Thomas Browne, in *Pseudodoxia
Epidemica*, 'to cut an Isthmus, that is, to take great pains, and effect
nothing, alludeth not unto this attempt [i.e. of divers Princes to
canalize the tract of land which parteth the Arabian and Mediter-
ranean Sea]: but is by Erasmus applyed unto several other, as that
undertaking of the Cnidians to cut their Isthmus, but especially that
of Corinth so unsuccessfully attempted by many Emperours. The
Cnidians were deterred by the peremptory disswasion of Apollo,
plainly commanding them to desist; for if God has thought it fit, he
would have made that Country an Island at first. But this perhaps
will not be thought a reasonable discouragement unto the activity of
those spirits which endeavour to advantage nature by Art, and upon
good grounds to promote any part of the universe; nor will the ill-
success of some be made a sufficient determent unto others; who
know that many learned men affirm, that Islands were not from the
beginning, that many have been made since by Art, that some
Isthmuses have been eat through by the Sea, and others cut by the
spade: And if policy would permit, that of Panama in America were
most worthy the attempt: it being but few miles over, and would
open a shorter cut unto the East Indies and China.'

Page 16²—An island . . . fairly commodious:
¶ Such an island as Odysseus' Ithaca, twelve miles long
by four at its broadest; or as Delos, once afloat until
Zeus tethered it to the sea-bottom. But all depends on
the recluse; for barren and rocky Patmos—where, alone
with his visions, St. John the Divine lived in a cave—is
only a fraction of their magnitude, and but three miles
of sea divide it from the mainland.

Page 17¹—That notorious little three-cornered island:
¶ Ptolemy, among the twenty-seven maps he drew of
the world of his day (A.D. 140), included one of Great
Britain; and the British Museum treasures others made by
Matthew Paris about 1250. But the first printed map—

Nova Descriptio—of the British Isles made by an English-man was published at Rome in 1546, the work probably of George Lily, the domestic chaplain of Cardinal Pole: *Britannia Insularum quae in Europa continentur maxima, a meridie in septentrionem protenditur, forma triquetra.* It is a charming scene to study: its three ships flaunting their pennons in the breezes, and a whiskered monster devour-ing a fish in the haunts of *vitulus marinus,* south of *Orchides Insulae XXXI,* neighboured by *Hebrides Insulae XLIII.* Clear to be seen are *Gymnasia item celebria duo, Oxonium et Cantabrigium,* while to westward lies Ireland, beatifically vacant, with its few cities, its eel-like rivers, its scattered groves, its musters of sugar-cone-shaped mountains, and, to the N.W., an obscure, yawning cavern—amid the wild waters of Lough Derg?—designated Pvrgatorivm s. patricii—with what might be an effigy of the saint him-self in the entry.

Vanished, never to return perhaps, are the days of the maps which even at a glimpse almost stifle one with the sense of space, mystery, silence and wonder they convey —solely by means of the beauty and simplicity of their imaginative cartography. The map, for example, of about 1655, of part of the eastern states of America, with its inset view of New York—her windmill a little loftier than her gallows-tree, and her gallows-tree all but out-topping her windmill. Bears, deer, beavers, turkeys, rabbits, foxes, otters, (?) racoons and storks in reverie diversify its shadings, and there is an unforgettable little diagram to the west denoting *Modus muniendi apud Mahikanenses.*

But yet again *any* map is romance in shorthand, though in most examples of these latter days that shorthand needs very close scanning. It is like a little dry seed that must be soaked long in the dews of early morning before the green sprout appears. Once, however, that spearhead has thrust itself up into the imagination, the jungle soon becomes profuse.

Page 17²—Merchant adventurers:

❡ Even though the phrase, the romance of Commerce, is now a *cliché*, the maps in a commercial atlas neatly cut up, coloured, analysed and diagrammed, are a rich feast for the fancy. To *see* where not only castor, camphor, colocynth and cocaine come from, but whence also the emerald, the chrysoprase, the topaz and the tourmaline; where impregnable forests brood, and the yellow fever skulks, and the Buddhist abounds; where those tempests called cyclone, hurricane, typhoon rise up and travel and pass away; what Penang lawyers, supplejacks, bdellium and carambola may be; and what precise delicacies have their origin in Jipijapa, Rosario and Trebizond—all this can scarcely be acquitted of a romantic flavour.

There is, too, a vast sweep of imaginative as well as of historical reference in the fact that the tide of trade which in ancient times set in from east to west turned at last about and now as steadily flows from west to east; that the discovery of America was at first chiefly important in that it brought east the silver of Mexico and Peru, and that for 'thousands of years' pepper and spices were by far the most profitable commodities. The first direct cargo of these condiments, indeed, of 1497, from India to Lisbon, made possible by Vasco da Gama, brought in a profit of 6,000 *per cent.*

Pepper—who would now, even in full view of the punctured pot that appears on every breakfast-table, guess that these syllables fell as tunefully on the ear of our ancestors as, say, those of radium or of vitamin fall on our own. 'A fruit or berrie it is (call it whether you will) neither acceptable to the tongue nor delectable to the eye; and yet for the biting bitterness that it hath, we are pleased therewith, and we must have it fet forsooth as farre as India.' For as the author of *A Greene Forest* explains:

The Pepper tree groweth in Indie, and upon the side of the hill Caucasus right opposit to the Sunne. His leafe is much like the Iunipers leafe. It groweth amongst the Groves and Woods, such as

103

the Serpents inhabit: But to be free from any their kinde of endamaging, the inhabitants of that countrie, saith Isidore, when the fruites hereof ripen, doe set the whole Grove on fire, and by that meanes the deadly Serpents flie, and are driven away. So that the fire hath two effectes in so working: the one to their terrour and feare: the other to make black and becolour the Carnels as it were most browne: when as both they and the residue of their fruit by naturall growth and proper colour are all white. It taketh also in this fiering, not onely blacke colours, but wrinckles also, as we may see upon his upper skin. They that will be Craftes maysters in this marchandise, have proufe of both olde and new thus. If it be light, they judge it olde: if more weightie, then take they it to be newe. But herein sometime the Merchants play the verie Marchants. For they intermeddle now and then amongst their olde Pepper the froth or sinders of Silver or Leade, and such like, to make it waye heavie.

But the romantic—as this passage might prove—is not a thing to be clutched at or waylaid or bargained for. Like wisdom itself, it cannot be gotten for gold and its price is above rubies. Even 'the depth saith, It is not in me: and the sea saith, It is not with me'. It is an enrichment, a radiance—like the breaking of sunshine on a wooded hill— conferred by the mind or the imagination in a state of intense activity of interest. A delight in beauty, memory, association, all these and much else may influence one's intuitive recognition of what is romantic and what is not. And that recognition is the outcome of a species of *interest* which is no more stable—is usually less stable—than other species of interest. But whether one's prevalent interest in the universe be materialistic, scientific, philosophical, mystical, or sensual in kind and direction—and it may be coloured with all these—that universe itself depends upon such interest, and that, on the life within us. It is fitful. It veers. To keep a working shred of it may entail a desperate struggle. But if it perish, existence becomes a mere mocking shadowland, and to continue to live as impracticable as it would be if one *acted* in the belief that all is predetermined. For this reason, perhaps, the word *romantic* is apt not to ring quite true when, in conjunction with 'service', one chances on it in a trade circular. Its effect there may be hardly more animating than the indisputable assertion that the cod is 'a genus of bony fishes, which includes the cod proper'.

'What have we here?' says Trinculo, 'a man or a fish? Dead or alive? A fish: he smells like a fish; a very ancient and fish-like smell; a kind of not of the newest Poor-John. A strange fish!'

Page 18¹—It is but a cabalistic picture in the flat:
¶ In this connection it may be mentioned that of Mercator's original globes more than ten specimens have been discovered since 1880; that the compass was first referred to in print by Alexander Neckam in the twelfth century; and the loadstone by Roger Bacon.

Apart from astronomy, the first universal text-book of navigation was *Tractatus de Sphaera mundi*, by the mathematician John Holywood *alias* Sacro Bosco, in the thirteenth century. It may also be again recorded that Alonzo Sanchez de Huelva is the name of the pilot who was supposed to have discovered America before Columbus.

The first rutter (or ruttier, i.e. 'instruction for finding one's course at sea') in English, 'with the lawes of the Yle of Auleron', was a translation of *Le Routier de la Mer iusques au fleuve de jourdain*, of 1528. In 1536 appeared the next. Its lively and sonorous title runs:

'The Rutter of the Sea, with the havens, rades, and soundyngs, kennynges, wyndes, floodes, and ebbes, daungers and costes of dyvers regions, with the lawes of the Yle of Auleron, and the iudgements of ye sea. Lately translated into Englyshe. Imprinted at London in Poules Chyrche yard, at the sygne of ye Maydens Hed, by me, Thomas Petyt. The yere of our Lorde God M.D.XXXVI. The xxviii daye of Marche.'

Many such references, enticing to the jackdaw, will be found in Captain Albert Markham's Notes to the Hakluyt Society's edition of the voyages of John Davis (1880).

Page 18²—A prodigious mass of uninviting matter:
¶ We may therefore conceive of the earth as consisting of a central unoxidised metallic nucleus, around which are arranged the basic rocks, the siliceous, and finally the stratified, each zone being placed

according to the relative density of its component parts in a state of intense heat.

So wrote Sir William Dawkins in 1873. Nor are we much better off to-day. 'The lithosphere', says Dr. H. R. Mill, has as a whole 'a rigidity approximately equal to that of steel'. Where now the subterranean joys and terrors, seas and monsters conjured up by that prophetic wizard of my boyhood, Jules Verne? And what of that other dream of even earlier days—this 'sedentary Earth', 'Built of circumfluous waters calm, in wide Crystalline ocean', and the vision of the waters of that ocean for ever pouring in enormous cataract into Space over the lip of a world shaped like an infinite saucer? How often in childhood from some aerial perch in the inane have I watched that gigantic amphitheatre, quiet as the heavens around me in the lullay of its roar.

Those waters are not yet silent, but I know now they are not of this world. And we must accept, at any rate for the time being, what authority tells us. Namely, that this zonal globe is not only solid and unstable, but that it is also round. The only redeeming merit left, in fact, to the cause of the Flattist is that it is now one of the causes called forlorn. It became so finally, it seems, on March 7th, 1870. On that day Alfred Russel Wallace—a master of Islands—won a wager of £500 by scientifically demonstrating on the Old Bedford Canal the rotundity of the earth. Why is it that men of science of our own day allow this happy precedent to remain so sterile? Why should not the hospitality of the National Sporting Club be extended to the heavy-weights and fly-weights not merely of brawn but of intellect? The loser by the venture referred to was 'John Hampden, Esq., of Swindon'. He had been previously led astray 'from a belief in Newton's *theories* to a knowledge of Nature's *facts*' by a friend named William Carpenter, a journeyman printer, who, after Wallace's experiments were over, not only wrote a lively and jocular pamphlet describing them, but persisted in his heresy.

He begins his account with a quotation from 'history'

concerning Copernicus, who with his dying breath thanked Heaven that he had been 'enabled to dispel an error of five thousand years' duration':

It was the morning of the 23rd of May, 1543; heaven was still lighted with stars; the earth was fragrant with flowers; all Nature seemed to sympathize with the great revealer of her laws; and soon the sun, rising above the horizon, shed its earliest and purest ray upon the still, cold brow of the departed, and seemed in its turn to say, 'The king of creation gives the kiss of peace, for thou hast been the first to place him on his throne'.

How one's heart goes out to the wistful ghost of the old old fallacy still smiling out at us in that word 'rising'! But William Carpenter was no sentimentalist. His tract incorrigibly concludes:

MR. WALLACE! by the fact . . . that, in the end, you will have to 'rely' upon *the Truth* . . . we counsel you to REFUND, at all events, the sum of *five hundred pounds* which was awarded to you by MR. WALSH [the umpire], and which you received on the First of April, 1870; and, with all gracefulness, admit that WATER IS NOT CONVEX: and the EARTH, NOT A GLOBE!

However, the £500 had by then been handed over, and, except probably to John Hampden himself, the First of April must have seemed a suitable day for the transaction. And this was merely William Carpenter's swan-song.

The earth, then, is a solid steel-like orb—its mass, say, six thousand trillion tons. It is so old that for several thousand million years it has been capable of supporting 'life'. On its extreme rind we humans crawl. It is rotating with a (fortunately) unimaginable velocity; it is revolving— 'though proof of this is less simple'—round the sun; and it is so utterly isolated that, according to Sir James Jeans, if, on self-extinction intent, it lay in wait in space for a star to shatter it to less than atoms, its suicidal suspense by the wayside might continue for 1,000,000,000,000, 000,000 years. In spite of all these noughts, could solitude be less eloquent? Viewed otherwise, of course, our earthly refuge may be merely a bauble for the amusement of the physicist and the mathematician.

But though it be accepted as all it is said to be, in an

ethereal sea, might one perhaps be forgiven for wishing —merely wishing—that it were almost any other shape than the shape it is—if only for the very inadequate reason that a sphere is 'perfect'? Tulip, or gourd, or grape-cluster, or hourglass-shaped; or (as it was anciently surmised) cylindrical, or conic, or a three-dimensional spiral, an octahedron or a polyhedron, or like a loose string of beads, or an intricate nest of Chinese boxes, conducting the discoverer, as the ages pass, from one strange and lovely layer into another and another, stranger and lovelier yet? The old Chinese, indeed, to whom the insignificant remainder of their then vaguely known world was but a region of barbarism, imagined the heavens to be round, the earth square, and their empire, with its provinces, four-cornered. Let that empire be but one side of a cube, what then would be the prospect at sea or in the desert of Gobi, when ship or caravan was navigating one of its right angles? The chief defect common to all such shapes as these is that they would give us a world which, like our own, would be bound in the long run—man being the bold and restless creature he is—to be completely explored. Not so if that world were of the Juan Fernandez disc pattern, indefinitely extended—with numberless ranges of mountains, enormous forests, oceans, seas, waters, wastes, wilds and wildernesses, 'antres vast', on, and on, and on; with its known and its unknown and its incalculable; with its races, nations, and civilizations of innumerable orders, degrees, kinds and ages; its beauties and oddities and rarities; and perhaps at one remote lip that oceanic everlasting avalanche of water!

Alas, if it weren't for the superficial charms of this oblate spheroid how could one really wish to be here? Even as an object of science it is a somewhat humiliating abode for the spirit of that castaway, Man. The ignoramus scans with avidity as much as he can digest of the information available about it; yet still some antique voice within sings on that it cannot be true. Not exactly like that. Has not Mr. Yeats declared that 'everything that can be seen, touched, measured, explained, understood, argued over, is to the imaginative artist nothing more than a means'? And is it not—in Coleridge's words, though he might scorn to see them used in such a connection—'is it not on the *immediate* which dwells in every man, and on the original intuition, that all the certainty of our knowledge depends'? Perhaps, then, the novice and the greenhorn may comfort himself with the thought that much of this science is only a delicious nosegay of exquisitely retrieved data in some at present inconceivable relation to truth. Surely, too, one may—with their own connivance, and at a certain risk, and holding tight to their distinction from fancies—do what one likes with one's *facts?* I wonder.

'I am afraid, sir,' says the young author in *Lavengro*, 'it was very wrong to write such trash, and yet more to allow it to be published.' 'Trash! not at all;' replies his publisher, 'a very pretty piece of speculative philosophy. Of course you were wrong in saying there is no world. The world must exist, to have the shape of a pear; and that the world is shaped like a pear, and not like an apple, as the fools of Oxford say, I have satisfactorily proved in my book. Now, if there were no world, what would become of my system?'

Moreover, as Hamlet realized, there are degrees of incredulity:

To the celestial, and my soul's idol, the most
beautified Ophelia. . . .
In her excellent white bosom, these, &c. . . .
Doubt thou the stars are fire;
Doubt that the sun doth move;
Doubt truth to be a liar;
But never doubt I love.
O dear Ophelia! I am ill at these numbers:
I have not art to reckon my groans; but that I
love thee best, O most best! believe it. Adieu.
Thine evermore, most dear lady, whilst
this machine is to him,
HAMLET.

And that appears to be the first use of the word machine in this sense, and the only use made of it by Shakespeare.

But what if that machine be out of order? 'I asserted that the world was mad,' exclaimed 'poor Lee', Coleridge's friend, 'and the world said, that *I* was mad, and confound them, they outvoted me.'

Page 18³—Man's ingenious ditch at Panama:
❡ Sir Thomas Browne's mere reference to it as being most worthy the attempt scintillates with the romantic. And the actual achievement is a page in romantic history. But as time goes on and those great dams and locks become at last, maybe, obsolete—choked, dismantled—then there will gather over their masonry the romance of the old and abandoned, and they will be at one with the great pyramid of Cheops—and with that superb gesture of Vasco de Balboa's when, on September 26th, 1513, having surveyed the South Sea from the mountains of Darien, he waded into its waters above his thighs and took possession of it in the name of his sovereign, Ferdinand of Spain. This is all of a piece, too, with the tale of Pizarro, who was with him there that day, and who for lack of iron during his conquest of Peru is said to have shod his horses with gold and silver. As for the feast of the naked and gilded Amazonian princesses described by Raleigh in his account of the 'Empyre of Guiana', it stands out in one's memory of the reading of books as may the appearance of one's first comet or snowfall or sight of the sea. Such things, however remote they may be, seem to belong to some dream life of our own, as if we had once actually participated in them!

Page 18⁴—An island worthy of romantic respect:
❡ Charles Darwin as a young man had the joy of feasting his eyes on most of the world's islands. And they were eyes not only indefatigably faithful in the service of science, but no less eager in delight at every revelation of that world's peace and beauty. It ravishes him. He stands at gaze drinking in the scene before him, unable to express his joy in it. 'It is not possible,' he says somewhere, 'to give an adequate idea of the higher feelings of wonder, astonishment, and devotion, which fill and elevate the

mind.' So, too, Katherine Mansfield: 'I could weep like a child because there are so many flowers, and my lap is so small, and all must be carried home'.

But Darwin, like all true devotees, had the sharpest of preferences; and even islands sometimes failed to please him. 'These miserable islands' is his reference to the Falklands, once called, more prettily, by Richard—the son of the great Sir John—Hawkins's Maiden Land; and, more prettily yet, by the Dutch, the Sibaldines, and by the Spanish, the Malvinas. Darwin's only good word is for their *carne con caero*, 'as superior to common beef as venison is to mutton'.

And again: 'Farewell, Australia!', runs his prophetic apostrophe on March 14th, 1836. 'You are a rising child, and doubtless some day will reign a great princess in the south; but you are too great and ambitious for affection; yet not great enough for respect. I leave your shores without sorrow or regret.'

Page 19¹—The Isle of Wight:
¶ This is the feeble tribute of a mere transitory passenger on a very few of England's ferries. But even so intent, hospitable and visionary a pilgrim as Mr. H. M. Tomlinson treasures a fond memory of *his* first island, and that also is not far to seek:

'To reach felicity we must cross the water.' There is no reason for this, but we know it is true, for felicity is where we are not. We must cross it to an island, and a small one. . . . I remember a shape on the horizon, which often was visible from a Devonshire vantage, though sometimes it had gone. Its nature depended, I thought, on the way of the sun and wind. It was a cloud. It was very distant. It was a whale. It was my imagination. It was nothing; it was unapproachable. But one morning at sunrise I put my head out of the scuttle of a little cutter, and the material universe had broken loose. The tiny ship was heaving on a ground-swell, vast undulations of glass, and over us titanic masonry was toppling in ruin—I feared the explosions of surf would give a last touch to a collapsing island, and Lundy would fall on us. We landed on a beach no larger than a few bushels of shingle. It was enclosed by green slopes and high walls of rock; and we climbed a track from the beach that mounted amid sunlight and shadow. The heat of the upper shimmering platform of granite and heath above the smooth sea, and its smell and look of antiquity, suggested that it had been abandoned and forgotten, and had remained apart from the affairs of a greater and more important world since the creation. That was my first island, and I still think its one disadvantage is that it is only twelve miles off-shore.

Page 20¹—¶ Spice Islands:
>   The isles Ternate and Tidore
>   Whence merchants bring their spicy drugs;

and not without risk: 'So the sixteenth of May we passed the line, where many of our men fell sick of the scurvy, calenture, bloody flux, and the worms; being left to the mercy of God, and a small quantity of lemon-juice every morning. . . '. So runs the narrative of the voyage of Sir Henry Middleton to Bantam and the Maluco Islands in 1604-6. And then, 'This day we had sight of all the clove islands, that is to say Maquiam, Motir, unpeopled, but with great store of cloves, Tidore and Ternate, all of them picked [peaked] hills in form of a sugar-loaf'.

And, for merchandise in view, besides cloves; pepper —including, we may hope, Selkirk's Malagita, very good against 'griping of the guts', and mace and nutmegs; also China-silk, indigo, ambergris, musk, civet, bezoar stones (of sovran account in physic), camphor, benjamin (fragrant benzoin), 'buxrace' or cinnamon, and in addition, 'a small quantity of china dishes or light trifles, not exceeding the value of three pounds, or not bearing above the bulk of a small chest', which the merchants or seamen might want to take home with them.

Drake had passed that way thirty years before, and the king of Ternate had pleasant memories of him. These, however, did not entirely allay his apprehensions at sight of the English ships now lying off his shores.

The General caused them to entreat the king to come into the ship, who came in trembling, which the General seeing thought he was a-cold, and caused his men to fetch him a black damask gown laid with gold lace, and lined with unshorn velvet, which the king put upon his back but never had the manners to surrender it again but kept it as his own.

But the bad manners were not always on the side of the

islanders. Take that chieftain, 'the *tabriqui*, Meta', of one of the Solomons who, unlike the king of Ternate, had never seen a white man before. He came out in his canoe to the Spanish admiral's ship, decked for the occasion with bracelets of bone and stags' teeth and coral, and sat there with such gravity and dignity as we could not but admire in a savage. . . . He remained for a while looking at us, his cheek resting on his hand, and, although I called him he did not reply; when we laughed at his gravity, feeling himself inclined to laugh he cunningly covered his mouth with his hand. . . . Then he asked me if I wished to kill him, as he was much frightened.

Times have changed: with our '57 kinds' available at the nearest grocer's we would not nowadays sell our souls for a nutmeg. And when Mr. H. M. Tomlinson recently visited Ternate, civilization had been there before him. 'One day, on Ternate, I passed through the shade of a nutmeg grove, and came upon a lane at the back of the village. I could smell vanilla, and looked about for that orchid, and presently found it growing against a sugar palm. Behind that odorous shrubbery was a native house, and beyond the house, and far below it, the blue of the sea. Nobody was about. It was noon. It was hot. The high peak of Tidore across the water had athwart its cone a cloud which was as bright as an impaled moon. I saw no reason why this earth should not be a good place for us, and, thanking my fortune, idled along that lane till I saw another house, set back among hibiscus,' and nailed up on a board along the veranda he read this legend in Malay: THE COMMUNIST PARTY OF INDIA.

So again a recent visitor to the Society Islands tells me that when one still tropical night—all hushed, and the moon like hoarfrost spread—he landed on remote and lofty Bora Bora, a faint peculiar buzz fell on his ear, sounding on even above the boom of the breakers on the reef. It was the *whrr* of a movie apparatus. The gentle natives were being entertained with a European prize-fight—and were much amused. Not so with the movie melodrama that followed. At this they were shocked. But,

113

as the poet says, 'Progress is the law of life; man is not man as yet'. Moreover,

> where the vanguard camps to-day
> The rear shall rest to-morrow.

Page 21¹—Engelant:

¶ One of the very earliest, if not the earliest, of medieval treatises on geography is the *Libro del Conoscimiento*, or, in resounding English, *The Book of the Knowledge of all the Kingdoms, Countries and Lordships that there are in the World.* Its pages bravely adorned with royal ensigns, it was the work, about 1350, of a Spanish Franciscan. He was the first European to mention in writing and to name the Canary Isles, the Madeiras and Azores, to fix the whereabouts of Prester John, and to report on the centre of Africa, and he affirms that he had been entertained in the Castle of Magog.

'Know,' he says of England, 'that it is a very well populated country and that it contains eleven great cities,' which he names. He continues, 'I left Inglaterra in a boat, and reached the island of Irlanda which is a short crossing of a mile. [Though it must be confessed that at times it doesn't seem so!] They say that formerly it was called Ibernia. Know that it is a well peopled island with a good climate, and there are three great cities in it.' Five are actually mentioned—Strangford, Limerick, Ros, Waterford and Dublin. 'In this island there are no snakes nor vipers, nor toads, nor flies, nor spiders, nor any other venomous things. . . . The women are very beautiful though very simple. It is a land where there is not as much bread as you may want, but a great abundance of meat and milk.' The dearth of *fauna* is due, it is said, to the fact that Ireland was severed from England long before England itself was enisled by the sea. But whence came that rare beauty, and those voices, as low and musical as the chimings of a brook?

All but two centuries after the *Libro del Conoscimiento,* Andrew Boorde's *Fyrst Boke of the Introduction of Knowledge* appeared. Boorde was a man of Sussex. He was born at

Board Hill on the southern verge of what was then the great Forest of Pevensel, and he loved England. He was a 'physicke doctour', and a great traveller, and while in his early thirties, it seems, was made suffragan bishop of Chichester, though he never fulfilled the office. 'I have travayled rownd about Chrystendom, and out of Christendom,' he avers, but 'yf I were a Iewe, a Turke or a Sarasin or any other infidele, I yet must prayse and laud [my country], and so would every man, yf they dyd know of every countrey as well as England.'

He is none the less a candid critic and specifies that country's 'seven evils': the neglect of fasting, the prevalence of heresies and swearing, the laziness of the young people, the want of training for midwives, that mere cobblers are its physicians, the mutability of his countrymen's minds, and, last, their lust and avarice. When in his travels he came to the 'Dukedom-ship of Sasony', he marvelled greatly how the Saxons could have conquered England, since Saxony is but a small country compared with it. 'For I think, if al the world were set against Englond, it might never be conquerid, they beyng treue within them selfe. And they that would be false, I praye God too manyfest them what they be.'

He considered English speech debased by comparison with Italian, Castilian and French; and himself indulged in Latinities. He decided that water is bad for us, ale natural to us, and beef good for us. He is lively, straightforward, curious and fond of a joke, good or bad; so his book makes excellent company.

Page 21²—Bintang:
¶ It was off an islet near Bintang that John Davis— ninety-nine years after Martin Behaim's death—met his end. His high hopes of the North-west Passage, after three vain attempts to find it, remained undaunted. On May 27th, 1595—two hundred and fifty years all but a week, that is, before Franklin set sail in the *Erebus*—he had addressed a letter to the Privy Council in introduction of

his *Worlds Hydrographical Description.* In this, after long argument with the noble, if insular, patriotism of his day, he concludes: 'all which premises considered there remaineth no more doubting but that the landes are disjoyned, and that there is a Navigable passage by the Norwest, of God for us alone ordained to our infinite happiness, and for the ever being glory of her majestie, for then her stately seate of London should be the storehouse of Europe: the nurse of the world: and the renowne of Nations'.

Nine years afterwards he sailed for the East Indies in the *Tigre* (240 tons) with a companion pinnace, the *Tigres Whelpe.* Off Bintang a leaking junk-load of 'Japonian' pirates—Davis himself having been 'beguiled with their humble semblance'—treacherously attempted to seize his ship.

At their first comming forth of the Cabbin, they met Captaine Davis comming out of the Gun-roome, whom they pulled into the Cabbin, and giving him sixe or seven mortall wounds they thrust him out of the Cabbin before them. His wounds were so mortall that he dyed as soone as he came into the waste. They pressed so fiercely to come to us, as we receiving them on our Pikes, they would gather on our Pikes with their hands to reach us with their Swords. It was neere halfe an houre before we could stone them backe into the Cabbin: In which time we had killed three or foure of their Leaders.

After they were driven into the Cabbin they fought with us at the least foure houres before we could suppresse them, often fyring the Cabbin, burning the bedding, and much other stuffe that was there. And had we not with two Demy-culverings, from under the halfe decke, beaten downe the bulke head and the pumpe of the ship we could not have suppressed them from burning the ship. This Ordnance being charged with Crosse-barres, Bullets, and Case-shot, and bent close to the bulke head, so violently marred therewith boords and splinters that it left but one of them standing of two and twentie. Their legs, armes, and bodies were to torne as it was strange to see how the shot had massacred them.

In all this conflict they never would desire their lives, though they were hopelesse to escape: such was the desperatenesse of these Japonians. Only one lept over-boord, which afterward swamme to our ship againe and asked for grace; wee tooke him in, and asked him what was their purpose?

He told us that they meant to take our shippe and to cut all our throates. He would say no more, but desired that he might be cut in pieces.

The next day, to wit, the eight and twentieth of December, we went to a little Iland to the Leeward off us. And when we were about five miles from the Land, the Generall commanded his people to hang this Japonian; but he brake the Rope, and fell into the Sea. I cannot tell whether he swamme to the land or not.

Maybe he succeeded in so doing, and there remains an island in these seas frequented by the ghost of a Japonian who, like Iago, would 'say no more', except only that he desired he might be cut in pieces. A few pages before the record of Davis's death we have a remarkable portrait of the Sultan Aladin, king of Achin, to whom the voyagers had presented a present of a looking-glass, a drinking-glass and a bracelet of coral, in hopes of pepper:

The King is called Sultan Aladin, and is an hundred yeares old, as they say, yet hee is a lustie man, but exceeding grosse and fat. In the beginning of his life he was a fisher-man: (of which this place hath very many; for they live most upon fish:) and going to the Warres with the former King shewed himselfe so valiant and discreet . . . [that] these twentie yeares he hath by force held the Kingdome, and now seemeth to bee secure in the same.

His Court is from the Citie halfe a mile upon the River, having three Guards before any can come to him, and a great Greene betweene each Guard; his house is built as the rest are, but much higher, hee sitteth where hee can see all that come to any of his Guards, but none can see him. The wals and covering of his house are Mats, which sometime is hanged with cloth of Gold, sometime with Velvet, and sometime with Damaske. Hee sitteth upon the ground crosse-legged like a Taylor, and so must all those doe that be in his presence. He always weareth foure Cresis, two before and two behind, exceeding rich with Diamonds and Rubies; and hath a Sword lying upon his lap. He hath attending upon him fortie women at the least, some with Fannes to coole him, some with Clothes to dry his sweat, some give him Aquavitae, others water: the rest sing pleasant Songs. He doth nothing all the day but eate and drinke, from morning to night there is no end of banquetting: and when his belly is readie to breake, then he eateth Arecca Betula, which is a fruit like a Nutmeg, wrapped in a kind of leafe like Tabacco, with sharpe chalke made of Pearle Oyster-shels: chawing this, it maketh the spittle very red, draweth the Rhume exceedingly, and procureth a mightie stomacke: this maketh the teeth very blacke, and they be the bravest that have the blackest teeth. By this meanes

117

getting again his stomacke, he goeth with a fresh courage to eating. And for a Change with a Cracking Gorge, hee goeth into the River, where he hath a place made of purpose, there getting a stomacke by being in the water. Hee, his great men and women doe nothing but eate, drinke, and talke of Venerie. If the Poet's Fables have any shew of truth, then undoubtedly this King is the great Bacchus. For he holdeth all the Ceremonies of Gluttonie.

As in all places of Europe the Custome is by uncovering the head to shew reverence, in this place it is wholly contrary. For, before any man can come to the Kings presence, he must put of his hose and shooes, and come before him bare-legged, and bare-footed, holding the palmes of the hands together, and heaving them up above his head, bowing with the bodie, must say, *Doulat*; which done, dutie is discharged. And so hee sitteth downe crosse-legged in the Kings presence. Hee doth onely spend the time in eating with women, and Cock-fighting. And such as is the King, such are his Subjects; for the whole Land is given to no other contentment.

If *Doulat* were the only need, duty would be as consolatory a term as Mesopotamia; but precisely how far went this unique 'contentment'? We moralizing Westerners seem to suffer from so many illusions.

Kings, however, come and go; but islands remain. An earlier glimpse of Achin will be found in the Travels of Friar Odoric. He had voyaged fifty days from Mobar, where lay the body of the blessed Thomas the Apostle; and he came to Lamore, the Lambri of Marco Polo. Here he says:

I began to lose sight of the north star, as the earth intercepted it. And in that country the heat is so excessive that all the folk there, both men and women, go naked, not clothing themselves in any wise. And they mocked much at me on this matter, saying that God made Adam naked, but I must needs go against His will and wear clothes. Now, in that country all the women be in common; and no one there can say, this is my wife, or this is my husband! But when a woman beareth a boy or a girl she giveth the child to whom she listeth of those with whom she hath consorted, and calleth him the father. The whole of the land likewise is in common; and no one can say with truth, this or that part of the land is mine. But they have houses of their own, and not in common.

It is an evil and a pestilent generation, and they eat man's flesh there just as we eat beef here. Yet the country in itself is excellent, and hath great store of flesh-meats, and of wheat and of rice; and they have much gold also, and lign-aloes, and camphor, and many other things which are produced there. And merchants come to this island from far, bringing children with them to sell like cattle to those infidels, who buy them and slaughter them in the shambles and eat them. And so with many other things both good and bad, which I have not written.

There, also, was a notorious idol—like that 'stuffed Judas called Copeca' of the Solomons. 'It is as big as St. Christopher [himself greatly revered at Padua], as commonly represented by the painters, and it is entirely of gold, seated on a great throne, which is also of gold. And round its neck it hath a collar of gems of immense value. And the church of this idol is also of pure gold, roof and walls and pavement.'

And here, with his own pretty additions, is what Sir John Mandeville made of this passage:

In the kingdome of Mobar there is a wonderfull strange idole, being made after the shape and resemblance of a man, as big as the image of our Christopher, & consisting all of most pure and glittering gold. And about the necke thereof hangeth a silke riband, ful of most rich & precious stones, some one of which is of more value than a whole kingdome. The house of this idol is all of beaten gold, namely the roofe, the pavement, and the sieling of the wall within and without. Unto this idol the Indians go on pilgrimage, as we do unto St. Peter. . . .

Traveling from thence by the Ocean sea 50 daies journey southward, I came unto a certaine land named Lammori, where, in regard of extreme heat, the people both men and women go stark-naked from top to toe: who seeing me apparelled, scoffed at me, saying that God made Adam and Eve naked. In this countrey al women are common, so that no man can say, this is my wife. Also when any of the said women beareth a son or a daughter, she bestowes it upon anyone that hath lien with her, whom she pleaseth. Likewise al the land of that region is possessed in common, so that there is not mine & thine, or any propriety of possession in the division of lands: howbeit every man hath his owne house peculiar unto himselfe. Mans flesh, if it be fat, is eaten as ordinarily there as beefe in our countrey. And albeit the people are most lewd, yet the countrey is exceeding good, abounding with all commodities, as fleshe, corne, rise, silver, gold, wood of aloes, Camphir, and many other things.

And to-day:

119

The coast at Achen head, and for about one mile to the eastward, is rocky and steep, beyond which it is sandy for the whole distance to Pedro point; with the exception of Achen head, which is steep-to, it may be approached by the lead, the bottom being composed of black sand for about 3 miles off-shore, with white sand and shells outside that distance.

In places especially near Kwala Gigieng, there are sandhills, within which the land is in great part morass, with but scanty vegetation, but occasionally there are trees of some height. The morass is intersected by creeks and lagoons, with footpaths connecting the several villages which are generally situated on the higher ground.

The villages are numerous and are usually surrounded by alang-alang woods, lofty coconut trees, or cultivated ground; many are seen from seaward . . . Kota Raja . . . lies in the great Achen valley. It is the capital . . . The old residence of the Sultan is a rectangular building surrounded by a wall and enclosed by a ditch. The river flows through it. The inner quarters are used for the Governor's residence . . .

> The fort over against the oak-wood,
> Once it was Briudge's, it was Cathal's,
> It was Aed's, it was Ailill's,
> It was Conaing's, it was Cuiline's,
> And it was Maelduin's;
> The fort remains after each in his turn—
> And the Kings asleep in the ground.

Page 22¹—Christopher Columbus:

¶ On that famous Thursday, October 11, 1492, his fleet sailed on through the highest seas they had yet encountered on their voyage. A flaming meteor, a branch of the wild rose in blossom floating on the blue-black waters, had been kindlier omens. After nightfall the crews, 120 adventurers in all, repeated, as was their custom, the *Salve Regina*. There would be no moon until an hour before midnight—and then only a moon in her third quarter. At ten o'clock Columbus, as he paced the poop of the 50-ton *Santa Maria*, saw a light dead ahead. It rose and fell, as if it were that of a lantern swung to and fro in the dark. Let us share, if we can, the perturbation of his soul. At dawn—a marvellous wilderness of colour—his doubts were set at rest. Man had discovered another island. But Columbus himself supposed it was Japan.

Page 22²—Our ideal pattern:
¶ It will vary with the kind of recluse. Iago abandoned alone on an island suggests the caged, insane and spotted pard, but though Mr. Pickwick's stay might be brief, his milk of human kindness would neither fail nor corrupt. Dr. Johnson would toil for his life there and die a stoic. Keats, like Emily Brontë, was a distant cousin of Robinson Crusoe himself. Young Wordsworth would have remained William. Jane Austen would have died a neat and natural death.

Primarily, of course, the proof of the maroon is in the eating. Food secured, is our island first and foremost something from which we cannot easily get away—a cage? Or is it that haven where it is blissfully seldom we shall be interrupted—a hermitage? That again depends on the recluse.

What precise climate shall be ours? Now bitter cold, to mark the full comfort of the great watch-fire of allspice wood we shall burn in cave-mouth or corral; and now piping hot for contrast to winter's rages, and to enrich the siesta in the cool shade of our woodlands? Or arid brassy noons and tropic rains? Or a perpetual sweet, fresh and smiling summer; bud, flower, fruit and leaf ever shining on the flanks of the hills and through the ravines and valleys to the fringes of the hungry sands; and there the long foam-capped combers plunging in from the blue—to fall 'in a thudding shower of light and snows'?

Exactly what distance from that other island called Home will suffice us? Or from our nearest neighbours, plain or coloured? What non-human company do we desire? Multitudes of sea-fowl, of course, the little parrot and the macaw; but small birds also of a very bright plumage, green, blue, silver, yellow and amethyst, and butterflies of every dye. And should these birds sing or be silent?

Shall there be dangers or only the appearance of them? Or nothing but safety arching over the scene? What necessities will be necessary, what little luxuries still more so? What books? Ink? How deep shall the ocean lie about our shores? Five thousand fathom, like that which neighbours the Philippines and the volcanoed islands of Japan, or shelving with serpentine seaweeds, static sponges, coral and sunken coloured rocks, such as Shelley delighted in? And shall it roar the livelong day in spouting billows, or utterly lull at times to rest as if at night we lay beneath the stars amid a sea of glass?

What calling, what craft, apart from a little knowledge, say, of seamanship, carpentering, and of the chase—and an instinct for the edible—shall prepare us for our long solitude? And how shall we spend our scanty leisure—for of labour we shall find the sum? Shall we sit and respond to the sea-mews solely with the sound of our own sweet voices? Or twang a lute? Or breathe into the loud bassoon?

But again and again the question of size returns. Great clumsy Baffinish islands are out of the question—they are all but a contradiction in terms. Since then, on or over our ideal island there will of a surety never hover airship or seaplane, unless quite a little one and that home-made, for we must not be overlooked; and since somehow the horse seems either an exotic or an anachronism in such surroundings, we shall keep to our feet. That being so, the more various our resort the better. A creek (or creeks), a spit of quicksand, dunes, caves, precipices, cataracts, streams, an unfathomable inland lake, morning mists, bright moons, an occasional spouting hurricane —all these seem desirable, and in certain of its tracts our island should be all but (and perhaps in one region, quite) inaccessible. Then its little realm will last out our full time there, and when we depart from it we shall leave some of its unknown still unknown behind us.

Islands, like most things, are very largely what they seem. We see, we build, we think and we imagine according to scale. We cannot else. And though in his endless ingenuity man constructs immense telescopes and so enormously enlarges the visible universe (the author of

Eos will tell us how many noughts are required), though he has discovered in the world of the infinitesimal not only all the *cocci* and their cousinry, but also that the mystery and workmanship of natural objects is ever more and more exquisite the more closely it is revealed, yet he remains physically and spiritually his own yardstick. And how deliciously complacent he can be about it, even when writing to the Press:

> . . . I am bold enough to say that we Englishmen, by gradual process of selective evolution, have, in the really well-bred horse, with adequate substance (not the racing weed), produced by far the most beautiful animal in all creation. . . .

Not so much as a nod of gratitude for the queer-toed, eleven-inches-high, Eocene Eohippus!

Mere space, at any rate, needs no flattery; 'that's partly what I meant by saying that magnitude, which up to a certain point has grandeur, has beyond it ghastliness'; and a child lost in wonder at the light on a daisy or a butterfly is brimmed with as much rapture as he can contain. So may his elders be if their eyes are as clear, their divination as adventurous, and their imagination as hospitable as his.

Man's own workmanship, on the other hand, less easily survives magnification. To excel in vastness the pyramids of the Pharaohs would be an easy feat to the engineers of our own day—the ambition, the incentive, the labour and the money being available. But there is no difficulty and little pleasure in imagining a city compared with which the topless towers of New York would be mere pygmy toy-work. It is not the power to achieve that matters, but the eventual good of *so* achieving.

> Crafty inventions, subtle past believing
> Now unto evil bring him, now to good . . .

And as with our modern excesses in locomotion and our vast unwieldy hoard of impersonalized 'scientific knowledge', what on our minds would be the effect of an architecture utterly disproportionate to our few inches of stature is as yet nothing more than a speculation.

There may be judgements on arrogance other than the doom of Babel. Men that live in crystal palaces seldom seem to live up to them. If, then, a brief lodging on a desert island restored nothing more than one's sense of proportion, it would not have been wasted. And to this end we may hope Providence will provide that in dimensions that island shall be, say, thirteen miles by four.

Page 23¹—Juan Fernandez:

¶ However minute an island may be—and islands, like human consciousness, are usually but the green or sandy tops of high hills or rocks hidden in the deeps below—it has wakened to as many daybreaks, dreamed beneath as many moons as have most of its grosser sisters. Islands that appear above the salt blue waters at dawn and vanish with the waning of their first moon are rare. One such, between 1845 and 1857, reared its head above the sea among the hundred and fifty Friendly Isles—so called because when Cook discovered them the natives went unarmed. It was called Wesley Island. It came, it vanished. But though there have been islands in actuality even of as short a stay as this, accounts of such phenomena are usually born of fantasy, or the islands themselves prove to be only basking leviathans. Rippled by the glass-clear waves that flank them, these lie harmlessly sunning themselves under heaven, and what wonder if at sight of them—

Seafarers imagine they are gazing with their eyes on some island. . . . So they fasten their high-stemmed ships with anchor ropes to this false land; they make fast their sea-horses as if they were at the sea's brink, and up they climb on the island, bold of heart; [while their] vessels stand, fast by the shore, surrounded by the stream. And then the voyagers, weary in mind, and without thought of danger, encamp on the isle. They produce a flame, they kindle a vast fire. Full of joy are the heroes, late so sad of spirit; they are longing for repose. But when the creature, long skilled in guile, feels that the sailors are securely resting upon him, and are keeping their abode there, in enjoyment of the weather, suddenly into the salt wave, together with his prey, down dives the Ocean-dweller and seeks the abyss; and thus, by drowning them, imprisons the ships, with all their men, in the hall of death.

Juan Fernandez, however, is real and stable enough, and its history subsequent to its occupation by the buccaneers has been an exceedingly chequered one. For seventy years from 1749 it was under Spanish sovereignty. In May 1751 during an earthquake an enormous tidal wave swept over it, drowning the governor, his family and thirty-five other souls. Fifteen other Spanish governors came and went. The island was converted into a state prison, became notorious for the misery of its inmates, and was abandoned in 1814. Chili seized it, deporting thither her political malcontents. Once more horror reigned, and again, in 1822, the island was abandoned. So runs the story on.

In 1835, when an English adventurer named Sutcliffe was governor, another vast seismic wave from out of the sea swept over it, and was followed at night by an eruption of flames and smoke out of deep water a full mile from the beach. The island was again abandoned, and for ten years was peopled only by waifs and strays. It reverted to the vile conditions of a penal settlement. Then once more—man being what man is, and especially in South America—horror and bloodshed; then abandonment. And the island breathed in peace again.

A ship chandler named Flint leased Más-á-tierra in 1867. He failed, as did his successor. In the following year a tablet to the memory of 'Alexander Selkirk Mariner' was erected by the commander and the officers of the *Topaze*. The intention was no doubt excellent, and yet, such is man, it somehow affects one's visionary view of the island much as the handsome effigy in stone of Mr. Palmer, armed with his high hat and umbrella, affects the sensitive visitor to that ancient city of many parliaments —Reading. We feel he was worthy of memorialization, but not quite like that.

In 1895 only fifty-three inhabitants were found on the island, eking out their lives by exporting cod, dog-fish, seal-pelts and goatskins. Its police-force then consisted of four invalided pensioners, and in spite of them its social life was denounced as 'discreditable'.

In 1915 the vast cold searchlight of the War momentarily settled upon it. For on March 14th of that year the *Dresden*, having escaped disaster in the Falklands, was there scuttled by her captain, thus sparing the *Glasgow* and *Kent* that office. Chili resented English intervention. But His Majesty's Government deeply regretted that 'any misunderstanding should have arisen', and were prepared 'to offer a full and ample apology'. With that offer, the curtain has descended again for the time being on Selkirk's hermitage.

As for islands that have come and gone, the Governments of England and Norway were only recently at odds concerning an island which neither could afterwards locate. Even in these days the oceans remain spacious enough for that. But that a complete archipelago, no less than six hundred miles long by three hundred miles wide, should have vanished from civilization's ken for two whole centuries after its discovery, and should have remained unfound, though sought for, is an event that is, alas, hardly likely to recur.

This was the fate of the Solomon Islands; and even as lately as 1901 they were still unprospected and largely unexplored. In 1567 an expedition for 'the discovery of certain islands and a continent' set sail from Peru under Alvaro de Mendaña. The number of all that embarked on this voyage was 150 men, including, besides the soldiers and sailors, four Franciscan friars and the slaves. Mendaña's two ships sailed on Wednesday, 19th November. 'Early in December we noticed the flight of the birds that passed us in the morning and evening, and whence they came, and whither they went towards the setting sun. All this was no certain guide.' By January they had begun to doubt whether they would ever see land. 'But I always told them that, if God was with them, it would be His pleasure that they should not suffer ill.' It is Hernando Gallego, Mendaña's chief pilot, who is speaking.

One thousand four hundred and fifty leagues from Peru they sighted a small island six leagues away. Though

Gallego wished to reach it, he decided, such was its situation, that 'it would not be wise to run the risk of losing all our lives for an island so small', and consoled the malcontents, who were weary of the voyage and unwilling to leave even so poor a haven as this, with the promise that he would 'give them more land than they would be able to people'. He named it the Isle of Jesus. But this island has not yet been rediscovered.

On they sailed, and on the 7th of February, the eightieth day since they had set out from 'the port of the City of Kings', they sighted land, 'very high':

Every one received the news with feelings of great joy and gratitude for the favour which God had granted them through the intercession of the Blessed Virgin, the Glorious Mother of God, whom we all believed to be our mediator; and the *Te Deum laudamus* was sung.

A small force was landed, which forthwith burned 'many temples dedicated to the worship of snakes, toads and other insects'. A wounded soldier died of tetanus, and the evil seed of vengeance was sown. These savages 'are tawny and have crisp hair. They go naked, wearing only short aprons of palm leaves. . . . They are, in my opinion, a clean race, and I am certain that they eat human flesh.' While the Spaniards were celebrating Mass on shore on the 15th of March canoes arrived, and the cacique in command sent Mendaña 'a present of a quarter of a boy, including the arm and hand, together with some roots'. These remains Mendaña conspicuously buried; at which the gift-bearers 'were abashed and hung their heads'. The expedition sailed on from island to island, north-west to south-east, leaving behind them not peace but enmity and hatred. On their return voyage, their daily rations were reduced to half a quartern of stinking water. Scurvy spread. Some went blind. A dead body was thrown overboard every day. A soldier gambled away his ration of water, and went mad. The hundred of them that survived reached Peru on June 19th, 1568.

Anxious, for the glory of Spain, that these islands should be colonized, Mendaña called them 'The Islands of

Salomon', deliberately baiting the name, so it appears, with the hint that here was to be found the Ophir of Solomon. Years went by, and Drake appeared upon the South Sea. Mendaña's scheme was abandoned for the time being, and Gallego's Journal suppressed—it remained, as a matter of fact, in manuscript, until the second quarter of the nineteenth century. 'Commandement was given, that [the islands] should not be inhabited, to the end that such Englishmen, and men of other Nations as passed the Straits of Magellan to goe to the Malucos [Moluccas], might have no succour there, but such as they got of the Indian people.'

News of the islands reached the English through a Portuguese prisoner, Lopez Vaz, but nothing came of it. In 1595 there arose a new viceroy in Peru, and under his auspices Mendaña (now aged 53), accompanied by his wife, and with de Quiros for chief pilot, set sail for St. Christoval. When about half-way across the Pacific they believed they had found the Solomons. But Mendaña soon discovered his mistake, and he called these new islands Las Marquesas de Mendoza. They voyaged on, and after a prodigious rainstorm in which the *Almiranta*, with a hundred souls on board, vanished, never to be seen again, they discovered within a league of them yet another large island. Once again Mendaña was disappointed, for this was Santa Cruz. He determined to seek no further; but to rest content and to colonize that. But disaster followed disaster. He himself sickened and died a few hours after a total eclipse of the moon. The superstitious Spaniards hailed it as an evil omen. His successor followed him. The rest took to their ships, and in their search for that 'clumsy tub', the *Almiranta*, missed by but a few hours the mountain-tops of St. Christoval itself. Only two of the four ships that had set sail from Peru reached the Philippines. The *Fragata* was found long afterwards 'driven ashore with all her sails set and all her people dead and rotten'.

De Quiros tried again, in 1605, and once more by a mere

mischance missed his quarry. Yet again in 1614, having presented no fewer than fifty memorials to the king—'Acquire, sire, since you can, acquire heaven, eternal fame, and that new world with all its promises'—he made preparations for another attempt. They were not to be fulfilled. He died at Panama on his way home. Had he lived to carry out his project, Queensland might well have become a new Peru.

It was not until 1766, and in part owing to the fact that European astronomers were anxious to secure an appropriate site from which to observe the transit of Venus in 1769, that Captain Carteret, in the *Swallow*, chanced upon the long-lost islands—whose very existence he himself had doubted—and even then he was unaware that he had succeeded. After him came Bougainville and others. But Mendaña? Quiros? 'The brave navigator goes and returns not; the seekers search far seas for him in vain . . . and only some mournful and mysterious shadow of him hovers long in all heads and hearts.' As for the Solomon Islanders, three centuries of isolation have left them unchanged, except that, like the rarer English wild flowers, they are rapidly dwindling in numbers, and in time, perhaps, will be gone.

Page 23²—Marooned:

¶ The word maroon, says the dictionary, is said to be a corruption of the Spanish *cimarron*—wild, from *cima*—mountain-top, and ultimately the Greek, *kuma*—wave. Its earliest use recorded in the N.E.D. is of 1626. According to R. C. Dallas, the author of *The History of the Maroons*, it meant in Jamaica 'hog-hunters'. These maroons were fugitive negro slaves of the Spaniards, who during their domination over the island, once the headquarters of William Morgan and the buccaneers, had stamped out the original natives who were themselves descendants of the gentle and romantic race of Guiana encountered by Raleigh during his quest of El Dorado.

For over a century, from 1650, these runaway negroes

defended their freedom against the English by force of arms, the odds in men immeasurably against them. Under their chiefs, Cudjoe, Accomping, Johnny, and others, they 'defied the choicest troops of one of the greatest nations in the world, kept an extensive country in alarm, and were at length brought to surrender only by means of a subvention still more extraordinary than their own mode of warfare'.

Their strongholds were of volcanic origin—wide ravines with precipitous sides, and negotiable only by way of steep shelved narrow alleys of rock, through which their assailants could march only in single file—sheer fissures debouching into luxuriant and primeval forest glades. They were called cock-pits.

In Dallas's time (1803) a negro slave in Jamaica, he tells us, incidentally, was worth a round £50 sterling. He worked from dawn till sunset—with two hours' rest in the heat of the day. For comparison it may be mentioned that the white maid-of-all-work in Victorian times, who enjoyed an occasional 'evening out', was paid about £10 a year— then roughly equivalent to a capital sum of £300 —and that this was the price of a female slave in Virginia before the Civil War.

Jamaica is the island of a hundred rivers, and apart from the vagaries of Nature (one of which has been recently described by Mr. Richard Hughes in his *High Wind in Jamaica*), it is delectable, though hot. 'The twilight is brief,' says Dallas, 'the nights are beautiful, the planet Venus shines so luminously in its pellucid night-skies as to cast a shadow from trees, like another moon.' Not many years ago, says my encyclopaedia, there was such a plague of rats in Jamaica that the mongoose was imported to get rid of them. The rats vanished. So the agile mongooses began to exterminate the harmless snakes, the small birds and the lizards, and there followed a pestilent plague of insects, especially of ticks. It reminds one of the bumble-bees and the clover and the cats; also of Mr. Ralph Hodgson:

130

> . . . I saw in vision
> The worm in the wheat,
> And in the shops nothing
> For people to eat;
> Nothing for sale in
> Stupidity Street.

Page 28¹—Goats' flesh, broiled or boiled:

¶ The most obvious reason why records of the castaway are so few is this odd obligation we all labour under as mortals to be continually converting what is without into the within. We must have water; we must find food:

> 'A loaf of bread,' the Walrus said,
> 'Is what we chiefly need . . .'

else we abandon without long delay even the pleasantest of retreats.

> Now when they got as far as the Equator
> They'd nothing left but one split pea—

that is the situation—as it is related, more soberly, in the record of an expedition to the South Seas in 1591, under the command of Thomas Cavendish:

> But after we came neere unto the sun, our dried Penguins began to corrupt, and there bred in them a most lothsome and ugly worme of an inch long. This worme did so mightily increase and devoure our victuals, that there was in reason no hope how we should avoide famine, but be devoured of these wicked creatures: there was nothing that they did not devoure, only yron excepted: our clothes, boots, shooes, hats, shirts, stockings: and, for the ship, they did so eat the timbers as that we greatly feared they would undoe us by gnawing through the ships side. Great was the care and diligence of our captaine, master, and company to consume these vermine, but the more we laboured to kill them the more they increased; so that at the last we could not sleepe for them, for they would eate our flesh and bite like Mosquitos. In this wofull case, after we had passed the Equinoctiall toward the North, our men began to fall sick of such a monstrous disease, as I thinke the like was never heard of. . . . Our captaine with extreme anguish of his soule was in such wofull case that he desired only a speedie end, and though he were scarce able to speake for sorrow, yet he perswaded them to patience, and to give God thankes, and, like dutifull children, to accept of his chastisement. For all this, divers grew raging mad, and some died in most lothsome and furious paine. It were incredible to write our misery as it

was : there was no man in perfect health but the captaine and one boy. The master being a man of good spirit with extreme labour bore out his griefe, so that it grew not upon him. To be short, all our men died except 16, of which there were but 5 able to moove.

Could any man desire better word of himself than that about the 'master'? His like is to be found throughout the history of the sea; and, in fiction, in Conrad's *The Secret Sharer* and in Mr. Humphrey Jordan's *The Prevailing Wind*.

To perish for want of *drink* must, for an Englishman, be a more unusual experience. He has, at any rate, no word, equivalent to *starve*, that signifies this process.

In his book on *Galápagos: World's End*, a book resembling a tropical island in its wealth of exotic life, Dr. William Beebe repeats a story that was related to him by a taxi-cab driver, named Christiansen, whom he met by chance the day after his return to civilization and New York. Christiansen had sailed from New South Wales bound for Panama in a Norwegian barque, when a boy of nineteen, seventeen years before. This was in November. In early May his ship was still becalmed in the Pacific, and at last, her stores of food and fresh water being nearly exhausted, her master gave up all hope of preserving the lives of himself and all on board if they remained inactive. He summoned the crew and candidly gave them the choice between staying on the ship or making in open boats for some islands—'off here to the north-west of us'. All chose the islands. They lit the barque's running lights, 'nailed notices to the cabin door', ran up the Norwegian flag and abandoned her, setting off in two boat-loads, ten men to each. Christiansen was in the captain's boat.

On the twelfth day they sighted land. It was Indefatigable Island. 'Nothing but lava. So there we was.' For months this little band of derelicts managed to keep life in their bodies by drinking turtles' blood— 'Boy, that's sweet. It turned *me*. I didn't want any'—and a little brackish water found among the rocks. They scooped out the rich yellow fat of these turtles with their hands. Their boat having been smashed to tinder, they wandered on over the lava beaches of the island, pining for water and searching for food. Inland, among unapproachable volcanic hills, streamed down a blessed rain from the clouds above. 'We could see [it] falling every day,' but, 'after a while we got so we didn't even talk about it any more.'

Two whole months had gone by and they had tasted nothing but raw turtle and similar delicacies, seal-meat being 'awful tough and fishy', when the ship's carpenter, who for the liveliest of reasons had divested himself one afternoon of the two flannel shirts he wore, discovered a box of damp matches which had remained hidden in an inner pocket the whole eight weeks! 'Baby. We laid them out in a row . . . and watched them dry.' And the lava of Indefatigable Island warmed to a fire.

Some of them fell sick and some of them died. 'Nights was the bad time . . . Nights was the worst!' In a bay at the foot of precipitous cliffs they came at length on rotted relics of previous castaways, including two pairs of ladies' slippers and some magazines dated 1894. Here they found water 'not exactly fresh' but in plenty. 'Funny, after we got to that beach, we hardly talked at all. . . . We just sort of grunted and held out our hands when we wanted something, or made some kind of a signal. Seemed like it was too much trouble to talk.' Of what they *thought*, when they thought at all, little is related. 'One day we was all eating. I can see us now. . . . My whiskers and my hair was long and I was grease all over, and then, suddenly, a cry, "Ship! Ship! Ship!" '

In earlier times similar experiences might be enjoyed much nearer home. When the Earl of Cumberland's expedition to the Azores, etc., was returning home to England:

it befell, that we kept a colde Christmas with the Bishop and his clearks (rockes that lye to the Westwards from Sylly, and the Western parts of England): For soone after, the wind scanting came about to the Eastwards . . . in such sort, that we could not fetch any part of

England. . . . In the meane time, we were allowed every man three or foure spoones full of vinegar to drinke at a meale: . . . With this hard fare (for by reason of our great want of drinke, wee durst eate but very little), wee continued for the space of a fourtnight or thereabouts: Saving that now and then wee feasted. . . . And that was when there fell any haile or raine: the haile-stones wee gathered up, and did eate them more pleasantly then if they had bene the sweetest Comfits in the world: The rainedrops were so carefully saved, that so neere as wee coulde, not one was lost in all our shippe.

But to return from fact to fiction, a motionless veil of the imagination hangs over the story of Arthur Gordon Pym—a banquet of horrors such as very few tales of this genre can have excelled. One may even suspect that Poe, with his passion for rivalry, embarked upon his story with this maximum in mind. Four young men named—a little oddly for their peculiar circumstances—Arthur, Peters, Parker and Augustus, are the only survivors on board a water-logged ship in mid ocean. They are starving. Turn and turn about they dive again and again, with a chain fixed to the ankle for ballast, in an attempt to reach the flooded storeroom with its locked door. In these straits a Dutch hermaphrodite brig, painted black and with a tawdry gilt figure-head, looms into view, sails set, and draws near over the sea. They dance and yell in a frenzy of rapture—even though to the eyes of these anguished castaways there is a trace of the odd in the motions of her steersman. When she has come rocking on, not only within hail but into sharp close view, they realize there is no help in her. She is at the mercy of the winds, for the body of the steersman is without mind or intended motion, and it is the flutterings of a sea-gull glutting itself upon his liver that occasion his erratic movements at the helm. The bird heavily flies up, then wheels; and there drops from its beak a fragment of its spoil at their feet. They eye it and, furtively, one another. The decks of the brig are strewn with corpses, male and female, their skins saffron in hue, owing, it would seem, to the ravages of yellow fever.

One of the four perishes. The three left, now *in extremis,* draw lots to decide which of them shall be sacrificed for the maintenance of the other two. This they do by means of splinters instead of the usual straws. Arthur's state of mind, as with outstretched hand he sits stark while the two anatomies at his side draw out in turn their chosen splinters from between his fingers, can be compared only to that of the gentlemen seated round the green-baize table in Stevenson's story of the Suicide Club; and this not to Poe's disadvantage. In the course of these extremities Augustus shrinks in weight from a hundred and twenty-seven pounds to about forty-five. The voyagers of the sixteenth and seventeenth centuries shared conditions scarcely less abject; but, owing in part to Poe's peculiar concern with the phenomena of putrefaction, their records are easier to digest.

An open boat brought three passengers almost as much reduced, but far more dangerous, to Axel Heyst's paradise in Joseph Conrad's *Victory*. Phthisical, emaciated Mr. Jones—with his 'used-up, weary, depraved distinction'—because perhaps he is the most civilized of them, is by far the most sinister, and that guileless and familiar name becomes as densely dyed with his evil influence as the staves of a rum-keg are with rum.

Page 28²—Turnips:

❡ Selkirk at first lost all appetite; he missed acutely bread and salt, but he was soon well off for vegetables. Besides his turnip-greens and his cabbage-trees, he had parsley, purslain, 'sithes' (? chives) and a herb with a very cordial and grateful smell resembling that of balm. He was about twenty-six when he was marooned, and had dreamed that the leaky ship he was on would soon be lost—a dream that came true. He was 'the best Man in her'; and very welcome to Rogers, who nicknamed him 'the Governour'.

Apart from the Mosquito Indian, and prior to Selkirk's sojourn there, Basil Ringrose, the buccaneer, mentions a shipwrecked sailor who was five years alone on Juan Fernandez before he was taken off by a passing ship. A much briefer solitude was that of a gunner who deserted from Dampier and swam off to the island of Gorgona, between Corsica and Leghorn. He was a man of action and resource:

> He cut down two small trees, which he dragged to the Water side, and bound together with Twigs. On these he fixed a little Mast, and of two Shirts which he had with him, made a small Sail. Having a large Bag he filled it with Oysters, and made it fast to the two Trees, and, early in the Morning, put off from the Island, on this desperate Equipment, and so passed the Night on the Ocean.

He landed the next afternoon. For another *kind* of hermit there is the 'painted prince' whom Dampier brought home to England. 'Being reduced to low circumstances, he sold Prince Jeoly, who', poor soul, was then 'carried about for a Shew, till he died of the Small-Pox at Oxford'.

Page 30¹—Selkirk:

❡ Steele's, though the best, was only one of no fewer than four contemporary published accounts of Selkirk, and there are two narratives of his life beside. Steele himself frequently talked with Selkirk. He believed that even if he had been ignorant of Selkirk's story, he would still have detected the ravages of solitude in his 'aspect and gesture'. He 'showed a certain disregard to the ordinary things about him, as if he had been sunk in thought'.

Like Gulliver, Selkirk regretted his return to the busy world. Possessed of £800 in prize money—his share of the 'hundred Ton of Gold' which was the value of the rich Acapulco ship seized by *The Duke* and *The Duchess*—he was not so happy, he said, as when he hadn't a farthing. After a few months' absence Steele met him again 'in the street, and though he spoke to me I could not recall that I had seen him. Familiar discourse . . . had taken off the loneliness of his aspect, and quite altered the air of his face'.

Selkirk returned eventually to Largo and to his parents, but, shunning the haunts of men, constructed a cave in their garden, 'where he sought repose in solitude'. He fished, he rambled, and in these solitary self-communings often encountered a young girl named Sophia Bruce tending a single cow. For hours as she sat singing he watched her innocent face, unseen, and at length they eloped to London. It was a brief idyll, for there he seems to have abandoned her.

He returned home, once more offended the elders of his native kirk by engaging in a broil, and, after visiting Bristol and Liverpool, went again to sea. And at sea he died—in 1723. He is said to have bequeathed his effects to 'sundry loving females'—including two who claimed to be his widows. But of this episode Defoe made no practical use.

Finally, 'by this one may see', and it may be the Scots elders would have agreed, 'that solitude, and retirement from the world, is not such an unsufferable state of life as most men imagine, especially when people are fairly thrown into it unavoidably, as this man was'.

In a neat little volume, with smudgy cuts and a map, and entitled *Providence Displayed*, Isaac James records the experiences of a few other castaways. Between 1525 and 1555, for example, a seaman named Peter Serrano swam ashore when his ship was wrecked off the coast of Peru, and found himself on a sandy island where there was neither water, wood nor grass, only raw cockles, shrimps, turtles and rain-puddles. To secure fresh water he made cisterns of his turtle shells, emptying the smaller ones into the greater until he had accumulated a fair supply. To make fire he dived for pebbles as there were none in his sand, chipped them to an edge, and used threads of his shirt for tinder. He was three years 'in this state'. And in that time his hair had grown like bristles all over his body.

A second castaway then took refuge on his island. Serrano thought he was a devil until, as this stranger bounded on in hot pursuit of him, he overheard him reciting the Apostles' Creed! They quarrelled, they separated, they made it up, and lived afterwards together in amity for four years.

After his rescue Serrano kept his gigantic beard as a souvenir and for proof of his long seclusion, and Charles V, then Emperor of Germany, bestowed on him a pension of 4,800 Peruvian ducats a year. Serrano then cut down his beard because it incommoded him in bed.

In 1614 two survivors of an abandoned passage boat between England and Dublin found themselves on an island 'towards the Extremities of Scotland', their only shelter at first being a kind of cromlech. They, too, had no water but the rain. At the end of six weeks one of them vanished during the night. His companion lived on alone for eleven months in all, and when snow fell—a rare phenomenon in island stories—he caught sea-mews by means of a little stick baited with sea-dog's fat, which he stuck out of a crevice in the hut he had built out of drift-wood.

Isaac James tells also of a seaman (somewhat on the outskirts of this particular theme) who was condemned to death, reprieved, and marooned on the then deserted St. Helena. He dug up the coffin of one of the ship's officers who had been lately buried there, launched it in fair weather, and paddled out to his ship. She lay becalmed a league and a half away. Whether one credits this story or not, it is pleasant to hear that all was forgiven and forgotten.

Increase Mather—part author of surely one of the *blackest* books in English—tells of yet another anchoret who was cast away on the isle of Roncador in the Caribbean Sea. He had fish, fowls, flint and fire. When he was rescued, though only two years had gone by, 'the man having in so long a time conversed only with Heaven, looked . . . very strangely, and was not able at first Conference promptly to speak and answer'. But the 'very strangely' is too vague and the 'Heaven' too explicit.

And, last, Isaac James gives a brief account of a young woman, of the Western Dog-ribbed tribe of Indians, who was found on the 11th of January, 1772, on the south side of the Athapupuskow Lake in that vast tract of country west of Hudson Bay where of late three snow-bound explorers came to so tragic an end. She had escaped from a hostile tribe that had taken her prisoner. When her deer sinews failed she made snares of the sinews of rabbits and clothes of their skins 'which were not only of real Service, [but] showed great Taste, and exhibited no little Variety of Ornament'. She had twisted willow-bark fibres into twine for fishing-nets, and had made snow-shoes by means of five or six inches of hoop-iron for a knife, and the shank of an arrow-head for awl, having never seen iron before. Thus she had spent in solitude the dark icy months of winter. And though it is a long, far call, the name of Emily Brontë springs to mind.

The record of yet another castaway is cited by Dr. William Beebe from Captain David Porter's *Journal of a Cruise made to the Pacific Ocean* (1822). His name was Patrick Watkins, and of his own will apparently he abandoned the English ship that had carried him to the Galápagos and became the first resident on Charles Island.

Captain Porter described this hermit merely by hearsay —he himself was the commander of an American frigate that busied itself (a little unconscionably) with the capture of English whaling ships. His appearance 'was the most dreadful that can be imagined; ragged clothes, scarcely sufficient to cover his nakedness, and covered with vermin; his red hair and beard matted, his skin much burnt, and so wild and savage in his manner that he struck everyone with horror'. For several years he lived alone. Then he was outmanoeuvred by a negro whom like Friday he intended to make the subject of his sole monarchy, and in consequence was mercilessly whipped by the captain of the English smuggler of which the negro was one of the crew, was robbed of his money, potatoes and pumpkins, and once more marooned on the island, but in handcuffs. He rid himself of these by means of an old file which he drove into a tree.

When ships touched at the island he would waylay

one of the crew, drench him with rum and keep him in servitude. He thus secured four more or less willing prisoners.

Wild and savage though his appearance might be, even at the end of his sojourn on the island he could indulge in as choice a sentence as, 'I have been a long time endeavouring, by hard labour and suffering, to accumulate the wherewithal to make myself comfortable', and, at the end of his letter, could fall back into his ease again with 'Do not kill the old hen; she is now sitting and will soon have chicks'. Patrick at last set sail with his subjects in an open boat, but he arrived alone at Guayaquil. He explained there had been a shortage of water on the voyage! A tawny damsel then entering the tale, romance goes out of it, and what finally became of 'fatherless Oberlus', the pseudonym with which Watkins signed his letter, is not related.

Page 30²—¶ Defoe
or De Foe, or simply Foe, as his grandfather was content to call himself, and *he* kept a pack of hounds. Defoe relates that in his own day there was a family of Norman descent in Warwickshire named De Beau-Foe (possibly, thinks Wilson, de Beaufoy), and that members of it who had retained only 'the latter part of their sirname' were scattered about the country. But he seems to have left merely as an inference what it would obviously have pleased him to claim as a fact.

Page 30³—The life . . . of Crusoe:
¶ The copy of the first edition of Robinson Crusoe in the library of the British Museum is in enviable company; it shares a case with *The Compleat Angler, Paradise Lost, Pilgrim's Progress* and *Gulliver's Travels*, while under the next pane of glass lie *Tottel's Miscellany*, Sidney's *Apologie for Poetrie*, Bacon's *Essays*, Herrick's *Hesperides* and *The Faërie Queene*. If only some April evening one might surprise the shades of these ten authors hobnobbing around that case.

Page 32¹—Money is money's worth:

¶ It is also one of the problems that resemble the porcupine, particularly in its relation to the author and the artist. One of Dr. Johnson's best-known axioms is, 'No man but a blockhead ever wrote except for money'. Another is his remark to Dr. Strahan: 'There are few ways in which a man can be more innocently employed than in getting money'. He was then in his sixties, but when, in the last year of his twenties, his poem 'London' was published, it included this couplet:

> Turn from the glittering bribe thy scornful eye,
> Nor sell for gold what gold could never buy.

The view changes a little if after 'wrote' in the first quotation (which does not imply that those who write only for money are never blockheads) we add *well*; after 'money', in the second quotation, *innocently*, and alter the 'could' in the third to *should*. You may contract with a poet to supply you with a grammatical and technically competent or even a new sonnet; it is when you bargain with him for an original, a beautiful, or even a good sonnet that doubts and difficulties begin. Excellent authors have written for a living; their excellence depends on how much of life itself has gone into their writing.

Page 32²—Fortunate Hannah:

¶ In 1722 Defoe invested about £1,000 in an estate called Kingswood Heath in Colchester for her benefit, money, it appears, that had been invested in the South Sea Company. Hannah, then thirty, was one of a family of two sons and four daughters. Of the eldest daughter, Maria, who 'married a person of the name of Langley', 'further particulars are wanted'. On April 30th, 1729, Sophia, the youngest, married a Mr. Henry Baker. 'Always happy in each other,' they lived together thirty-two years. Hannah after her father's death—her portion in his estate having been retrieved, it seems, from her brother—went to live at Wimborne in Dorsetshire. Like her other sister, Henrietta—whose only grandson, William, as a boy went to sea and was drowned—'she was considered a sensible woman but of peculiar habits'. But these are not specified. She died on April 25th, 1759, and her body lies interred in the beautiful minster.

A great-grandson of Defoe named John Joseph was hanged at Tyburn on January 2nd, 1771, for a highway robbery; another, David, was bound apprentice to a watchmaker, but he too ran away to sea and became cook to the gentlemen of the gun-room of the *Savage*, sloop-of-war. Yet another was brought up a caulker, and a fourth became a boxmaker and undertaker. This great-grandson had eight children of whom four died in infancy. Other descendants followed the callings of haberdasher, tick merchant, schoolmaster and print-seller.

'Curiosity,' says Wilson in introducing these particulars, 'will be naturally awake to learn the fate of a family that descended from so ingenious a writer.' But when Curiosity is (though, perhaps, inadequately) satisfied and turns away, we may find that she has left a gentler and younger sister in our company, named Compassion. For one cannot look along life for many generations anywhere with complete composure, any more than one can so regard the monuments to dead strangers in a church. The faint red thread of the odd yet apposite, of the curious and predestined, in the grey fabric of what looks so commonplace—how moving it becomes in retrospect: so much busyness, so much trouble, so many hopes and sorrows and interests and delights, and always the steadily descending quiet dust on what is past and gone, the dust whence springs the most narcotic of all earth's poppies, oblivion.

Page 33¹—Seven other publications:
❡ The other four are *Charity still a Christian Virtue; A Letter to the Dissenters; Some Account of the Life and Most Remarkable Actions of Henry Baron de Goertz*, who died a noble death on the scaffold; and *A Friendly Rebuke to One Parson Benjamin*, that parson being Benjamin Hoadley, then Bishop of Bangor.

Page 33²—Dickory Cronke:

¶ Dickory Cronke was the son of a tinner of St. Columb's, in Cornwall, and was nicknamed Restoration Dick because he was born on the day of King Charles's return to his kingdom. It was not until he was three years old that his parents discovered he was dumb. He was a precocious little scholar, was adopted by a 'Welch gentleman' and retired finally to St. Helens (in Cornwall).

Defoe wrote him up. He was accustomed to writing things up. He informed his readers that Dickory was in the habit of rising and retiring all the year round with the sun—thus saving on the swings what he lost on the roundabouts; that he enjoyed walking; that he lived on bread and milk—'a quantity of a pint and sometimes more'—which suited him so admirably 'that he never slept out of a bed, and never lay awake in one'.

No less admirable habits of mind accompanied these wholesome habits of body; for Dickory—Defoe adds with unction—was never heard to complain except at the oaths of the tinners or when he saw them drunk. He then made sorrowful sounds of reproach, and next day would present the culprits with a little essay on the subject of the misuse of language or of alcohol. Lastly, he was never idle. He was, in fact, a paragon, though one may suspect Defoe of gilding the lily, his motives in so doing being irreproachable. 'If,' he says, 'the world could be persuaded to look upon him [Dickory] with candour and impartiality, and then to copy after him, the Editor has gained his end.'

But as with Defoe's treatise on Marriage, even excellent motives may cast a shadow. Having justified the candour of this particular treatise, Defoe concludes: 'With this satisfaction he [the Editor] comfortably prays for its success'. And, to judge from its chapter headings, he cannot have prayed in vain.

Page 33³—Sir John Mandeville:

❡ Sir John Mandeville or Syr John Maundeville—or to give him what seems to have been his real name, John of Burgundy, or John with a Beard—has for many years been the victim of a fiercely debated literary problem, though now apparently it is agreed that the *Travels* attributed to him are a magpie's nest of other men's silver spoons and gewgaws, and that the shadowy jester— *un menteur à triple étage*—who was responsible for building it was a notary public of Liége named Jean d'Outre-meuse, who died in 1400.

But the book's the thing, whatever its origin or author-ship, and in its kind in English the *Travels* cannot be ex-celled—its avidity, its ingenuousness, the quality of its light and colour. What wonder it has been a perennial joy from the end of the fourteenth century, when it first appeared, until our own day; and its pages, of course, are almost as thickly inlaid with islands as the floor of heaven is with patines of bright gold. For example:

And there is also a great yle that men call Java & the kinge of that countrey hath under hym seven kinges, for he is a full mightie prince. In this yle groweth all maner of spyces more plenteously than in any other place, as ginger, clowes, canell [or cinnamon], nutmyge and other, and ye shall understande that the nutmyge beareth the maces, & of all thing therein is plenty savinge wine. The King of this lande hath a riche palace and the best that is in the worlde, for all the greces of his hall and chambres are all made one of gold & another of silver, & all the walls are plated with fine gold and silver, & on those plates are written stories of knightes, and batayles, and the pavimente of the hall and chambres is of golde and silver, and there is no man that woulde beleve this riches that is there except hee had sene it. . . .

And this:

. . . Whoso goeth from Cathay to Inde the high and the low, he shal go through a kingdome that men call Cadissen & it is a great lande, there groweth a maner of fruite as it were gourdes, & when it is ripe men cut it a sonder, and men fynde therein a beast as it were of fleshe and bone and bloud, as it were a lyttle lambe without wolle, and men eate the beast & fruite also, and sure it semeth very strange. Neverthelesse I sayd to them that I held y^t for no marvayle, for I sayd that in my countrey are trees y^t beare fruit y^t become byrds flying, and they are good to eate, & that that falleth on the water liveth & that that falleth on earth dyeth, & they marvailed much thereat.

There is again the 'yland' of the giants, 'xlv or L fote long, & some sayd L cubits long', with their sheep like young oxen, that 'beare great wolle'. Orell and Argete, too:

There are more eastward two other yles—ye one is called Orell and the other Argete of whom all the land is mine of gold & silver. In those yles many men se no sters clere shining, but one starre y^t is called Canapos and there many men se not ye Mone but in the last quarter. In that yle is a great hyll of golde that pismyres, or ants, kepe, & they do fine golde from the other that is not fine golde, and the pismyres are as great as houndes, so that no man dare come there for dread of pismyres that should assayle them; so that men may not worke in that gold nor get thereof but by subtiltie, and therefore when it is righte hote the pismyres hide them in the earth from undern to none of the daye, and then men of the countrey take Cameles and dormedaries and other beastes & go thither and charge them with gold and go away fast or the pismyres come out of the earth. And other times when it is not so hot y^t the pismyres hide them not, they take mares that haue foles, and they lay upon these mares two long vessels, as it were two small barels and the mouth upwards and drive them thether and holde theyr foles at home; and when the pismyres se these vessels they spring therein, for they haue of kinde to leue no hold nor pyt open, and anone they fyl these vessels with golde, and when men think that the vessels be full they take the foles and bring them as nere as they dare, and then they whine, and the mares heare them, and anone they come to theyr foles and so they take the gold, for these pismyres will suffer beastes for to go among them, but no men.

About three centuries divide Mandeville from Defoe; and rather more than three Hakluyt and his voyagers from ourselves; and, apart from Mandeville's fantastic fabrications, it is curious to realize how sharp a change has taken place in human consciousness since his day and theirs in its outlook on the world of the actual. In Mandeville there is as naive and greedy a delight in *things* as there is in *Crusoe*, but for their rarity, their strangeness, their preciousness. Their use, their age and their marketableness seem not very much to have interested him.

What still enthralls us, as it must have enthralled his earliest readers, is the remoteness of his romantic *'yles'*.

They lie beyond verification. Their distance is incomputable. And if we accepted as our unit of measurement of the distance between two places the amount of vivid experience derivable from the journey between them, no modern inventions would succeed in dwarfing *our* world. But one cannot glean a very rich harvest of that at a thousand miles an hour. A page or two of *Arabia Deserta*, however, will restore one's imaginative yard-measure, or even a glance at a map of the vast sterile State of Nevada—which drinks up its own rivers, and whose inhabitants now number less than two to the square mile.

Still the ascertained has to a great extent destroyed the strange and the marvellous with the fabulous and the apocryphal. And this though the most enthusiastic globe-planer of us all can have actually set eyes on but a small fraction of the earth's surface. Our newspapers are so persistently concerned with the great powers and countries of the globe, they are so reticent about the others, that we are apt to forget or to ignore the never-mentioned, and so fail to realize how immense and how various, how strange and how remote these regions and the races that inhabit them remain.

Civilized man, we are told, is on the point of vacating his nursery and will presently, poor soul of endless gallantries, set out to his preparatory school. Precisely how happy he will be there or what conception of the world awaits the intelligent occupant of it when yet another three centuries have been humanly occupied is not within easy speculation. It may prove to be that of another kind of 'Mandeville'—a romantic poet, aged, in terms of civilization, not five, but, say, eleven—and yet, the gulf between! He may himself be the product of the biologist. Or are dark ages lying in wait for him? To what degree again will he share our sense of wonder, of beauty, our waning desire for peace, silence, solitude?

However that may be, a leader-writer in *The Times* lately assured his readers that 'the days of the traveller's tale are done'. But how recent is the completion of this process, for though only a few months ago a great explorer was relating how in the shadow of the Great Wall of China he had found in the dead calm that dreams there the footprints in the sand left by his dog eight years previously, and how he had picked up full in the light of the sun a scatter of coins that must have fallen from the money-bags of a caravan that had passed that way (I think), before Caesar landed in Britain; and though news from Ur and elsewhere is no less romantic, where now are the fond dreams of my infancy—those wild, icy, bear-infested haunts of Aurora, the North and the South Poles? They have followed the unicorn—not into extinction, but, far worse, into disrepute. Power-stations multiply in darkest Africa. The lion amid his harem sits to be snapshotted by a naturalist with a 'Brownie' in a Ford. The haunts of the once famous gorilla will soon, it seems, be dumb. 'The more primitive sense of wonder, the pure gape, is no longer' gratifiable.

Alas, 'tis true 'tis pity, and pity 'tis 'tis true, for to some of us gaping is still one of the most enjoyable methods of inhaling the breath of life.

Page 33[4]*—The 'Farther Adventures':*
¶ Bitter controversy followed its publication; but 'Defoe had been so long accustomed to the ill usage of the world that he must have been prepared for its assaults whenever they should overtake him. Whether he appeared abroad as a politician or a moralist, provoking resentment by his satire, or furnishing matter for calming the passions, scandal was still at his heels.' One such assault was an anonymous pamphlet—the work of Charles Gildon who had the privilege of appearing in *The Dunciad*. It consists of eighteen small pages, and the title (of the second edition) runs thus:

The Life and Strange Surprizing Adventures of Mr. D- De F-, of London, Hosier, who has liv'd above fifty Years by himself, in the Kingdoms of *North* and *South Britain*. The various Shapes he has appear'd in, and the Discoveries he has made for the Benefit of his Country. In a Dialogue between *Him, Robinson Crusoe*, and his Man *Friday*. With Remarks, Serious and Comical upon the Life of Crusoe.

147

It is a coarse but amusing skit—far more amusing at any rate than the epistle to Defoe by the same author that follows it—its scene being laid in a 'great field betwixt Newington Green and Newington Town', and at one o'clock in the morning. Defoe enters in full moonlight armed with a brace of pocket pistols, and congratulating himself on having obeyed a '*Secret Hint*' that had warned him not to go home that night, and so ensured his safety from the 'unsanctified Paws' of the footpads. Anticipating Pirandello, however, two gigantic rogues suddenly pounce out on him—'airy Fantoms' no less notable than Robinson Crusoe and his man Friday. They have come to revenge themselves on their creator for having made them such mountebanks in his book.

'Why,' says Defoe, 'are you not my Creatures? mayn't I make of you what I please?'

'Not so,' says 'dear Son Crusoe'; and having heard his Robinson's charges against him Defoe turns to Friday:

'How the Devil have I injur'd you?' he asks.

'Have injure me,' says Friday, 'to make me such Blockhead, so much contradiction, as to be able to speak *English tolerably well* in a Month or two, and not to speak it better in twelve Years after; to make me go out to be kill'd by the Savages, only to be a Spokesman to them, tho' I did not know, whether they understood one Word of my Language; for you must know, Father D—n, that almost ev'ry Nation of us *Indians* speak a different Language.

Defoe's self-defence is, of course, his own indictment.

First, he begins, you must know, that by speaking favourably of Popery, I lay up a Friend in a Corner . . . and should the Fox Hunters prevail, that Religion must be the Mode; if it never does, I at least pass for a Moderate Man . . .

and so on. But all in vain. These fantoms take their revenge. They cram down his throat for a purgative bolus, first the Adventures, then their sequel, and conclude by tossing him in a blanket:

And so good Morrow, Father D—n. *Past three a Clock and a Moon light Morning.*

And 'D——l *solus*' awakes.

148

Page 34¹—Captain Singleton:
¶ The dates refer to publication as they are given in a *Chronological Catalogue of the Works of Daniel Defoe* by William Lee, 1869. The closer one considers them the more inexplicable they become. Such an achievement, however it was managed, was magnificent, but surely it ought not to be literature? Yet there it is, and presumably every word of it is Defoe's; for although he was much and often concerned with the world of spirits he makes no mention, so far as I know, of that kind of ghost which is said nowadays to haunt the library of the British Museum. Nor, it seems, was this term and the charge it implies ever levelled against him by his detractors—a more likely eventuality. Can it be that he had been 'hoarding' his fiction?

Page 35¹—Crusoe on his island:
¶ Few are the things one is apt to treasure so fondly as the crumbs of knowledge one has remembered since infancy. The manual of geography in use at my dame's school was always referred to as the little yaller book. I learned in it that an island is 'a piece of land surrounded with water'. What joy, what reassurance, then, was mine when, on looking up the word recently in a dictionary, I found that this was still perfectly true: 'Island . . . piece of land surrounded by water.' And *land*, what of that? Why not make sure of that too? Well, land is 'the solid part of earth's surface'. And water? Water is a 'colourless, transparent, tasteless, scentless compound of oxygen and hydrogen in liquid state convertible by heat into steam and by cold into ice'.

What a procession of negatives! It began to appear that the meaning of a word denoting an object is the least possible meaning it means. No wonder definitions aridify arguments. And how far away from my own little personal idea of an island the dictionary was leading me. The countenance, now a little forlorn, of Robinson Crusoe looked out of my mind at me. And as he gazed he seemed to be a sort of *man*. What, then, is a man? A lump of carnality surrounded by air? No. Man, says the dictionary, is a 'human being . . . person'. And human means, 'Of, belonging to, man'. And 'person'? A person is an 'individual human being (contempt[uously] *who is this* p. ?)'.

Poor old Robinson Crusoe. A slight vertigo seemed to have come upon his shade. He had sighted the spume-smoked shoals of the Meaning-of-Meaning. But let us away from such abstractions:

> And then up spoke the little cabin-boy,
>   And a pretty little boy was he;
> 'Oh! I am more grieved for my daddy and my mammy
>   Than you for your wives all three.'
>
> Then three times round went our gallant ship,
>   And three times round went she;
> And three times round went our gallant ship,
>   And she sank to the bottom of the sea.

> *And the raging winds did roar,*
> *And the stormy winds did blow,*
> *While we jolly sailor boys were up into the top,*
> *And the land-lubbers lying down below, below, below,*
> *And the land-lubbers lying down below.*

Page 38[1]—Easter Island and its . . . images:
¶ East of the central portico in the cobbled courtyard of the British Museum stand two of the smaller of these colossal basaltic figures. That on the left—formidable company enough for a solitary traveller when darkness is falling—is Hoa-Haka-Nana-Ia. He was rooted up from his own place in 1869, and presented to the museum by Queen Victoria.

When one looks at a map of the known world of the fifth century B.C., its Persian Empire bounded on the east by 'unknown deserts', its northern Europe the abode of Hyperboreans, only the fringe of Northern Africa revealing itself in the south with the Erythraean Sea to the south-east, and, on the west, a narrow drift of the Atlantic with Ierne to the north, the Cassiterides and the south-west tip of Al-fion a little below it, and the Fortunate Islands the only sea-marks to the south—one may forget that the 'known' then applied only to such a traveller as

Herodotus—and strangely enough even he does not once mention the name of Rome. And one may forget also that scattered over the world of which he was unaware were races and nations and outlandish peoples with *their* limited 'known', and with his known *un*known.

HOA-HAKA-NANA-IA, for example. He or his like may have been for centuries gazing from hollow eye-sockets out to sea when Herodotus was in his cradle.

Whether or not, twenty-two hundred years went by before, on Sunday, April 5th, 1722, Hoa's shrine was 'discovered' by Mynheer Jacob Roggeveen. In calm, thick, showery weather, at about the 10th glass of the afternoon watch, it was sighted, low and flattish, away over the water; and though dusk soon swallowed it up, it was at once given the name of *Paásch Eyland*—that particular Sunday being Easter Day. The aim of Roggeveen's expedition was to find the great Southland referred to by Dampier in his *Voyage*. But this was 'as yet out of sight', and remained so; and Easter Island was his sole reward.

His discovery proved to be an island of a pleasing shape—an obtuse-angled triangle—about ten sea miles long and five wide at most, and with quieted craters at its three corners, about 800 to 1,000 feet high. One can share the Dutchman's satisfaction. But how many guineas would one give to share exactly in what the first of its islanders who came aboard the *Thienhoven* more or less consciously *thought*, first, of his own ancestral images, and next, of these strange, clothed Dutchmen and their ship.

All that we are told is that the 'hapless creature seemed to be very glad to behold us'. He exhibited 'the greatest wonder'. He *felt* over all he saw with minute attention, and when suddenly in a scrap of looking-glass he espied his own reflection he was seized with dismay; and then— as I have seen a cat do—he looked round the edge of it towards the back of the glass. Roggeveen and his men after having 'sufficiently beguiled' themselves with this savage, sent him off with some blue beads, a little mirror, scissors and other trifles.

151

One feels a stab of regret, a stab of remorse—even at this late day!—on reading that the Dutch seamen who were afterwards left in charge of the boats of a landing party were 'moved to discharge their muskets'. They feared the islanders were about to attack them as some of them had snatched up stones. In one volley they killed ten or twelve of these well-set-up, sallow-skinned, exquisitely painted, good-humoured, thievish and harmless natives. After that, however, orders were 'promptly obeyed with reverence'.

Roggeveen does not appear to have been much impressed by the images—but he did not go close enough to get a clear view of them. He admired the fifty-feet-long windowless native huts with their stoops of faced uncemented stone. And with the island itself he was enraptured—even though it had no trees, no birds and, apparently, no insects. 'It might be made into an earthly paradise,' he said.

Don Felipe Gonzales, who rediscovered the island in 1770, was more enraptured by the natives. 'There are no halt, maimed, bent, crooked, luxated, deformed or bowlegged among them. . . . I believe . . . it would be easy to convert them to any religion that might be put before them.' He seems to have intended no irony, and adds that they were quite content with any old rags, ribbons, coloured paper, etc., which the sailors cared to give them. As with children, that is, and all other imaginative folk, very simple and coloured objects gave them an inordinate amount of pleasure.

They would have been the happier for being left to their own remote solitude. No less than eighteen hundred miles from Pitcairn, the refuge of the ill-starred *Bounty* mutineers, Easter juts up out of that ocean 'beyond reach of man's mind for vastness'—the Pacific, so named by that supreme navigator, Magellan, because apart from its slow vast swell he encountered no storms in traversing it. In the fine old phrase, he was the first to 'girdle the earth in one continuous round'.

He was about fifty when on August 10th, 1519, he sailed from Seville in quest of the Spice Islands by way of an as yet hypothetical strait south of America, and achieved his object though he died on the voyage home. Five vessels set sail. Two returned. About 270 men went in them, including one Englishman. Only thirty-one survived the voyage. Magellan rounded the Cape of the Eleven Thousand Virgins and sailed gallantly on into the unknown waters that have since borne his name.

In 1909 the one European on Easter island was an old French sailor named Pont, who had lived there for a quarter of a century and had heard nothing of the rest of the world for twenty-four months. Five years afterwards the German war vessel the *Prinz Eitel Friedrich* put ashore upon it nearly fifty prisoners of war—English and French sailors—and left them to shift for themselves. The natives, ravaged by tuberculosis, had then dwindled from an original 2,500 to a tenth of that number. They are now reported to be 'restless, dirty and uncouth, and incorrigible thieves'.

As for their ancient images, the following account of them is taken with kind permission from *The Mystery of Easter Island:*

It bears no resemblance to the ideal lotus-eating lands of the Pacific; rather, with its bleak grass-grown surface, its wild rocks and restless ocean, it recalls some of the Scilly Isles or the coast of Cornwall. It is not a beautiful country nor even a striking one, but it has a fascination of its own. All portions of it are accessible; from every part are seen marvellous views of rolling country; everywhere is the wind of heaven; around and above all are boundless sea and sky, infinite space and a great silence. The dweller there is ever listening for he knows not what, feeling unconsciously that he is in the antechamber to something yet more vast which is just beyond his ken. . . .

The whole situation was not only one of striking beauty, but brought with it an indescribable sense of solemnity. Immediately above the camp towered the majestic cliff of Raraku, near at hand were its mysterious quarries and still erect statues; on the coast below us, quiet and still, lay the overturned images of the great platform of Tongariki, one fragment of which alone remains on its base, as a silent witness to the glory which has departed. The scene was most wonderful of all when the full moon made a track of light over the sea, against which the black mass of the terrace and the outline of the standing fragment were sharply defined; while the white beams turned the waving grass into shimmering silver and lit up every crevice in the mountain above. . . .

Looked at from the landward side, we may, therefore, conceive an *ahu* as a vast theatre stage, of which the floor runs gradually upwards from the footlights. The back of the stage, which is thus the highest part, is occupied by a great terrace, on which are set up in line the giant images, each one well separated from his neighbour, and all facing the spectator. Irrespective of where he stands he will ever see them towering above him, clear cut out against a turquoise sky. In front of them are the remains of the departed. Unseen, on the farther side of the terrace, is the sea. The stone giants, and the faithful dead over whom they watch, are never without music, as countless waves launch their strength against the pebbled shore, showering on the figures a cloud of mist and spray. . . .

Page 38²—'Utopia':

¶ Sir Thomas More's concern in his *Utopia* (i.e. Nowhere) was not with the imaginary delights and dangers of a *desert* island. His book is a witty, mellow, shimmeringly ironical essay in the ideal, and is written in a prose style as limpid and fluent as Spenser's in verse.

Moreover, the domain told of by Raphael Hythloday, who by his looks and habit appeared to be a seaman, and whom 'Mr. More' met by chance in Antwerp, was originally part of the mainland and had been converted into an island by its king, Utopus. 'He caused fifteen miles space of uplandish ground, where the sea had no passage, to be cut and digged up; and so brought the sea round about the land.'

With its fifty-four great cities, it is a conception on the grand scale, and, as a niggardly reference in the *New Atlantis* proves, Bacon himself had scanned its entry.

The island of Utopia is in the middle two hundred miles broad, and holds almost at the same breadth over a great part of it; but it grows narrower towards both ends. Its figure is not unlike a crescent: between its horns, the sea comes in eleven miles broad, and spreads itself into a great bay, which is environed with land to the compass of about five hundred miles, and is well secured from winds. In this bay there is no great current, the whole coast is, as it were, one con-

tinued harbour, which gives all that live in the island great conveni-
ence for mutual commerce; but the entry into the bay, occasioned by
rocks on the one hand and shallows on the other, is very dangerous.
In the middle of it there is one single rock which appears above water,
and may therefore be easily avoided, and on the top of it there is a
tower in which a garrison is kept, the other rocks lie under water and
are very dangerous.

Even to have strayed through its chief city (though
only in print) is to have breathed an ampler air.

The city is compassed about with a high and thick wall, full of
turrets and bulwarks. A dry ditch, but deep and broad and overgrown with bushes, briers, and thorns, goes about three sides or
quarters of the city. To the fourth side the river itself serves for a
ditch. The streets are appointed and set forth very commodious and
handsome, both for carriage and also against the winds. The houses
be of fair and gorgeous building, and in the street side they stand
joined together in a long row through the whole street without any
partition or separation. The streets be twenty feet broad. On the
back side of the houses, through the whole length of the street, lie
large gardens, which be closed in round about with the back part
of the streets. Every house has two doors; one into the street, and a
postern door on the backside into the garden. These doors be made
with two leaves, never locked or bolted, so easy to be opened that
they will follow the least drawing of a finger and shut again by
themselves. Every man that will may go in, for there is nothing within
the houses that is private, or any man's own. And every ten years
they change their houses by lot.

They set great store by their gardens. In them they have vineyards,
all manner of fruit, herbs, and flowers, so pleasant, so well furnished,
and so finely kept, that I never saw thing more fruitful nor better
trimmed in any place. Their study and diligence herein comes not
only of pleasure, but also of a certain strife and contention that is
between street and street, concerning the trimming, husbanding, and
furnishing of their gardens, every man for his own part. And verily
you shall not lightly find in all the city any thing that is more commodious, either for the profit of the citizens, or for pleasure. And
therefore it may seem that the first founder of the city minded
nothing so much as he did these gardens.

Fair indeed and commodious; and so serene and sooth-
ing is the prose that it lulls away criticism. Yet one may
look a little askance at that 'nothing within the house
that is private or one's own', and openly rebel at that en-
forced change by lot. As for the dice and the dogs in the

passage that follows, inability to comprehend a pleasure is not a conclusive argument against its existence, and the butchering huntsman, at this taunt against his beloved music, *might* remember his Hippolyta in *A Midsummer-Night's Dream:*

Among those foolish pursuers of pleasure, they reckon all that delight in hunting, in fowling, or gaming; of whose madness they have only heard, for they have no such things among them. But they have asked us, what sort of pleasure is it that men can find in throwing the dice? For if there were any pleasure in it, they think the doing of it so often should give one a surfeit of it: and what pleasure can one find in hearing the barking and howling of dogs, which seem rather odious than pleasant sounds? Nor can they comprehend the pleasure of seeing dogs run after a hare, more than of seeing one dog run after another; for if the seeing them run is that which gives the pleasure, you have the same entertainment to the eye on both these occasions; since that is the same in both cases: but if the pleasure lies in seeing the hare killed and torn by the dogs, this ought rather to stir pity, that a weak, harmless and fearful hare should be devoured by strong, fierce, and cruel dogs. Therefore all this business of hunting is, among the Utopians, turned over to their butchers; and those, as has been already said, are all slaves; and they look on hunting as one of the basest parts of a butcher's work. . . .

But how ancient are most novelties in ideas:

They look upon freedom from pain, if it does not rise from perfect health, to be a state of stupidity rather than of pleasure. . . . They almost universally agree that health is the greatest of all bodily pleasures; and that as there is a pain in sickness, which is as opposite in its nature to pleasure as sickness itself is to health; so they hold, that health is accompanied with pleasure; and if any should say that sickness is not really pain, but that it only carries pain along with it, they look upon that as a fetch of subtilty, that does not much alter the matter.

Then again:

In choosing their wives they use a method that would appear to us very absurd and ridiculous, but it is constantly observed among them, and is accounted perfectly consistent with wisdom. Before marriage some grave matron presents the bride naked, whether she is a virgin or a widow, to the bridegroom; and after that some grave man presents the bridegroom naked to the bride. We indeed both laughed at this, and condemned it as very indecent. But they, on the other hand, wondered at the folly of the men of all other nations, who, if

156

they are but to buy a horse of a small value, are so cautious that they will see every part of him, and take off both his saddle and all his other tackle, that there may be no secret ulcer hid under any of them; and that yet in the choice of a wife, on which depends the happiness or unhappiness of the rest of his life, a man should venture upon trust, and only see about a hand's-breadth of the face, all the rest of the body being covered, under which there may lie hid what may be contagious, as well as loathsome. All men are not so wise as to choose a woman only for her good qualities; and even wise men consider the body as that which adds not a little to the mind: and it is certain there may be some such deformity covered with the clothes as may totally alienate a man from his wife when it is too late to part with her. If such a thing is discovered after marriage, a man has no remedy but patience. They therefore think it is reasonable that there should be good provision made against such mischievous frauds.

But might not the word of the grave matron have sufficed? And last:

There be divers kinds of religion, not only in sundry parts of the Island, but also in divers places of every city. Some worship for God the sun; some the moon; some some other of the planets. There be that give worship to a man that was once of excellent virtue or of famous glory, not only as God, but also as the chiefest and highest God. But the most and the wisest part (rejecting all these) believe that there is a certain godly power unknown, everlasting, incomprehensible, inexplicable, far above the capacity and reach of man's wit, dispersed throughout all the world, not in bigness, but in virtue and power. Him they call the father of all. To him alone they attribute the beginnings, the encreasings, the proceedings, the changes, and the ends of all things. Neither do they give divine honours to any other than to him. . . .

They are almost all of them very firmly persuaded that good men will be infinitely happy in another state; so that though they are compassionate to all that are sick, yet they lament no man's death, except they see him loth to depart with life; for they look on this as a very ill presage, as if the soul, conscious to itself of guilt, and quite hopeless, was afraid to leave the body, from some secret hints of approaching misery. They think that such a man's appearance before God cannot be acceptable to Him, who being called on, does not go out cheerfully, but is backward and unwilling, and is, as it were, dragged to it. They are struck with horror when they see any die in this manner, and carry them out in silence and sorrow, and praying God that He would be merciful to the errors of the departed soul, they lay the body in the ground; but when they die cheerfully, and full of hope, they do not mourn for them, but sing hymns when they carry out their bodies, and commending their souls very earnestly to God: their whole behaviour is then rather grave than sad, they burn the body, and set up a pillar where the pile was made, with an inscription to the honour of the deceased. . . .

Page 39[1]—Gulliver's Lilliput:

¶ The island of Lilliput, with its neighbouring Blefuscu, separated from it, in accordance with Swift's 'ten times' device, by a channel only eight hundred yards wide, lies somewhere off the west coast of Australia, and south-west of Sunder Strait, in latitude 30° 2″. But Gulliver's sailing directions, alas, are unlikely to locate it.

Like fat Jack, he set sail from Bristol City. His ship the *Antelope* was wrecked on Guy Fawkes Day, 1699—'the beginning of summer in those parts'. Driven upon a rock, she immediately split, and 'six of the crew, of whom I was one, having let down the boat into the sea, made a shift to get clear of the ship and the rock.'

. . . In about half an hour the boat was overset by a sudden flurry from the north. What became of my companions in the boat, as well as of those who escaped on the rock, or were left in the vessel, I cannot tell; but conclude they were all lost. For my own part, I swam as fortune directed me, and was pushed forward by wind and tide. I often let my legs drop, and could feel no bottom; but when I was almost gone, and able to struggle no longer, I found myself within my depth; and by this time the storm was much abated. The declivity was so small that I walked near a mile before I got to the shore, which I conjectured was about eight o'clock in the evening. I then advanced forward near half a mile, but could not discover any sign of houses or inhabitants; at least, I was in so weak a condition that I did not observe them. I was extremely tired, and with that, and the heat of the weather, and about half a pint of brandy that I drank as I left the ship, I found myself much inclined to sleep. I lay down on the grass, which was very short and soft, where I slept sounder than ever I remembered to have done in my life, and, as I reckoned, above nine hours; for when I awaked it was just daylight. I attempted to rise, but was not able to stir; for, as I happened to lie on my back, I found my legs and arms were strongly fastened on each side to the ground; and my hair, which was long and thick, tied down in the same manner. I likewise felt several slender ligatures across my body, from my arm-pits to my thighs. I could only look upwards; the sun began to grow hot, and the light offended my eyes. I heard a confused noise about me; but in the posture I lay could see nothing except the sky. In a little time I felt something alive moving on my left leg, which advancing gently forward over my breast came almost up to my chin; when, bending my eyes downward as much as I could, I perceived it to be a human creature not six inches high, with a bow and arrow in his hands and a quiver at his back. In the meantime, I felt at least forty more of the same kind (as I conjectured) following the first. I was in the utmost astonishment, and roared so loud that they all ran back in a fright; and some of them, as I was afterwards told, were hurt by the falls they got by leaping from my sides upon the ground. However, they soon returned, and one of them, who ventured so far as to get a full sight of my face, lifting up his hands and eyes by way of admiration, cried out in a shrill but distinct voice, *Hekinah degul!* The others repeated the same words several times, but I then knew not what they meant.

Crisp, alert, not a word too much or wanting, what a marvel of matter-of-fact imaginativeness this fragment is! That half a pint of brandy, that grass, those slender ligatures, the offending light. And the sky, the bending of the eyes and then, signal, complete, *created*, the tiny warrior himself.

And *Brobdingnag:*

On the 16th day of June, 1703, a boy on the topmast [of the *Adventure*] discovered land. On the 17th, we came in full view of a great island, or continent (for we knew not whether), [it proved to be a peninsula]; on the south side whereof was a small neck of land jutting out into the sea, and a creek too shallow to hold a ship of above one hundred tons. We cast anchor within a league of this creek, and our captain sent a dozen of his men well armed in the long boat, with vessels for water, if any could be found. I desired his leave to go with them, that I might see the country, and make what discoveries I could. When we came to land, we saw no river, or spring, nor any sign of inhabitants. Our men therefore wandered on the shore to find out some fresh water near the sea, and I walked alone about a mile on the other side, where I observed the country all barren and rocky. I now began to be weary, and seeing nothing to entertain my curiosity, I returned gently down towards the creek; and the sea being full in my view, I saw our men already got into the boat, and rowing for life to the ship. I was going to holla after them, although it had been to little purpose, when I observed a huge creature walking after them in the sea, as fast as he could: he waded not much deeper than his knees, and took prodigious strides; but our men had the start of him half a league, and the sea thereabouts being full of sharp pointed rocks, the monster was not able to over-take the boat.

This I was afterwards told, for I durst not stay to see the issue of that adventure, but ran as fast as I could the way I first went, and then climbed up a steep hill, which gave me some prospect of the country. I found it fully cultivated; but that which first surprised me was the length of the grass, which, in those grounds that seemed to be kept for hay, was about twenty feet high.

I fell into a high road, for so I took it to be, though it served to the inhabitants only as a footpath through a field of barley. Here I walked on for some time, but could see little on either side, it being now near harvest, and the corn rising at least forty feet. I was an hour walking to the end of this field, which was fenced in with a hedge of at least one hundred and twenty feet high, and the trees so lofty that I could make no computation of their altitude. There was a stile to pass from this field into the next. It had but four steps, and a stone to cross over when you come to the uppermost. It was im-possible for me to climb this stile, because every step was six feet high, and the upper stone above twenty. I was endeavouring to find some gap in the hedge, when I discovered one of the inhabitants in the next field, advancing towards the stile, of the same size with him whom I saw in the sea pursuing our boat. He appeared as tall as an ordinary spire's steeple, and took about ten yards at every stride, as near as I could guess. I was struck with the utmost fear and astonish-ment, and ran to hide myself in the corn, from whence I saw him at the top of the stile looking back into the next field on the right hand, and heard him call in a voice many degrees louder than a speaking-trumpet; but the noise was so high in the air, that at first I certainly thought it was thunder. Whereupon seven monsters, like himself, came towards him, with reaping-hooks in their hands, each hook about the largeness of six scythes. . . .

When, after touching bottom and wading a mile—'the declivity was so small'—Gulliver gets to shore on Lilliput, he is still in one's mind's eye his natural human stature. Somewhere between that point and the end of the passage quoted above—and it is difficult to be quite certain where —he becomes gigantic; and, if anything, the tiny crea-tures that storm his body then become *less* than their given six inches. So he remains until he boards the ship that carries him home—with his Lilliputian sheep and black cattle in his pocket. On Brobdingnag's shores, how-ever, the sea beats in storm as it beats elsewhere, and not in proportionate billows a wondrous forty to fifty feet high. And here, as soon as the huge-boned gigantic reapers discover Gulliver skulking under a furrow amid their corn, he becomes a pigmy. Nine-year-old Glumdalclitch is never surely in one's fancy forty feet or so tall; the rat is no sabre-toothed tiger; the monkey no ogre twice as high as a lamp-post; and Gulliver's house, though it was built in proportion to his stature, is never much bigger than a good-sized box.

The ten-times device, then, is by no means so simple in effect as it would appear likely to be. Swift's satire is in consequence, none the less, the more effective—at both extremes.

Not even a close reader, either, when carried away by his fancy, always pays heed to his author's definite statements. How many lovers of *Kubla Khan*, for example, have *realized* that the instrument on which the Abyssinian maid is accompanying her song about Mount Abora is a *dulcimer?* And who has set inward eye on the *other* two 'gallants', whom the Ancient Mariner accosts on their way to the bridegroom's wedding feast? The fact is, that until one has read again and again and with extreme care such poems, for mere example, as the odes *To Psyche* or *To Melancholy*, it is impossible to realize how *strange* a thing poetry is, how miraculous was 'the working brain' of John Keats, and how absurd—with the loveliness that is preterrational—are the secrets of the imagination and the soul.

Swift's chapters on 'Laputa, etc.' are in a different tone and temper. The child in him died out in them. But the island on which Gulliver first lands in these parts is as actual as words could make it, and intensely happy must Swift have been in so using them, and in all that they tell of.

This island was at a greater distance than I expected, and I did not reach it in less than five hours. I encompassed it almost round, before I could find a convenient place to land in; which was a small creek, about three times the wideness of my canoe. I found the island to be all rocky, only a little intermingled with tufts of grass, and sweet-smelling herbs. I took out my small provisions, and after having refreshed myself, I secured the remainder in a cave, whereof there were great numbers; I gathered plenty of eggs upon the rocks, and got a quantity of dry sea-weed and parched grass, which I designed to kindle the next day, and roast my eggs as well as I could, for I had about me my flint, steel, match, and burning-glass. I lay all night in the cave where I had lodged my provisions. My bed was the same dry grass and sea-weed which I intended for fuel. . . . The day was far advanced. I walked a while among the rocks, the sky was perfectly clear, and the sun so hot, that I was forced to turn my face from it: when all on a sudden it became obscured, as I thought, in a manner very different from what happens by the interposition of a cloud. I turned back, and perceived a vast opaque body between me and the sun, moving forwards towards the island: it seemed to be about two miles high, and hid the sun six or seven minutes; but I did not observe the air to be much colder, or the sky more darkened, than if I had stood under the shade of a mountain. As it approached nearer over the place where I was, it appeared to be a firm substance, the bottom flat, smooth, and shining very bright from the reflexion of the sea below. . . . I waved my cap (for my hat was long since worn out) and my handkerchief towards the island; and upon its nearer approach, I called and shouted with the utmost strength of my voice, and then looking circumspectly, I beheld a crowd gathered to that side which was most in my view. I found by their pointing toward me and to each other, that they plainly discovered me, although they made no return to my shouting. But I could see four or five men running in great haste up the stairs, to the top of the island, who then disappeared. . . .

In his fourth voyage Gulliver set sail from Portsmouth as captain of the *Adventure*, 'a stout merchantman of 350 tons'. There is a mutiny on board, set about by recruits from Barbadoes and the Leeward Islands, who had been buccaneers. The mutineers shut him up in his cabin, and on May 9th, 1711, amidst, to him, unknown parts of the ocean, put him into a boat and after rowing about a league marooned him at low tide upon an island and returned to the ship.

In this desolate condition I advanced forward, and soon got upon firm ground, where I sat down on a bank to rest myself, and consider what I had best to do. When I was a little refreshed, I went up into the country, resolving to deliver myself to the first savages I should meet, and purchase my life from them by some bracelets, glass rings, and other toys, which sailors usually provide themselves with in those voyages, and whereof I had some about me. The land was divided by long rows of trees, not regularly planted, but naturally growing; there was great plenty of grass, and several fields of oats. . . .

Having travelled about three miles, we came to a long kind of building, made of timber, stuck in the ground, and wattled across; the roof was low, and covered with straw. I now began to be a little comforted; and took out some toy . . . in hopes the people of the house would be thereby encouraged to receive me kindly. The horse made me a sign to go in first; it was a large room with a smooth clay floor, and a rack and manger, extending the whole length on one side. There were three nags and two mares, not eating, but some of them sitting down upon their hams, which I very much wondered at; but wondered more to see the rest employed in domestic business. . . .

The 'toy' is Swift in essence. The only feature that troubles me in this charming scene is how any intelligent nag could persuade itself to sit upon its hams. A most uncomely equine attitude.

Page 40¹—This wanton attempt:
¶ The Preface to the *Serious Reflections,* indeed, is a succession of icy douches:

I ROBINSON CRUSOE [and let his own capitals enforce his statement] being at this Time in perfect and sound Mind and Memory, Thanks be to God therefore; do hereby declare, their [i.e. his critics'] Objection is an Invention scandalous in Design, and false in Fact; and do affirm, that the Story, though Allegorical, is also Historical; and that it is the beautiful Representation of a Life of unexampled Misfortunes. . . . All . . . parts of the Story are real Facts in my History, whatever borrow'd Lights they may be represented by; namely, the footprint, the old goat, the thing in the bed, the dream, the landing, the ship on fire, Man Friday, the parrot— they are all litterally true. . . . In a Word, there's not a Circumstance in the imaginary Story, but has its just Allusion to a real Story, and chimes Part for Part, and Step for Step with the inimitable Life of *Robinson Crusoe.*

And last:

Besides all this, here is the just and only End of all Parable and Allegorical History brought to pass, *viz.* for moral and religious Improvement.

Worse and worse, as Christian said; the fact being, perhaps, that Defoe was led on by his enemies into these excesses. Even if they better him as a moralist, which is debatable, they do him little service as an artist. The *Serious Reflections* have been dismissed as unreadable—a harsh word, and one also in the nature of a boomerang. Still it appears to be comparatively easy to write what may prove to be very difficult to read. So also with the bore and his listener. Not that the *Reflections* have no better parts. The chief mystery here is not so much that our 'Rob. Crusoe' is hostile to solitude, except that of retiring into one's self in serious meditation—'There is no need of a Wilderness to wander among wild Beasts, no necessity of a Cell on the top of a Mountain . . . if the Soul be truly Master of it self all is safe'; but that he is positively contemptuous of—desert islands!

His chapter on solitude none the less is not only the wisest but also the most enjoyable in the *Reflections*. They afterwards ramble off into a sermon on honesty and similar themes—prolix, sententious, laboured, with a digression that in passing scornfully dismisses the arts and courtesies of the Chinese, even their porcelain—'if we had the same Clay we should soon outdo them'. As for their silks, gold and silver, 'they have nothing but what is not common with our ordinary poor Weavers'. A sublime insularity.

With the *Vision of the Angelic World*, the scene brightens and the prose takes life—in, for example, as rhythmically sustained a passage as:

I return to my Share of these Things. It was after my conversing with my learned Friend about the heavenly Bodies, the Motion, the Distances, and the Bulk of the Planets, their Situation, and the Orbits they move in, the Share of Light, Heat and Moisture, which they enjoy, their Respect to the Sun, their Influences upon us, and at last, the Possibility of their being habitable, with all the Arcana of the Skies; it was on this Occasion, I say, that my Imagination, *always given to wander*, took a Flight of its own; and as I have told you that I had an invincible Inclination to travel, so I think I travelled as sensibly, to my understanding, over all the Mazes and Wastes of infinite Space, in Quest of those Things, as ever I did over the Desarts of *Karakathay*, and the uninhabited Wasts of *Tartary*, and perhaps may give as useful an Account of my Journey.

Having handsomely acquitted the devil of 'the Thousands of Crimes we lay to his Charge that he is not guilty of', Crusoe—though the voice we hear now bears no resemblance to his familiar tones, but is solely Defoe's—continues:

> But the more particular Discoveries of this Converse of Spirits, and which to me are undeniable, are such as follows: namely, Dreams, Voices, Noises, Impulses, Hints, Apprehensions, Involuntary Sadness, etc.,

a promising catalogue with an echo of Burton in it. And then this prophetic onset: 'Dreams are dangerous things to talk of . . .' But the interest declines, there is little of the visionary in what follows and less of the angelic. Indeed he himself dismisses visions as making only 'a Heaven of Sense':

> My Meaning is this, all Visions, or propounded Visions either of Heaven or Hell, are meer Delusions of the Mind, and generally are Fictions of a waking bewildred Head; and you may see the Folly of them in the meanest of the Descriptions, which generally end in shewing some glorious Place, fine Walks, noble illustrious Palaces, Gardens of Gold, and People of shining Forms, and the like. Alas! these are all so short, that they are Unworthy of the Thoughts of a mind elevated two Degrees above Darkness and Dirt. . . . Let us cease to Imagin concerning it, 'tis impossible to attain, 'tis criminal to attempt it.

Here and there a sentence rings solemnly: 'And what Heart could support here its future State *in* LIFE, much less that of its future State *after* LIFE even good or bad?' But though the intention of what follows may be equally serious, the effect is less moving. The preacher was perhaps too sure of his congregation.

Page 40²—The pines are not trees, but humans:
¶ Not so the beings whom Baron Holberg's hero, Niels Klim, encounters in his *Journey to the World Underground*. This famous Danish author, who died at the age of seventy in 1754, is renowned not only for his comedies but as a historian and a philosopher, and during his career occupied what a tongue-tied Englishman might assume to be the somewhat uncomfortable Chair of Eloquence at the

University of Copenhagen. The *Journey* was written in Latin; and no more than *Crusoe* or *Gulliver* was it intended as a book for boys; it is at once a satire and 'a complete system of Ethics'.

Its hero, armed only with a boat-hook, descends into the nether world by way of an orifice in the 'Weathercock Mountain'. The rope by which he is suspended snaps, and, like Milton's archangel, he falls—and falls. He finds himself at last in a region where all the inhabitants are trees —the best and cleverest of them being distinguished by the greatest number of branches. They can move sluggishly from place to place. They are endowed with speech and they are of the usual two sexes. This he discovers to his cost, for at his entry into this pleasant land he is pursued by a furious bull, takes refuge in the branches of what unfortunately proves to be the wife of the sheriff of a neighbouring city, and is shut up in consequence in the local Bridewell. It is assumed that Klim himself, clothes and all, is a species of ape; *Pikel Emi*, he is called, i.e. the outlandish baboon.

The strangest feature of the book is that the author should have thought so well of his readers as to suppose them capable of really sharing the company of his talking tree-humans. Apart from this difficulty, the *Journey* is, roughly, *Gulliver* with its chief charm omitted. The satire is frequently acute and at times amusing, though the geography is (for a novice in such matters) nothing but confusion.

Time has converted many of the Baron's neatest little pleasantries into the commonplace. His contemporaries must have been vastly amused at the notion of a virgin named Palmka enjoying the dignities of a Chief Justice in her native city Kokleku, and of a province inhabited by Juniper-Trees, where all the most important offices were held solely by Juniperettes. Nowadays in Denmark women sit in both the national assemblies; and perhaps nobody notices any difference.

Persons convicted of crime in the nether world are

ordered to be bled—the darker the issue of blood the worse the offence; 'it is always considered an ignominy to be sentenced by the council to be phlebotomized': and we remember *Erewhon*. Mention of Avarice-powders, too, and of 'drops' for the cure of pride and arrogance, and of sermons used as purgatives, also bring Samuel Butler to mind.

In Potu it is forbidden by law to expound the sacred writings. Controversialists on spiritual matters are immediately phlebotomized. Could Mrs. Eddy also have enjoyed the company of Niels Klim?

The denizens of the Land of Reason consider it necessary that in a well-regulated state at least half of the inhabitants should be fools. This, too, has a familiar ring. In Spelek they are assured of living to a very advanced age—centuries; and so, careless of the future and with the present only before their eyes, they indulge in every vice of which they are capable—which is Swift's and Mr. Shaw's Methuselah problem from a rather novel angle.

In another of the cities of the nether world it is more unusual to meet a man than a doctor. Klim himself comes across a 'little boy-Tree' in the street who is 'crying lists of births and deaths to sell'. He discovers to his amazement that in the preceding year the local death-rate four times exceeded the birth-rate. He runs, literally, for his life. But, then, doctors have always been the butt of waggery. In Miho, again, 'the New Sparta', the rich being forbidden to spend and enjoy their riches, the common people, having no employment, sleep away their lives in indolence and complete poverty, whereas in Liho, the rich being given a free hand, the arts and sciences, trades and professions all flourish, the citizens are encouraged to work and none is in want but by his own fault.

Klim continues on his travels. Birds and animals in the new provinces of the nether world take the place of the trees he has left behind him—and even musical instruments. At length, owing to his military sagacity, he is made emperor of a state whose subjects, the Quamites, are 'perfectly of the human form, and the only real men' whom he has yet encountered in his travels. They are stupid people who take him for an envoy from the sun, and he leads them in war against the surrounding provinces, peopled by tigers, bears, cats and cocks. In one of these expeditions he chances on a book entitled *Tinian's Supra-terraneous Travels; or, a Description of the Empires, Kingdoms, and Countries on the Earth, and particularly of those in Europe.* It is an ingenious and original device, but the result is a little heavy, and the reflection in the looking-glass too closely resembles what has gone before. Nothing escapes the author's mockery—from religion, the academies and poetry to wigs, coffee and carriages. The brief passage on England is neatly pointed:

The *English* prefer their liberty to everything else; and none are in this nation slaves, with the exception of the married women. In matters of religion, they reject to-day that which they professed yesterday. This changeableness I attributed to the situation and climate of the country; for as they are islanders and seamen, their fluctuating element has, in all probability, some effect upon their minds. They are incessantly inquiring after each other's health, so that a stranger might easily take them all to be physicians; but the question *How do you do?* is a mere phrase—a simple sound without the least signification. The inhabitants of this island file, point, and sharpen, their understanding and imaginative faculty to such a degree, that numbers of them in the end will not infrequently lose their senses altogether.

Niels Klim eventually 'with the velocity of lightning' falls back up to the surface of the earth again, to find himself 'amidst a number of barren rocks; which, to my utter astonishment, I recognized as the same, whence, some years before, I was precipitated into the subterraneous regions.'

Nothing except perhaps 'a complete system of ethics' becomes so tedious at last as satire inadequately diluted. That Giant-the-Jack-Killer, the satirist, should deal in tinctures as well as essences. 'To decide who is wise and who is not, requires a person to be wise himself.' And

168

satirists who have been *wise* both in heart and head are uncommon. The *Journey* may be taken as an entertaining attempt to clear the ground for a site whereon man may afterwards erect some kind of Utopia. But out of what? Out of bricks that will somehow have to be made of *this* scoffed-at rubble? The general process is so devastating that the resultant scene is distinctly forbidding. And one falters at a Utopia governed by an oligarchy of converted satirists.

The author of the *Journey* had sharp eyes and sharp wits and the confidence to express in spade-for-spade terms his destructive opinions of mankind. This entails a state of being almost as solitary as Robinson Crusoe's, but his reflections, I fancy, will prove most enjoyable if taken in small doses.

Page 41¹—The patriarch:
¶ George Pine had actually left England with his master in 1589 in *The India Merchant*, one of four vessels that set out with the intention of settling a factory in the East Indies. All bearings lost, in a sea 'very stormy and tempestuous', they sight land, high and rocky, and somewhere off the coast of *Terra Australis Incognita;* and then they are wrecked:

> For when we came against the rocks, our ship having endured two or three blows, being now broken and quite foundred in the waters, we having with much ado gotten our selves on the bowsprit, which being broken off, was driven by the waters into a small creek, wherein fell a little river, which being encompassed by the rocks, was shelter'd from the wind, so that we had opportunity to land ourselves, though almost drown'd, in all four persons, beside the Negro—

a prose as disjointed as the experience must have been. They light a fire, build a tent of 'sail-clothes', and the negress, 'being less sensible [in the old sense of the term] than the rest', stands sentry. They have ample provisions; cocks and hens that have escaped from the wreck, a plentiful supply of fruit and nuts and shell-fish, a bird like a swan that cannot fly, and a beast about the size of a goat; and since too the climate is never colder than it is in

169

England in September, they have much to be thankful for. Of George Pine's wives, his master's daughter, Sarah England, who was fourteen when *The India Merchant* set sail, has fifteen children; Mary Sparkes and Elizabeth Trevor have, the one, thirteen, the other, seven; and the 'blackmore', Philippa, has twelve. An insular Utah. And yet jealousy seems never once to have shown its green-eyed visage in this situation—a tribute to all concerned.

After forty years the population of the island has increased to 565; after fifty-nine years, when George Pine, now of a very ripe age, abdicates in favour of William, solemnly bestows his Bible upon him, charging that it shall be read once a month at a general meeting, and expires, it has increased to 1,789. Yet another twenty years, and the warren is ten to twelve thousand strong.

What became of the Dutch ship which discovered it in 1667 still 'speaking good English', what—a more tantalizing question—became of the island and all its little Englands, Sparkeses, Trevors and Phils, is not related.

Settlements after Henry Neville's pattern are infrequent in fiction, the nearest to our own day being Miss Rose Macaulay's *Orphan Island* (late *Smith Island*). Since 1923, when Mr. Thinkwell, a lecturer in sociology in the University of Cambridge, having been marooned on it with his family, was elected its premier, no tidings of it have been wafted eastwards. He found it amply occupied, for, nearly seventy years before his arrival, Miss Charlotte Smith, a clergyman's daughter, having embarked in her twenties for San Francisco with some fifty orphans, had *en route* suffered shipwreck on its lovely shores.

Apart from the forty surviving orphans, who, as she sits on the sand, congregate about her crinolined person like chicks around a hen, the ship's doctor, an Irishman, and a Scots maid were then her only human company. They somehow 'managed'. At length, and in spite of Mr. O'Malley's intemperate habits and his Latin tags, Miss Smith contracts what she fondly supposes to be a lawful union with him. Ten children follow, their birthdays being recorded with extreme brevity, and then the veil of oblivion descends on the island until the Thinkwells arrive.

Miss Smith, though but an early Victorian by birth, is completely Victorian in 'piety and prudery', mind and morals. Freed in 1870, by a shark, of a husband who with almost his last breath vindictively assured her that he was no husband, this old nonagenarian (and by no means a model one), with her first-born, Albert, as her vice-regent, rules her little kingdom with a rod of iron. The Smiths, however faint the tinge of their blue blood, are its ruling caste; the down-trodden orphans are nobodies—they merely keep the shops and do all the hard work. And they deserve to, for there must have been a time when *their* average age was, say, twenty-two, while the ten fatherless young O'Malley-Smiths were from fifteen down to five.

Such a situation, rampantly Victorian in politics, religion, class distinction and so on, and this in full and isolated bloom, is naturally a rich and honeyed feast for Mr. Thinkwell—and for Miss Macaulay.

His daughter Rosamond, however, prefers islands to be solitary. How—for this and for much else—my heart goes out to her as on that coral strand she dances her ringlets to the whistling wind! In this lagooned and tropic paradise she has everything a dreamer could desire— humming-birds and birds of paradise, cloves and spices, sugar-cane, frangipani, candle-nuts and cockatoos—except only the absence of too much company.

The days passed slowly by. Slowly . . . because each was so new, so delightful, so many-coloured, and so strange. Like some lovely fruit that puts forth, ripens, and tumbles, over-mellow, to the ground, between dawn and nightfall, so each lovely day rose from the sea, small and gold and exquisite, ripened to a hot and fragrant noon, and slid rosily into the sea again, leaving the island afloat beneath the myriad eyes of a vast and purple night.

And again:

Huge, pale, landless, the Pacific stretched to a dazzling horizon, an ocean of shimmering silvery haze. . . . What loneliness, in which time and space seem drowned, God and man lost, sun, moon and earth a passing tumbler's show.

Miss Macaulay can at need survey her island with something less than indifference—and our own England also:

It is cold; it rains; it has large towns; its vegetation is poor, its sea poorer. It has, in short, few advantages over Orphan Island, beyond mere novelty and size.

But in the cadence of that 'tumbler's show' one seems to catch a homesick echo. Miss Macaulay's satirical intention was to put Miss Smith and her bastards firmly in their place—a benighted Victorian family group entrenched around a crinoline. But was that proper place a coral island? It saddens one to think of yet another oceanic solitude gone 'white'. And now, alas, she has washed her hands of it. 'Across the future of Orphan Island . . . is hung a curtain of mist. . . .' It is any fate's for the asking.

Miss Smith landed on Orphan Island in the 'fifties. *Sir Edward Seaward's Shipwreck, as written in his own Diary* (which begins on December 30th, 1724) was published in 1831—a full six years before Victoria came to the throne. None the less this romance is so quintessential a piece of Victorianism that it sets one speculating when precisely that wondrous exotic in English life began to bloom. According to its title-page, the Diary was 'edited by Jane Porter'; its actual authorship has been attributed to an elder brother. In that case Jane must have been an exceedingly active editor. She was also the author of *The Scottish Chiefs*, a romance which not only won her a European reputation, but was proscribed by Napoleon and was said to have inspired the Waverley Novels.

Like most other castaways in fiction, Edward can boast 'neither pedigree nor learning'. He merely came of 'loyal and honest parents'. None the less his niceness of behaviour in relation to his island and his Eliza neither blue blood nor culture could surpass. Newly wedded, and in the green of their youth, they are so ready to be wrecked on a desert island that within a few hours of their landing they are busily planting seeds from their yams and their coccos. Like Crusoe, they are never idle—except on Sundays. Unlike Crusoe's, their industry is nauseating. On Sundays they rest, 'go for walks', dress in their best clothes—it is many weeks before Eliza takes to trousers *à la Turque*—and each, unnoticed by either, takes a cold sea-sluice on deck, for fear of sharks. Nothing surprises them, not even the discovery of a treasure of 20,000 gold doubloons and, among other piratical plunder, thirty-six gold crucifixes. No mention, alas, of ruby, emerald or orient pearl.

Negroes arrive, and, before even one has noticed they are black, they have been caparisoned in smart check shirts and white duck trousers. On Eliza's twenty-first birthday they are regaled with coffee, wine, and cigars. But as usual, when solitude goes, romance goes with it. After marrying off his blacks and investing his doubloons in three per cents, Edward returns to England, showering largesse wherever he goes; and Queen Caroline, much attracted by his modest Eliza, not only circumvents Sir Robert Walpole on his behalf, and, blade in hand, bids him 'Rise up, Sir Edward Seaward', but at the same time appoints him Commandant and Governor of the islands he has left behind him. The young couple shine in these surroundings. But even on their island they could amuse themselves by 'turning common occurrences into causes of pleasantry'—one of the little secrets of success in polite society.

As bellicose Commandant defying Spain, Edward is even less entertaining company than when he was alone on his island with his Eliza and her Fidele, a King Charles's spaniel! Perhaps the chief attraction of his narrative is the food—such delicacies as iguana, snook, calipeavar, and chaddocks cooked in Cork butter, while its style resembles another dish favoured by this happy pair, 'cold pumpkin pie sprinkled with a little sugar and lime juice'.

Edward and Eliza themselves attract for other reasons. They are specimens of prigs many years before the term came to the meaning we now give it, and of snobs long before Thackeray adopted the cult. 'I had the honour of handing her Ladyship to her carriage, which bore the royal arms'—almost as giddy a position to keep one's balance in as Thackeray's in his imaginary jaunt down Piccadilly with a duke on either arm. Still, Edward was not a snob in the Naaman sense. He spoke to and treated his slaves quite kindly, even though they cost him only fifty pounds apiece; and this in the 1720's.

Page 41²—A problem novel:
¶ Not that Defoe disapproved of marriage; witness his *Religious Courtship* and *A Treatise.* He was fully as much interested in wives as in tradesmen. And he faced—one might say, he outfaced—many of the 'problems'. As the subtitle of her history genially informs the reader, Moll Flanders was 'five times a wife (whereof once to her own brother)', while Colonel Jack was 'five times married to four whores', a piece of arithmetic which his narrative will explain.

There is a sly furtive studious fiction that peeks about in the shadowy and unsavoury corners of life's farmyard, skirting the gilded puddle that beasts would cough at, and that other where the green fly drones over the sow's blood that hath eaten her nine farrow. Not so Defoe's. Chanticleer *in excelsis,* it flew up and perched on the very summit of the loftiest dunghill within reach, and clapped its wings and crowed and crowed again. And there is a glint of the sun in its bold round eye and a wind from over People's Common stirs the burnished plumes of its tail feathers. Not that even the friendliest of his admirers could wholly acquit Defoe of pandering at times to his great public. But of *lilies* that fester he is innocent.

Page 41³—Benamuckee:
¶ This word, like Glumdalclitch, may be an anagram; it *may* refer to a definite deity of the Oroonoque: I cannot say. Caliban's disjointed prattle on the Patagonian Setebos (with his odd and capricious distaste for pronouns) very faintly resembles Friday's on Benamuckee,

but the 'blossoming' of *his* 'rank tongue' might be rather too copious in the solitude of a desert island.

In *Pippa Passes* there is an island—one of the group that neighbours the coast of Rhapsody—Jules' and Phene's:

> To Ancona—Greece—some isle!
> I wanted silence only; there is clay
> Everywhere. One may do whate'er one likes
> In Art: the only thing is, to make sure
> That one does like it—which takes pains to know
>   Scatter all this, my Phene—this mad dream!
> Who, what is Lutwyche, what Natalia's friends,
> What the whole world except our love—my own,
> Own Phene? But I told you, did I not,
> Ere night we travel for your land—some isle
> With the sea's silence on it? Stand aside—
> I do but break these paltry models up
> To begin Art afresh. Meet Lutwyche, I—
> And save him from my statue meeting him?
> Some unsuspected isle in the far seas!
> Like a god going through his world, there stands
> One mountain for a moment in the dusk,
> Whole brotherhoods of cedars on its brow:
> And you are ever by me while I gaze
> —Are in my arms as now—as now—as now!
> Some unsuspected isle in the far seas!
> Some unsuspected isle in far-off seas! . . .

There are other enamoured references to islands in Browning:

> Now, one morn, land appeared—a speck
> Dim trembling betwixt sea and sky. . . .

> 'Our isles are just at hand,' they cried,
> Like cloudlets faint in even sleeping. . . .

> And now some islet, loosened from the land,
> Swims past with all its trees, sailing to ocean. . . .

But for a truly Olympian gesture in relation to islands we must go to Act V, Scene ii of *Antony and Cleopatra:*

> *Dolabella.* Most noble empress, you have heard of me?
> *Cleopatra.* I cannot tell.
> *Dolabella.*   Assuredly you know me.
> *Cleopatra.* No matter, sir, what I have heard or known.

175

You laugh when boys or women tell their dreams;
Is't not your trick?
Dolabella.   I understand not, madam.
Cleopatra. I dream'd there was an Emperor Antony:
O! such another sleep, that I might see
But such another man.
Dolabella.   If it might please ye,—
Cleopatra. His face was as the heavens, and therein stuck
A sun and moon, which kept their course, and lighted
The little O, the earth.
Dolabella.   Most sovereign creature,—
Cleopatra. His legs bestrid the ocean; his rear'd arm
Crested the world; his voice was propertied
As all the tunèd spheres, and that to friends;
But when he meant to quail and shake the orb,
He was as rattling thunder. For his bounty,
There was no winter in 't, an autumn 'twas
That grew the more by reaping; his delights
Were dolphin-like, they show'd his back above
The element they liv'd in; in his livery
Walk'd crowns and crownets, realms and islands were
As plates dropp'd from his pocket. . . .

'Behold, the nations are as a drop of a bucket, and are counted as the small dust of the balance: behold, he taketh up the isles as a very little thing.'

Page 43[1]—'The Tempest':
¶ When the play opens, twelve years have passed away since Prospero, Duke of Milan, with his small daughter Miranda, was set adrift at sea in a rat-forsaken, 'rotten carkasse of a Butt', sans rigging, tackle, sail or mast. It was only by the grace of that noble Neapolitan, Gonzalo, that it contained, apart from food and fresh water, certain 'rich garments, linens, stuffs', and some books from Prospero's library that he prized above his dukedom. But no commentator seems even to have guessed at their titles.

The island, with its branching coral and its yellow sands, its sea-nymphs and phantom voices, is in the main part bare. Trinculo can find neither bush nor shrub for shelter from the storm 'brewing i' the wind'; and Prospero (though this may be only a courtesy) can welcome his guest to naught but his 'poor cell'.* Caliban, too, though in gratitude for Prospero's kindness in ministering to him with water with berries in it, and teaching him how to name the sun and moon, could in return show him only the island's fresh springs, brine pits, its barren and fertile places; he himself being 'styed in the hard rock'. It is the more astonishing, then, how in the mere reading of the play the sweet influences, the solitude and the beauty of the island are ever in our minds, conjured there, apart from these few particulars, solely by its verbal music:

> . . . The isle is full of noises,
> Sounds and sweet airs, that give delight, and hurt not.
> Sometimes a thousand twangling instruments
> Will hum about mine ears; and sometime voices,
> That, if I then had waked after long sleep,
> Will make me sleep again. . . .

With far-away *Twelfth Night*, *The Tempest* is the most lyrical of the plays and therefore perhaps the nearest its author. Its text in the folio was probably printed, Mr. Dover Wilson concludes, from a prompt-copy in the dramatist's manuscript, it 'has been clearly abridged' and 'in the main by Shakespeare himself'. And it 'was quite possibly the last play that he wrote for the theatre'. Can one forbear the hope that this was so—though hopes have singularly little to do with the matter?

We are then left with these two insoluble problems: one, that of Shakespeare's subsequent silence—a man not yet in his fifties; the other, how next his inexhaustible genius might have flowered. For could there have been (though, if a purely personal confession may be forgiven,

* The stage direction for the second scene of the first act in the Cambridge edition runs as follows:
> The Island. A green plat of undercliff, approached by a path descending through a grove of lime-trees alongside the upper cliff, in the face of which is the entrance of a tall cave, curtained.
The whole play is unusually rich in stage directions, e.g. 'Enter Ariel, loaden with glittering apparel', etc. This one, however, has been distilled by the Editors from the scene itself and over those lime (or 'line') trees the Commentators have raged together even a little more furiously than usual. The *species* of tree is a little unexpected.

I feel almost as much daunted in Prospero's company as in the presence of Blake's horrific patriarchs)—could there be a more pregnant and significant Farewell? The experts have concluded that the rhymed epilogue is by another hand, and it has been explained as an apology to James I for Prospero's dabbling in witchcraft, yet that too has curiously apt overtones:

> . . . Gentle breath of yours my sails
> Must fill, or else my project fails,
> Which was to please. Now I want
> Spirits to enforce, art to enchant;
> And my ending is despair,
> Unless I be reliev'd by prayer,
> Which pierces so that it assaults
> Mercy itself and frees all faults.
> As you from crimes would pardon'd be,
> Let your indulgence set me free.

As for the island itself, whatever its original may have been, whether—'though all its fairies of the rocks were but flocks of birds' and all its 'divels' 'heards of swine'—it was that 'enchaunted, uninhabited, aboundantly fruitfull, richest, healthfullest, pleasing, meerely naturall island', Bermuda, with its 'shawes of goodly Cedar', its 'snaules and skulles' and Sea Owles, as it was described by Jourdain, and by William Strachey also, who, 'it is not impossible', was the friend whom Shakespeare 'got quietly in the corner and milked'; or whether it was the Lampedusa (about mid-way between Malta and Tunis) of Ariosto's *Orlando;* or *any* other, matters not. It is now and for ever, like workaday Crusoe's, an island that never was but always is. There dwell for ever, in their own peace, the Wizard, Miranda, Caliban and Ariel.

> From that daie forth the Isle has beene
> By wandering sailors never seene.
>   Some say 'tis buryed deepe
> Beneath the sea, which breakes and rores
> Above its savage rockie shores,
>   Nor ere is knowne to sleepe.

Page 43²—Its goats:

❡ 'Now it happened,' says Richard Walter, the editor, and co-author with Lord Anson, of *A Voyage Round the World* (1744), 'that the first goat that was killed by our people at their landing [on Juan Fernandez] had his ears slit, whence we concluded that he had doubtless been formerly under the power of Selkirk. This was indeed an animal of a most venerable aspect, dignified with an exceedingly majestic beard, and with many other symptoms of antiquity'—a collateral descendant no doubt, from Fiction out of Fact, of that 'most monstrous, frightful, old he-goat' which Crusoe found 'just making his will, as we say', in the cave.

A goat here and there is seen peacefully browsing, too, in the panoramic plate of the island included in Anson's handsome quarto. It depicts a tranquil undulating lawn or savanna dotted and encircled with myrtle trees; mountains beyond them rise into jutty peaks; twin streams of crystal water flow in the foreground; and there elegant gentlemen in eighteenth-century attire converse beside pavilions so dainty they appear to have been set up for some Belinda's wedding feast—'the Commodore's tent'. One looks—and looks again. Can *these* be Selkirk's wilds?

The author, who was chaplain of the *Centurion*, Anson's flag-ship in this expedition, admits that Juan Fernandez appears uncouth from the sea. So, too, Ringrose: 'As we approached,' he says (in 1680), 'both Islands seemed to us but one entire Heap of Rocks'. But *elegant* is the word used to describe the interior, and it precisely fits the chaplain's style. The island 'presented scenes of such elegance and dignity as perhaps would with difficulty be rivalled in any other part of the globe'. So multitudinous were the seals in Ringrose's time that his men were forced to kill before they could set foot on shore; and when afterwards they came to fill their casks, men had to be kept there to beat them off 'because the Seals covet hugely to lie in fresh water'.

When Anson sailed away from Juan Fernandez, he had set, for the benefit of those who came after him, kernels of peach and apricot in its kindly soil, and had sown lettuces, carrots and other garden plants. So may 'the actions of the just smell sweet, and blossom in their dust'.

Moreover, he left the goats, and the goat is a shag, grey- or green-eyed, vivacious animal that has less of a repute in England than it deserves. There it is usually seen tethered to an iron stake on a scrubby patch of no-man's-land. It has equivocal associations, of course. The devil is said to take its shape when he attends the Witches' Sabbath. A he-goat is emphatically a *he*-goat. To be a goat and to play the goat are neither of them reputable human activities. But Crusoe easily forgave or forgot all such frailties.

The first time I went out, I presently discovered that there were goats in the island, which was a great satisfaction to me; but then it was attended with this misfortune to me, viz. that they were so shy, so subtle, and so swift of foot, that it was the difficultest thing in the world to come at them.

Subtle indeed—enough, at any rate, in their natural surroundings, to keep themselves safe and fit and animated. Would that we could all claim an equal sagacity! It has been recorded that when two adult goats chance to encounter one another on a precipitous edge of rock whence any attempt to retire would be fatal, they keep their heads, they do not argue, nor do they fight for the right of way. They gaze steadily for a while each at each, and then at some secret understanding between them one of them gently lowers himself to a kneeling posture, the other as gingerly picks his way forward over his back— and trips on.

With such promising material it is curious that no castaway, in spite of ample leisure, ever seems to have tried to teach a goat to talk. 'Yet the memory of the Serpent,' as Sir Thomas Browne says, 'that spake unto Eve, the Dogs and Cats that usually speak unto Witches', might have afforded him 'some encouragement'.

The goat being an Old World animal it does not naturally consort with that other friend of the castaway, the coconut palm; though the illustrator of the Dutch *Crusoe*, possibly taking Tobago for his model, has sketched in a grove of them as if for luck. This particular tree shares with its cousin the date palm the ill fortune of being an object about which it is easy to be copiously informative. Sensible children, therefore, while otherwise as happy over its fruit as tomtits, learn to avoid all mention of it. Their elders, while realizing that if a coral island is ever to be their refuge, this one tree—whose nut may have bobbed nearly two thousand miles across the Pacific before it sprouted there—will supply them with drink, nourishment, greens, clothes, shelter, an anodyne and even oars, associate it with copra. And copra is the inevitable splash of local colour and evil smell in all modern blood-and-thunder tales of the South Seas. In them, for some reason unknown to the novice, the recluse never offers his visitor from the old country a draught of refreshing milk or a dish of jaggery from the coconuts hanging over his cabin—nor even a tot of *toddy* or of potent *arrack*, but at once resorts to the silver-mounted Tantalus on the sideboard.

Page 44¹—¶ He labours on
as no mortal man could who was the slave of that 'unnourishing island, a proud and arrogant heart'.

> God hath bid dwell far off all anxious cares. . . .
> To know
> That which before us lies in daily life,
> Is the prime wisdom: what is more is fume,
> Or emptiness, or fond impertinence. . . .

Page 45¹—He talks to himself:
¶ This habit, while it is also a symptom of insanity, seems to be the usual accompaniment of a prolonged solitude. There may too be solace in weeping. But not in listening to oneself laughing aloud among the rocks—Ha, ha, ha! Hoh, hoh, hoh! *Defienda me Dios de my! Audible* voices, too, such as Crusoe fancied he heard are an urgent warning.

A friend whose work committed him some years ago to spending much of his days alone in a very solitary part of the world once told me that in order to be certain of his mind there he used, during his walks abroad, to name aloud the different objects he saw. Yet another friend has confided to me that in similar circumstances he would frequently overhear himself talking to himself—a trinity in unity. One evening, too, as he sat alone, he heard his French servant, an ex-convict, who was at the moment engaged, unseen, in sawing up logs, suddenly clap down his saw and exclaim, 'Maintenant, *mon vieux Aragon, allez dans la cuisine et fumez une* BONNE cigarette!'.

Inward colloquies between self and self, or selves, are usual enough at all times and in all places. Prolonged adjurations in the second person are less so, though angry or scornful remarks on oneself out loud and of a defamatory kind are not uncommon. They are not always defamatory, though. Yet another friend happened once long ago to look in by chance on a room which at that moment was occupied only by one young man. He was intently examining his features in the looking-glass. At last,with a long sigh of satisfaction, he turned away, remarking aloud, 'Not handsome, perhaps, but distinguished!'

Page 46¹—At the sight of this money:
¶ The more the merrier:

The island . . . loomed large in the horizon. . . . They were just abreast of Mareciana, and beyond the flat but verdant Isle of La Pianosa. The peak of Monte Cristo, reddened by the burning sun, was seen against the azure sky. . . .

Edmond gazed most earnestly at the mass of rocks which gave out all the variety of twilight colours from the brightest pink to the deepest blue; . . . It was dark; but at eleven o'clock the moon rose in the midst of the ocean, whose every wave she silvered, and then, as she ascended, played in floods of pale light on the rocky hills of this second Pelion. . . .

The sun had nearly reached the meridian, and his scorching rays fell full on the rocks, which seemed themselves sensible of the heat. Thousands of grasshoppers, hidden in the bushes, chirped with a monotonous and dull note; the leaves of the myrtle and olive trees waved and rustled in the wind. At every step that Edmond took he disturbed the lizards glittering with the hues of the emerald; afar off he saw the wild goats bounding from crag to crag. In a word, the isle was inhabited, yet Edmond felt himself alone, guided by the hand of God. He felt an indescribable sensation somewhat akin to dread—that dread of the daylight which even in the desert makes us fear that we are observed. This feeling was so strong that at the moment when Edmond was about to commence his labour, he stopped, laid down his pickaxe, seized his gun, mounted to the summit of the highest rock, and from thence gazed round in every direction. . . . He then looked at the objects near him. He saw himself on the highest point of the isle, a statue on this vast pedestal of granite, nothing human in sight; while the blue ocean beat against the base of the island and covered it with a fringe of foam. . . .

He descended with a smile of doubt on his lips, and murmuring that last word of human philosophy, 'Perhaps!' . . . After having stood a few minutes in the cavern, the atmosphere of which was rather warm than damp, Dantes's eye, habituated as it was to darkness, could pierce even to the remotest angles of the cavern, which was of granite that sparkled like diamonds. 'Alas!' said Edmond, smiling, 'these are the treasures the cardinal has left; and the good abbé, seeing in a dream these glittering walls, has indulged in fallacious hopes'.

But he called to mind the words of the will, which he knew by heart. 'In the farthest angle of the second opening', said the cardinal's will. He had found only the first grotto; he had now to seek the second. . . .

[This] was lower and more gloomy than the other; the air, that could enter only by the newly formed opening, had that mephitic smell Dantes was surprised not to find in the first. He waited in order to allow pure air to displace the foul atmosphere, and then entered. At the left of the opening was a dark and deep angle. But to Dantes's eye there was no darkness. He glanced round this second grotto; it was, like the first, empty.

The treasure, if it existed, was buried in that dark corner. The time had at length arrived; two feet of earth removed, and Dantes's fate would be decided. He advanced towards the angle, and summoning all his resolution, attacked the ground with the pickaxe. At the fifth or sixth blow the pickaxe struck against an iron substance. Never did funeral knell, never did alarm-bell produce a greater effect on the hearer. . . . He approached with the torch the hole he had formed, and saw that his pickaxe had in reality struck against iron and wood. He planted his torch in the ground and resumed his labour. In an instant a space three feet long by two feet broad was cleared, and Dantes could see an oaken coffer, bound with cut steel; in the midst of the lid he saw engraved on a silver plate, which was

183

still untarnished, the arms of the Spada family; namely, a sword, pale, on an oval shield, like all the Italian armorial bearings, and surmounted by a cardinal's hat. . . . There was no longer any doubt—the treasure was there; no one would have been at such pains to conceal an empty casket. . . . Dantes inserted the sharp end of the pickaxe between the coffer and the lid and, pressing with all his force on the handle, burst open the fastenings. The hinges yielded in their turn and fell, still holding in their grasp fragments of the planks, and all was open. . . . Three compartments divided the coffer. In the first, blazed piles of golden coin; in the second, bars of unpolished gold, which possessed nothing attractive save their value, were ranged; in the third, Edmond grasped handfuls of diamonds, pearls, and rubies, which as they fell on one another sounded like hail against glass. . . . There were a thousand ingots of gold, each weighing from two to three pounds; then he piled up twenty-five thousand crowns, each worth about eighty livres of our money and bearing the effigies of Alexander VI and his predecessors, and he saw that the compartment was only half empty. Then he measured ten double handfuls of precious stones, many of which, mounted by the most famous workmen of that period, exhibited in their artistic setting a value that was remarkable even by the side of their intrinsic value. . . .

This is a translation and it is not too graceful; but young and greedy eyes will or should find nothing amiss with it. To more sophisticated ones, some of its details, though rich, are a little clumsy. Those three 'compartments'; the 'ingots'—so much, as the author acknowledges, the least attractive shape in which to dig up virgin gold; the cashier-like counting out of that round 'twenty-five thousand crowns'; the insistence on mere market value. I am even a little doubtful about the 'ten double handfuls of precious stones'. One feels unnecessarily stupid at having had to be told so much. A genuine glut of treasure is lavished upon us, but is there quite its equivalent in glamour?

These are merely nice if not pernickety questions, and *Monte Cristo* is one of the books it is well to swallow whole and early, leaving the imagination to brood over it in peace.

Still, even 'nice' questions may have a flavour, and the writer of any tale that intends to include moidores and doubloons in it has to face a good many of them before he begins. How long, for instance, can he legitimately play cat to his reader's mouse? To cheat him finally of the hidden treasure would be suicidal, however realistic—for this is a disaster which occurs often enough in actuality. At least two treasure-hunting expeditions only last year, one on land and the other submarine, came to nought. Alluring missives about the same time were circulated concerning the intentions of a little band of adventurers who were soon to be off in search of some piratical hoard— only, of course, to be found on islands—armed with a gold-detecting machine. A neat little mechanical device in lieu of the water-diviner's hazel twig. No news apparently has been heard of them lately.

But fiction is another matter, and though the tale-teller may well keep his reader on the sharpest of tenter-hooks, he is bound to disimpale him in the end. Even the temporary postponement of the coveted hour has its risks, though Stevenson gallantly faced them:

It was fine open walking here, upon the summit; our way lay a little down-hill, for, as I have said, the plateau tilted towards the west. The pines, great and small, grew wide apart; and even between the clumps of nutmeg and azalea, wide open spaces baked in the hot sunshine. Striking, as we did, pretty near north-west across the island, we drew, on the one hand, ever nearer under the shoulders of the Spy-glass, and on the other, looked ever wider over that western bay where I had once tossed and trembled in the coracle.

The first of the tall trees was reached, and by the bearing, proved the wrong one. So with the second. The third rose nearly two hundred feet into the air above a clump of underwood; a giant of a vegetable, with a red column as big as a cottage, and a wide shadow around in which a company could have manoeuvred. It was conspicuous far to sea both on the east and west, and might have been entered as a sailing mark upon the chart. . . .

We were now at the margin of the thicket.

'Huzza, mates, all together!' shouted Merry; and the foremost broke into a run.

And suddenly, not ten yards further, we beheld them stop. A low cry arose. Silver doubled his pace, digging away with the foot of his crutch like one possessed; and next moment he and I had come also to a dead halt.

Before us was a great excavation, not very recent, for the sides had fallen in and grass had sprouted on the bottom. In this were the shaft of a pick broken in two and the boards of several packing-cases strewn around. On one of these boards I saw, branded with a hot iron, the name *Walrus*—the name of Flint's ship.

All was clear to probation. The *cache* had been found and rifled: the seven hundred thousand pounds were gone!

Ben Gunn had seen to that. We suspected it—and yet at the dreadful moment one's young stomach went empty as a tub, if only for John Silver's sake. On landing in England Ben gets a niggardly £1,000 for his share of the pirate's booty. This 'he spent or lost in three weeks, or, to be more exact, in nineteen days, for he was back begging on the twentieth'. So, to the tune of *The Wrong Box* (which rings a little queerly here), he was 'given a lodge to keep, exactly as he had feared upon the island', and even 'a shuit of livery' perhaps, and he became 'a notable singer in church on Sundays and saints' days'.

But may it not be that in this one small particular his maker was mistaken? I have all but a conviction that Ben refused to be cajoled or decoyed on board the *Hispaniola*, and that he laid down his weary bones at last to be lost in the windy sands of his familiar island. For, after all, the author even of a tale of adventure can no more compel his puppets to be or to stay exactly what and where he intends them to be or stay than he can prevent echoes sounding in his prose; unless, that is, he is too astute to be quite honest. And for echoes, is there not a faint far-away rumour of *The Gold Bug* in that 'third tall tree', and of Gulliver in the reference to the manoeuvring company?

It is amusing to see, too, how even Stevenson, sedulous and sensitive craftsman though he was, falls a prey to the great original of all castaways when Ben makes his entry in chapter xv. Running under the pines, he had looked 'dark and shaggy'. Close to:

'Who are you?' I asked.

'Ben Gunn,' he answered, and his voice sounded hoarse and awkward, like a rusty lock. 'I'm poor Ben Gunn, I am; and I haven't spoke with a Christian these three years. . . .'

He was clothed with tatters of old ship's canvas and old sea cloth; and this extraordinary patchwork was all held together by a system of the most various and incongruous fastenings, brass buttons, bits of stick, and loops of tarry gaskin. About his waist he wore an old brass-buckled leather belt. . . .

Five pages afterwards we read:

'They have begun to fight!' I cried. 'Follow me.'

And I began to run towards the anchorage, my terrors all forgotten, while close at my side the marooned man *in his goatskins* trotted easily and lightly.

Could he possibly have paid our Robinson a more delicate compliment!

It is recorded of Mr. Gladstone, of all romantics, that he searched London for a copy of *Treasure Island* only to find that the first edition had been sold out. The tale itself was begun in a miserably wet summer at Braemar, its author in bed, and forbidden to speak until dinnertime. After breakfast, says Edmund Gosse, he would sit propped up on his pillows playing chess — a unique method surely of getting up steam for a story. This, as its chapters were completed, he read out every night after dinner. It was finished at Davos. 'And if'—as Stevenson told W. E. Henley, the original of the Sea-Cook—'if it don't fetch the kids, why, they have gone rotten since my day.'

That master piece of the story, Billy Bones's chest, was lifted, it is said, from a book of travel by Charles Kingsley, entitled *At Last;* but it was Stevenson's father who actually packed it, and a happy man he must have been.

The locale of Poe's *Gold Bug* (or *Gold Beetle*, as it more fastidiously appears in my little English edition of 1852) is also an island:

This island is a very singular one. It consists of little else than the sea sand, and is about three miles long. Its breadth at no point exceeds a quarter of a mile. It is separated from the main land by a scarcely perceptible creek, oozing its way through a wilderness of reeds and slime, a favourite resort of the marsh-hen. The vegetation, as might be supposed, is scant, or at least dwarfish. No trees of any magnitude are to be seen. Near the western extremity . . . may be found, indeed, the bristly palmetto; but the whole island, with the exception of this western point, and a line of hard, white beach on the sea-coast, is covered with a dense undergrowth of the sweet myrtle. . . . The shrub here often attains the height of fifteen or twenty feet, and forms an almost impenetrable coppice, burthening the air with its fragrance.

Glimpses of open nature like this are not the less welcome for being unusual in Poe. All is clear and precise; it is the music of the phrases that is the subtle charm. And here is the treasure:

The chest had been full to the brim, and we spent the whole day, and the greater part of the next night, in a scrutiny of its contents. There had been nothing like order or arrangement: everything had been heaped in promiscuously. Having assorted all with care, we found ourselves possessed of even vaster wealth than we had at first supposed. In coin there was rather more than four hundred and fifty thousand dollars—estimating the value of the pieces as accurately as we could by the tables of the period. There was not a particle of silver. All was gold of antique date and of great variety—French, Spanish, and German money, with a few English guineas, and some counters, of which we had never seen specimens before. There were several very large and heavy coins, so worn that we could make nothing of their inscriptions. There was no American money. The value of the jewels we found more difficulty in estimating. There were diamonds—some of them exceedingly large and fine—a hundred and ten in all, and not one of them small; eighteen rubies of remarkable brilliancy; three hundred and ten emeralds, all very beautiful; and twenty-one sapphires, with an opal. These stones had all been broken from their settings and thrown loose in the chest. The settings themselves, which we picked out from among the other gold, appeared to have been beaten up with hammers, as if to prevent identification. Besides all this, there was a vast quantity of solid gold ornaments;—nearly two hundred massive finger and ear-rings; rich chains—thirty of these, if I remember; eighty-three very large and heavy crucifixes; five gold censers of great value; a prodigious golden punch-bowl, ornamented with richly chased vine-leaves and Bacchanalian figures; with two sword-handles exquisitely embossed, and many other smaller articles which I cannot recollect. The weight of these valuables exceeded three hundred and fifty pounds avoirdupois; and in this estimate I have not included one hundred and ninety-seven superb gold watches; three of the number being worth each five hundred dollars, if one. Many of them were very old, and, as time-keepers, valueless, the works having suffered, more or less, from corrosion; but all were richly jewelled, and in cases of great worth. We estimated the entire contents of the chest, that night, at a million and a half of dollars.

How telling here is the inclusion of that of which there was none—'not a particle of silver', 'no American money', and the diamonds 'not one of them small'. How deftly set —rich as the Quetzal of the Aztecs—that one 'opal', the 'antique', the 'hammers', the 'avoirdupois', that 'if I remember', and the makeweight of superb gold watches! And since every man secretes a miser as well as a snob in his bosom, how one's heart warms to these gourmands over their chest, spending not only a whole day 'but the greater part of the next night' in gloating over its contents.

Fine though the shade of difference between Defoe's and Poe's verisimilitude may be, it is conspicuous. We absorb Defoe's particulars without checking them. Poe checks his own. He is more careful, logical, coherent and consequential. Moreover a slightly narcotic atmosphere is over all his fiction; it is full of the dark and even its stars are dangerous. Of this dreamlike atmosphere in Defoe, apart from the *Journal*, there is exceedingly little. The clarity of mind in Poe's stories is not quite normal either. Nor is the fine sharp edge of his senses, eye and ear. Compare Crusoe's terror at the footprint with the first few pages of *The Maelstrom*. Even the list of the islands in the horrific scene with which this tale opens is different in effect from any catalogue in *Crusoe*.

There is a sustained interest in Defoe; in Poe a continuous slight excitement. In both authors the matter-of-factness is only a device, effective even when it is found out. Defoe is more ingenuous, but Poe's is the subtler intellect. How far the literary critic's old friend Sincerity is here concerned is a nice point. Much depends on aim and object. Nothing could be more subtle, for example, than Newman's knowledge of the heart and how by means of words to influence his readers'. But by comparison with *his* deepest intention Defoe and Poe had none at all. None

189

the less the influence of Poe over the mind of his devotee is extreme—so long, at least, as his incantation lasts. On those who are out of sympathy with him it is worse than *nil*.

Page 46²—What a power they wield over the fancy:

❡ Indeed, mere simple good sense, when it is of Crusoe's variety, may shine like the face of sweet content itself; and there is a profound yet homely wisdom in it too, always ready for instant use and never worn out. When Mr. Betteredge, the kindly and sagacious old butler in *The Moonstone*, was dubious of the present, or needed comfort for the past, or sought counsel for the future, he invariably resorted to *Robinson Crusoe*:

> I am not superstitious; I have read a heap of books in my time; I am a scholar in my own way. Though turned seventy, I possess an active memory, and legs to correspond. You are not to take it, if you please, as the saying of an ignorant man, when I express my opinion that such a book as *Robinson Crusoe* never was written, and never will be written again. I have tried that book for years—generally in combination with a pipe of tobacco—and I have found it my friend in need in all the necessities of this mortal life. When my spirits are bad —*Robinson Crusoe*. When I want advice—*Robinson Crusoe*. In past times, when my wife plagued me; in present times, when I have had a drop too much—*Robinson Crusoe*. I have worn out six stout *Robinson Crusoes* with hard work in my service. On my lady's last birthday she gave me a seventh. I took a drop too much on the strength of it; and *Robinson Crusoe* put me right again. Price four shillings and sixpence, bound in blue, with a picture into the bargain.

Unfortunately, it was not until these pages were in the hands of the printers that I happened to recall Mr. Betteredge, and looked him up. Whereupon conscience began to murmur. Had I by any unhappy chance been guilty of positively misusing his panacea? There was no help for it: I must consult the oracle itself. That determined on, I took a pencil, carefully shut my eyes, opened *The Adventures* at random and firmly dotted the edge of the exposed right-hand page. Then I looked out of my eyes again, and—at line 29, page 95, *Everyman* edition—read these words: *I was obliged to let it lie where it was, as a memorandum to teach me to be wiser next time.* Could Apollo himself have spoken more incisively?

Lee gives a list of some of Defoe's favourite phrases, very few of which, he says, were common to other writers of his age. Among them are:—Let the World know; I say; Of which in its place; When it came to the Push; On that Foot; By the Way; In few Words; It must be confess'd; In short; To which he answers and says—nothing; Upon the whole; Says he; Be that as it will; In plain English; The hands of Justice; But of this by and by; At Home and Abroad; 'Tis true; And the like; Breaking in upon them; All Sorts; To come into their Measures; So nice a Juncture; The Shortest Way; One of Solomon's Fools; To talk Gospel to a Kettle Drum; Take this with you as you go.

They are for the most part rhetorical in purpose, easy, downright, assured and yet slightly cozening, buttonholing phrases; and the man can be read in them almost as clearly as in his handwriting or his face.

Page 48[1]—And in much far-sighted:

¶ After the model of the French Academy, instituted in 1635, Defoe proposed, as had Dryden before him, and as did Swift after him, the foundation of a society whose aim

should be to encourage polite learning, to polish and refine the English tongue, and advance the so much neglected faculty of correct language: also, to establish purity and propriety of style, and to purge it from all the irregular additions that ignorance and affectation have introduced; and all those innovations of speech, if I may call them such, which some dogmatic writers have the confidence to foster upon their native language, as if their authority were sufficient to make their own fancy legitimate.

At least half a century, too, before the term 'blue stocking' had made its way into the language Defoe was enrapturedly, and a little headily, singing the claims of woman to an education at least as comprehensive as man's—at *least:*

I cannot think that God ever made them so delicate, so glorious creatures, and furnished them with such charms, so agreeable and so delightful to mankind, with souls capable of the same enjoyments as men, and all to be only stewards of our houses, cooks, and slaves. . . . Women, in my observation of them have little or no difference, but as they are, or are not distinguished by education. Tempers, indeed, may in some degree influence them, but the main distinguishing part is their breeding. The whole sex are generally quick and sharp, I believe I may be allowed to say, generally so; for you rarely see them lumpish and heavy when they are children, as boys will often be. If a woman be well bred, and taught the proper management of her natural wit, she proves generally very sensible and retentive: and, without partiality, a woman of sense and manners is the finest and most delicate part of God's creation, the glory of her Maker, and the great instance of his singular regard to man, to whom he gave the best gift either God could bestow, or man receive: and it is the sordidest piece of folly and ingratitude in the world, to withhold from the sex the due lustre which the advantages of education give to the natural beauty of their minds.

The urbane cajolery of, 'I believe I may be allowed to say, generally so'!

Page 48²—Church Street:
¶ Stoke Newington, and *not* (a) at the 'Rose and Crown' in a back lane in Halifax, or (b) over a hairdresser's in a dingy little Harrow Alley in Whitechapel, or (c)—its author in concealment from his enemies, in a back chamber over the washhouse of the 'Duke William's Head', a small tavern at Hartley, near the little old market town of Cranbrook in Kent. Before Wilson wrote his life of Defoe all these places, and no doubt others, contested for the palm. At Stoke Newington Defoe's way of living was 'very genteel'. His flat handsome house, with its coach-house and stables, stood in four acres of garden which he characteristically 'turned to profit'.

Page 51¹—Why whiskers at all? :
¶ The duodecimo chapbook based on *Robinson Crusoe*, which at once followed its publication, is decorated with the crudest of cuts, such cuts as haunted Stevenson's memory when he was amusing himself in amusing his young friend, Lloyd Osbourne. They are like the pictures which a small boy scrabbles on the fly-leaf of a lesson

book for an antidote, yet they somehow convey the true spirit of *Crusoe*, its raw romance, more inwardly and winningly than can even art with a capital A. And the simple reason for this may be, that the *Adventures* are themselves so artless in effect.

One feels that Defoe, having brought his Crusoe to life, or life to his Crusoe, needed only to watch him enjoying that life, and always to his own secret amusement. That endearing mixture of modesty and vanity! If he did not confess his failures how could we share in his triumphs?

I searched for the cassava root, which the Indians, in all that climate, make their bread of, but I could find none. I saw large plants of aloes, but did not then understand them. I saw several sugar canes, but wild, and for want of cultivation, imperfect. . . . In short, I had made so little observation while I was in the Brazils, that I knew little of the plants in the field.

He spends two whole months in moiling and toiling before he succeeds in making two large earthen pots—and even then it is only an accident that suggests his not merely drying them in the sun, but burning them in fire. 'It would make the reader pity me, or rather laugh at me, to tell . . . what odd, misshapen, ugly things I made.' But we neither pity him, nor do we laugh at him. We merely love him dearly because we have most of us tinkered up a rabbit-hutch or hung a picture, and can share both his disappointment and his pride. So too with his tailoring:

Upon those views, I began to consider about putting the few rags I had, which I called clothes, into some order. . . . So I set to work a-tailoring or rather, indeed, a-botching, for I made most piteous work of it. However, I made shift to make two or three new waistcoats, which I hoped would serve me a great while.

Waistcoats! With these he was 'kept very dry'; and he at once, therefore, sets to work on a fantastic umbrella. The sheer generosity of his soul!

Whether, again, it be chance or design that achieves one of the most difficult of all literary feats in fiction—that of making the time go by—it is hard to say. Go by it does, however. 'I cannot say that after this, for five years, any extraordinary thing happened to me; but I lived on in the same course.' And the next minute we are actively occupying the five years that have *gone by*. And to such good purpose that, contrary even to his own specific statements, Crusoe never seems to grow a day older. We are told he was in his twenty-eighth year when he landed on his island, and nearly sixty when he left it. He arrives back in London, his farther adventuring over, aged about seventy-two. But what are mere dates in these matters? For my part he was just the more juvenile side of forty, say, thirty-eight, when he swam ashore from the wreck, and just the more juvenile side of forty he will ever remain.

Page 52[1]*—Distant horizons:*

❡ There is a treatise of many volumes which bears on its title-page the device ALL BEARINGS ARE TRUE. An ignoramus may confess (a) that he does not completely know what these words mean, and (b) that he does not intend to find out. They are an all-sufficing comfort as they stand.

Many sage and simple words of counsel follow: e.g. 'Instead of considering a coast to be clear unless it is shown to be foul, the contrary should be assumed'. We are warned, again, that 'in closing the land in fog' not even the shore horn is a sure safeguard from disaster. 'Large areas of silence have been found'—some of them 'quite close to the horn itself. . . . The lead is generally the only safe guide'. And a secret meaning seems to echo in the sound of that *lead* which needs searching out. Whether, however, it be transmutable into gold or not, every reader will agree at sight that in life, as at sea, the smallest of errors may 'put the ship ashore'.

But this book is not concerned with moral warnings. These are unintentional. Its *raison d'être* is solely marine. Its charm is that it tells of countless islands and islets, and these of every magnitude. Some spacious yet still empty of man. Others mere rocks needling out of the crystal of the sea; pretty to look at, but best to avoid. It is full of soundings and volcanoes and monsoons, of winds and currents, of fringing reefs and shoals and eddies and tide-rips and overfalls, of trees or mountains to steer by and discoloured waters to shun, and of beaches and groves and buoys. Here, there is 'a boat pier with a white lantern on it'. There, 'a private light is exhibited from a trellis-work structure near the flag staff of the governor's house'. Here, again, 'the depths are liable to change: the banks are low'.

These are but petty examples of its ordinary workaday facts. How is it, then, that the mere recital of them as instantly and insidiously communes with some stowaway skulking in one's consciousness as may music itself? Why is it that common words threaded together like this, and purely for utilitarian purposes, resemble incantations? It does not matter much about the answer. The hooting of an owl; the chattering of the autumnal wind on Egdon Heath in its withered harebells; a tiny dervish dance of dry leaves in winter; the rattle of drums; the rap of oar on rowlock from a phosphorescent sea—all these are similar decoys.

And it is not the only joy of this book that it consists of such *facts*—though it is a rare pleasure to be able to stone the realist occasionally with his own missiles. It deals also with the Here and the Now, as near the latter at any rate as 1921, and only a few thousand miles from the former. Yet, open it at random, and instantly the spirit is set free. 'There are quantities of snakes . . . on these banks.' 'Northward . . . the character of the bottom changes to globigerina ooze'—a lyric in two words, and, as fact, pure poetry.

A few pages on we encounter an island 'fresh and healthy'—few marshes, few mudbanks—and in length only nine miles short of the distance from London to York. But its east coast rises sheer from the sea to densely overgrown mountains whose summits and valleys are little fitted to provide means of 'human habitation. . . .

At many points the coast consists of a great wall of rock plunging precipitously into the sea, so that whole stretches of it [blissful tidings!] are totally uninhabited'.

Another island, rich, fertile and mountainous, in shape an oval of 3,380 square miles, is 'still one of the least known'. It is rapidly gaining on the sea; '*Fort Defensie* built a century and a half ago, close to the water, being now nearly half a mile inland'. 'It is peopled by a peculiar, effeminate and very timid race.'

Then again, well-watered, mountainous O—— (I omit what follows the O lest the S.P.R., armed with bell, book and candle, should set out in its direction). Forty-eight miles long, east and west, and twenty wide, it is as yet unexplored and ill charted; it has no roads or footpaths; and the few natives who land on its coasts rarely venture far inland—where they would meet none of their own kind —for it has 'the reputation of being haunted'.

By what? By whom? Beings, it would seem, sinister and formidable enough, if the densely wooded, sheer-cliffed coast south-west of O—— is similarly frequented:

A number of sugar-loaf summits, many of which are burnt bare, with leafless trees on their summits, give the land a singular appearance. There are white patches on the cliffs in places. Caves and tunnels have been worn in the rocks, making the aspect of the coast arresting to the eye; in these vaults the natives bury their dead, together with their weapons and household goods, with sacred images to watch over them. Blood-red marks are found on the white walls of cliff in the vicinity of the buried corpses, which are attributed to evil spirits, and sometimes appear at spots one would have thought to be inaccessible.

But there are less disquieting localities than these. Here are a few scraps for proof of it—all about islands and all of those islands different: 'It is nearly always fine in T—Bentuni'. 'The houses are connected to the shore by bamboo bridges more than a hundred yards in length.' 'Hogs, goats, fowls, and sweet potatoes can be procured, and there is a store kept by a Chinaman.' 'Earthquakes are frequent.' 'No dangers have been seen along this part of the coast.' 'To enter, keep the beacon in the form of a cross in line with . . .' but in 1921 we are told this beacon had disappeared. And Cape Valsche, also—'dangerous to approach since it is possible to run aground before it is sighted'.

And again: 'As the vicinity of these islands has not been examined they should be approached with caution'. 'The weather was hazy, especially between July and October, when the land could seldom be seen more than a few miles away, except in the early morning, and the tops of the mountains were generally in the clouds.' Verdurous, unattainable, delectable vision. In brief, here is Tom Tiddler's Ground, welcoming not only such pilgrims of the sea as Mr. H. M. Tomlinson, but even the landlubber. Yet it is only one drift of many drifts of islands, perpetually in wait for maroons, greedy for castaways, and saturated with all that the poor gregarious westerner in his innocence means by solitude.

'But are there no solitudes out of the cave and the desert?' Charles Lamb questions ironically. 'Or cannot the heart in the midst of crowds feel frightfully alone?' It can, yet dreams on; and if only, is its fond illusion, the cage in which it dwells might be left alone too, the bird within might sing the sweeter.

As for ignorance, the difficulty is to know where one's own begins, it being impracticable to discover where it ends. There is an ignorance of feeling and of conception no less than of facts and 'ologies. We may be rich as Croesus in those 'ologies and yet as insensitive as the covers of the textbooks that contain them. We may know but utterly fail to comprehend. And our knowledge may serve for little more than blinkers, or may be so self-satisfying that in the face of anything that conflicts with it we remain blandly incapable or incredulous. It is unfortunate that those who have shared much the same environment and education share also much the same kind, quality and quantity of knowledge. Not only are they therefore likely to be less entertaining to one another, but they are apt also to be amused at the ignorance of 'the outsider', rejecting with the complacency of the herd instinct what *he* has, and they have not.

Besides, is there anything else in the world so animating as somebody else's ignorance? Charles Darwin—surely one of the most lovable of English writers—tells us in his *Voyage of H.M.S. Beagle* that he stayed ten weeks at Maldonado, on the northern bank of the Plata:

> . . . On the first night we slept at a retired little country-house; and there I soon found out that I possessed two or three articles, especially a pocket compass, which created unbounded astonishment. In every house I was asked to show the compass, and by its aid, together with a map, to point out the direction of various places. It excited the liveliest admiration that I, a perfect stranger, should know the road (for direction and road are synonymous in this open country) to places where I had never been. At one house a young woman, who was ill in bed, sent to entreat me to come and show her the compass. If their surprise was great, mine was greater, to find such ignorance among people who possessed their thousands of cattle, and 'estancias' of great extent. . . . I was asked whether the earth or the sun moved; whether it was hotter or colder to the north; where Spain was, and many other such questions. The greater number of the inhabitants had an indistinct idea that England, London, and North America were different names for the same place; but the better informed well knew that London and North America were separate countries close together, and that England was a large town in London! I carried with me some promethean matches, which I ignited by biting; it was thought so wonderful that a man should strike fire with his teeth, that it was usual to collect the whole family to see it: I was once offered a dollar for a single one.

Page 53[1]—Mrs. Veal:

¶ Fourteen years after *Mrs. Veal*, and one year after *Crusoe*, Defoe published another ghost story. In it we watch that same queer questing glance of his to right and left which hints at so much closer a knowledge of the preternatural than is definitely set out. A schoolboy spends his days in melancholy and terror; he is haunted by the ghost of a woman who 'dyed about eight Years since'. She accosts him morning and evening on his way to and from school in a field called the *Higher-Broom* Quartils. When, in hope to be rid of her, he goes another way—by the 'under

Horse Road' and on through 'the Narrow Lane', so does she. And this 'was worse'. Is it to be wondered at that his misery at last becomes insupportable and he unbosoms himself to his brother William? Sad to relate, the 'Spectrum' is exorcised by a zealous young clergyman, and Defoe refrains from telling us what in their brief colloquy the ghost said to him.

Not that this was beyond him! Whatever he might have made her utter would have been no less convincing than the last words attributed to Jack Sheppard as they were recorded in the manuscript which he himself handed over to Defoe in the cart on his way to execution—the boy of twenty-two, the old journalist of sixty-four: 'Blueskin has atoned for his Offences. I am now following, being just on the brink of Eternity, much unprepared to appear before the Face of an angry God.' Jack Sheppard—with his diamond ring and a cornelian on his finger, in his light tye periwig of about seven pounds value—was a popular hero. The Thief-Catcher, Jonathan Wild, not so. And Defoe is accordingly more reticent about him.

Page 56[1]—Out of which poetry is made:
¶ Defoe's verse is of the metallic, incisive, epigrammatic order. Such lines, for example, as these from *The True-born Englishman*—they rap out like corks from a pop-gun:

> We challenge all our heralds to declare
> Ten families which English Saxons are. . . .

> From this amphibious, ill-born mob began
> That vain ill-natured thing, an Englishman. . . .

> So dull they never take the pains to think;
> And seldom are good natured but in drink. . . .

> Antiquity and birth are needless here;
> 'Tis impudence and money make a peer. . . .

> For fame of families is all a cheat.
> It's personal virtue only makes us great. . . .

Or,

> No man has tasted differing fortunes more,
> And thirteen times I have been rich and poor.

Or these, again, from his *Hymn to the Pillory:*

> Thou, like the Devil dost appear,
> Blacker than réally thou art, by far!
> A wild chimeric notion of Reproach;
> Too little for a crime, for none too much.
> Let none th' indignity resent;
> For crime is all the shame of Punishment!

He dared lofty themes—'The Sun: Parent of Light', 'Eternity', 'Faith'; but in his treatment of them tends to see-saw between the rhetorical and—the indescribable:

> Thine [Faith's] is the fiery Chariot, thine the Steeds,
> That fetch't *Elijah* from *Old Jordan's Plains;*
> Such a long journey, such a Voiture needs,
> And thou the steady Coach-man held the reins.

But poetry in his verse is rare—though it may gleam out of such a line as 'Immortal trophies dwell upon his brow'; or, 'May he be first in every morning thought!' or, 'Who would not sacrifice for Thee, All that Men call felicity!' or in 'Thy radiant Bright, unfaded Face'.

Of light and lightness, grace and sinuosity, there is, too, little in his prose. Not much either of that sudden strangeness which words may take to themselves, as in 'a crepusculous glance' or in 'There is no blew Tulip'. But he excels in the effect given by bare simple statement—one of the secrets of the peculiar magic to be found in the prose of the sea, e.g. 'There was yce towards the north, but a great sea, free, large, very salt, and blue, and of an unsearchable depth'. Like Cobbett's, Defoe's prose trudges along sturdily, and at times clumsily, on its two sound legs, while Pepys's, no less direct and unaffected and full of matter, glances with the ease and swiftness of the flight of a swallow—scintillating with vivacity:

(Lord's day.) May 26, 1667. My wife and I to church, where several strangers of good condition came to our pew. After dinner I by water alone to Westminster to the parish church, and there did entertain myself with my perspective glass up and down the church, by which I had the great pleasure of seeing and gazing at a great many very fine women; and what with that, and sleeping, I passed away the time till sermon was done. I away to my boat, and, up with it as far as Barn Elms, reading of Mr. Evelyn's late new book against Solitude, in which I do not find much excess of good matter, though it be pretty for a bye discourse. I walked the length of the Elms, and with great pleasure saw some gallant ladies and people come with their bottles, and basket, and chairs, and form, to sup under the trees, by the water-side, which was mighty pleasant; so home. . . .

The best perhaps that can be said of Defoe's prose (as of any other writer's) is that it fully served his multifarious purposes; but as he seems seldom to have attempted feats much beyond his workaday scope, it is apt to sink below a certain level rather than to rise above it.

In *Crusoe* there are occasional gobbets of latinity:

But it was impossible to prevail, especially upon the Englishmen, their curiosity was so importuning upon their prudentials, that they must run out and see the battle.

But for the most part it is an easy and various savanna of the monosyllabic.

I swam round her twice, and the second time I spied a small piece of rope, which I wondered I did not see at first, and by the help of that rope got up into the forecastle of the ship. Here I found that the ship was bulged, and had a great deal of water in her hold, but that she lay so on the side of a bank of hard sand, or rather earth, that her stern lay lifted up upon the bank, and her head low almost to the water. By this means all her quarter was free, and all that was in that part was dry; for you may be sure my first work was to search and to see what was spoiled and what was free.

One hundred and thirty words in all, and only ten of more than one syllable. The result—in this particular specimen—though clear enough to the eye, is a little flat to the ear (e.g. the eight *whats* and *thats*, the second *free*), but simply because it has no airs or graces, except such winning Defoeisms as the 'I wondered' and 'You may be sure', it has the *effect* of being absolutely trustworthy. Of the Ancient Mariner (whose fate was on the high seas and never, alas, among islands), we see little more than skinny hand and patriarchal beard. His glittering eye is hypnotic, but what hides behind it? Crusoe's cheerful whiskered face is as open and candid as the sun. We believe what he says partly because he looks so guileless and is so childishly communicative. He is not taking pains enough to be telling us lies. As Leslie Stephen said of Defoe's matter: 'He sought to gain piquancy by diverging from the common track in the name of common sense'; so of his manner. 'As to the plainness and coarseness' of it, says Defoe himself in *The Present State of Parties*, he would make 'no apology for it'. Other writers, that is, less intent on the truth, might decorate and elaborate, but he, the plain honest man? No.

So, careful and careless by turns, his style is as copious as easy talk, an occasional pedantry jutting up out of the raciest idioms. But such a sentence as 'And thus, having found two or three broken oars belonging to the boat, and besides the tools which were in the chest, I found two saws, an axe, and a hammer, and with this cargo I put to sea', is not infrequent and, with all due respect to careless raptures, scarcely shipshape. And when he tells of 'a little river, with land on both sides' even his most ingenuous reader—the ingenuous reader being his main-stay—is being rather superfluously provided for.

The only fault he can find in his cousin, the author of *Gulliver's Travels*, says Richard Sympson in his letter from 'the Publisher to the Reader', is that after the manner of travellers he is a little too circumstantial. 'The style is very plain and simple; . . . there is an air of truth apparent throughout the whole.' So assuredly with Crusoe. Richard Sympson does not state, however, whether or not he had carried out his cousin's express instructions to him 'to hire some young gentleman of either university to correct' that style. And though in Gulliver's prefatory letter all is plain, it is by no means so simple. Its irony glitters like metal out of a jagged lump of quartz.

. . . Is there less probability in my account of the *Houyhnhnms* or *Yahoos*, when it is manifest, as to the latter, there are so many thousands, even in this country, who only differ from their brother brutes in *Houyhnhnm-land*, because they use a sort of jabber, and do not go naked? I wrote for their amendment, and not their approbation. The united praise of the whole race would be of less consequence to me than the neighing of those two degenerate *Houyhnhnms* I keep in my stable; because from these, degenerate as they are, I still improve in some virtues, without any mixture of vice.

Do these miserable animals presume to think that I am so degenerated as to defend my veracity? *Yahoo* as I am, it is well known through all *Houyhnhnm-land*, that, by the instructions and example of my illustrious master, I was able, in the compass of two years (although, I confess, with the utmost difficulty), to remove that infernal habit of lying, shuffling, deceiving, and equivocating, so deeply rooted in the very souls of all my species, especially the Europeans.

Here perhaps Swift has laid rather too heavy a finger on the scales. His own gigantic shadow looms up above Lemuel's head. We are conscious of an almost unendurable bitterness; and the smile is as dangerous as it is wry. He seems to detest the sinner—the abhorred 'species'— more even than the sin.

Defoe also was an indefatigable moralist, but how much he wrote for the approbation of his fellow-*Yahoos* and how much for their amendment not he himself could have declared. Far from having any quarrel with these miserable animals or feeling any physical or spiritual repulsion at their mere naturalism, his interest in fiction was almost entirely with moral outcasts, rebels against the law and society. He understood their natures. They flaunt and flourish awhile with astonishing versatility, but remorse and disaster lie in wait for them all. In Charles Lamb's words:

Singleton, the pirate—Colonel Jack, the thief—Moll Flanders, both thief and harlot—Roxana, harlot and something worse—would be startling ingredients in the bill of fare of modern literary delicacies. But, then, what pirates, what thieves, and what harlots is *the thief*, *the harlot*, and *the pirate* of De Foe? We would not hesitate to say, that in no other book of fiction, where the lives of such characters are described, is guilt and delinquency made less seductive, or the suffering made more closely to follow the commission, or the penitence more earnest or more bleeding, or the intervening flashes of religious visitation, upon the rude and uninstructed soul, more meltingly and fearfully painted. They, in this, come near to the tenderness of Bunyan; while the livelier pictures and incidents in them, as in Hogarth, or in Fielding, tend to diminish that 'fastidiousness to the concerns and pursuits of common life, which an unrestrained passion for the ideal and the sentimental is in danger of producing'.

Defoe himself defended Moll's past by maintaining that if her penitence was to be lastingly impressive at the end of her story her wickedness had to be correspondingly heinous at the beginning! A simple sum by rule of three. Charles Lamb's views, too, are very far from being those held—in *Lavengro*—by the old apple-woman on London Bridge whose son is in Botany Bay. Not even for two bright crowns or 'bulls'—i.e. twenty 'turnoes'—can she be coaxed to sell the short, thick, precious volume over which, her pan of smouldering charcoal at her feet, she sits coddling —its pages bound in greasy black leather, yellow and dog's-eared.

'So you think there's no harm in stealing?'

'No harm in the world, dear! Do you think my own child would have been transported for it, if there had been any harm in it? and what's more, would the blessed woman in the book here have written her life as she has done, and given it to the world, if there had been any harm in faking? She, too, was what they call a thief and a cut-purse; ay, and was transported for it, like my dear son; and do you think she would have told the world so, if there had been any harm in the thing? Oh, it is a comfort to me that the blessed woman was transported, and came back—for come back she did, and rich too— for it is an assurance to me that my dear son, who was transported too, will come back like her.'

'What was her name?'

'Her name, blessed Mary Flanders.'

'Will you let me look at the book?'

'Yes, dear, that I will, if you promise me not to run away with it.'

Page 57¹—Dante himself:

❡ But Dante's objects, though thus observed with the acutest of senses, having been transformed by his imagination, appear, when referred to in words, of a profoundly different substance. A similar difference is observable in the apparent substance of objects, as compared with that of their originals, when seen in dream. We may recognize them as symbols, though we may not be able to interpret them as symbols. So Dante's objects resemble the characters in a rune, and only an initiated self, if any, can interpret that rune. Take these few lines, as translated by Dr. John Carlyle, from the *Inferno:*

But in my ears a wailing smote me, whereat I bent my eyes intently forwards. And the kind Master said: 'Now, Son, the city that is named of Dis draws nigh, with its grave citizens, with its great company'.

And I: 'Master, already I discern its mosques, distinctly there within the valley, red as if they had come out of fire'.

And to me he said: 'The eternal fire, which causes them to glow within, shows them red, as thou seest, in this low Hell'.

We now arrived in the deep fosses, which moat that joyless city. The walls seemed to me as if they were of iron. Not before making a long circuit, did we come to a place where the boatman loudly cried to us: 'Go out: here is the entrance'. Above the gates I saw more than a thousand spirits, rained from Heaven, who angrily exclaimed: 'Who is that, who, without death, goes through the kingdom of the dead?'

Dreams remembered on waking that continue to haunt the mind as if with an assurance of some secret meaning are unusual—at least in my own small experience. And nowadays it may be a little indiscreet to refer to them! But one such dream, and it occurred after the above lines had been written, may be an example.

I dreamed that I was standing beside a mound of dark loose tumbled earth—earth that had been tossed up by the mattocks of those who were digging there. And *they*, as I knew well, were exhuming the long-interred body of the great Napoleon. It was night; and yet I was not aware what caused the luminousness around me and the sharp shadows in the earth. Nor could I see the diggers—or rather I could see only one of them, a young girl, pale of feature, and of unusual beauty. She was dressed in some heavy, close-fitting cloth, the skirts of which hung loose and in straight full folds to her feet. A strand of her dark hair, loosed by her labours, lay across her brow and cheek. . . .

What next I remember is looking down on the remains of a coffin, the lid of which had fallen in at a sharp angle with the nearer rotted side. It was empty, and on seeing this the apprehension seized me that the grave had been already rifled. But this apprehension was not shared by my companion; with a serene solemn gesture of reassurance, she continued to dig. And presently afterwards the corse itself was exposed in the dark loose earth. . . .

Next I found myself standing, only a pace distant, confronting this lifeless shape as it itself stood propped up against some brightly lit neutral-coloured background—of what I could not see; perhaps a lime-washed wall. The attenuated body—that of the young Napoleon, not the hermit of St. Helena—was clothed to the feet in a long dark military coat, stained with damp and mould. I recall no buttons on the breast, or they were too much tarnished to be conspicuous. On the head was a three-cornered hat. The lower part of the ashy face beneath the ivory brows was narrowed and fallen in under the high cheek bones; and the two eyes in that head gazed out at me with a marvellous effulgence. I gazed back—those eyes that in life few men had ever dared to meet—then turned my head and spoke in astonishment to those who stood near me but whom I could not see, and said, 'Then his eyes were not blue, or grey-blue? They are bright brown.'

Then I turned again and met that intense yet unspeculating gaze once more. 'No, not brown,' I added in a low voice, and as if to myself, 'orange-brown'. But this too was inaccurate; flat, wide, unblinking, intent, they were far more red than orange—a clear lively red. And there passed through my mind as I continued to meet and bandy thoughts with them, vague tumultuous remembrances of this supreme egotist and man of genius, and of the glory that was gone. . . .

In searching afterwards for some germ of this dream, I recalled at once an unusually intelligent black cat, once an admired pet, named Caesar. It died some months ago, miserably shrunken, and, according to the vet that visited it, of congestion of the liver. A few hours before it died the colour of its eyes became changed to a curiously bright strange green. And now, as I look back, these eyes too had looked out at me—as I myself looked down in horror at the poor dying creature—like those of the dead Napoleon; as if there were some secret between us, as if in some way I shared the responsibility, the blame for what had passed.

Be it ours—

> . . . To see with reasonable eyes
> Of what the mind, of what the soul is made,
> And what it is, in sickness or in sleep,
> That makes us rise in terror and think we see
> Dead men whose bones Earth bosomed long ago. . . .

Page 58[1]—The facts and figures:

¶ Defoe's appetite for actualities, and particularly actualities of an odd, unusual or extreme kind, such as those with which every daily newspaper is packed, seems to have been insatiable. It is his choice and arrangement that mark them as his own, and this is no less apparent in the *Journal* than in his account of the great storm of 1720— 'the most violent tempest the world ever saw'.

By slyly stating at the outset that he intends to ignore merely trivial damages, and so will not trouble his reader with the multitude or magnitude of trees blown down, whole parks ruined, orchards laid flat and the like, he whets that reader's appetite. He then proceeds to relate how a Mr. Dyer, a plasterer, perished because after jumping out of his bed at the violent shaking of the roof over his head he stayed to strike a light; while a Mr. Simpson, a scrivener, met his end because he refused to get up at all. And just that tinge of the bizarre and of the very human appears which makes all tragic records of life so much more searching and arresting.

So, too, in the *Journal:* 'It is impossible to describe the variety of postures in which the passions of the poor people would express themselves. Passing through Token-House-yard, in Lothbury, of a sudden a casement violently opened just over my head, and a woman gave three frightful screeches, and then cried O! death, death, death! in a most inimitable tone, and which struck me with horror and a chilness in my very blood.' Was there ever a more effective 'and which'? 'There was nobody to be seen in the whole street, neither did any other window open, for people had no curiosity now in any case nor could anybody help one another; so I went on to pass into Bell-alley.' There a merchant, a deputy-alderman and very rich—'I care not to mention his name, though I knew his name too'—had that moment hanged himself.

The *Journal* was fiction, based solidly on fact, and here again, for comparison, is a fragment from Pepys's *Diary;* and were ever words so few packed more closely with human experience?

. . . The hottest day that ever I felt in my life. This day, much against my will, I did in Drury Lane see two or three houses marked with a red cross upon the doors, and 'Lord have mercy upon us!' writ there; which was a sad sight to me, being the first of the kind that, to my remembrance, I ever saw. It put me into an ill conception of myself and my smell, so that I was forced to buy some roll-tobacco to smell to and chaw, which took away the apprehension.

. . . Abroad, and met with Hadley, our clerk, who, upon my

asking how the plague goes, told me it increases much, and much in our parish; for, says he, there died nine this week, though I have returned but six: which is a very ill practice, and makes me think it is so in other places; and therefore the plague much greater than people take it to be. I went forth, and walked towards Moorfields to see (God forgive my presumption!) whether I could see any dead corpse going to the grave; but, as God would have it, did not. But, Lord! how everybody's looks, and discourse in the street, is of death, and nothing else; and few people going up and down, that the town is like a place distressed and forsaken. . . .

Up; and put on my coloured silk suit, very fine, and my new periwig, bought a good while since, but durst not wear, because the plague was in Westminster when I bought it; and it is a wonder what will be the fashion after the plague is done, as to periwigs, for nobody will dare to buy any hair, for fear of the infection, that it had been cut off the heads of people dead of the plague. . . .

Page 60[1]—¶ How still and clear:
. . . There is one pleasure still within the reach of fallen mortality —and perhaps only one—which owes even more than does music to the accessory sentiment of seclusion. I mean the happiness experienced in the contemplation of natural scenery. In truth, the man who would behold aright the glory of God upon earth must in solitude behold that glory. To me, at least, the presence—not of human life only— but of life in any other form than that of the green things which grow upon the soil and are voiceless—is a stain upon the landscape—is at war with the genius of the scene. I love, indeed, to regard the dark valleys, and the grey rocks, and the waters that silently smile, and the forests that sigh in uneasy slumbers, and the proud watchful mountains that look down upon all—I love to regard these as themselves but the colossal members of one vast animate and sentient whole—a whole whose form (that of the sphere) is the most perfect and most inclusive of all; whose path is among associate planets; whose meek handmaiden is the moon; whose mediate sovereign is the sun; whose life is eternity; whose thought is that of a God; whose enjoyment is knowledge; whose destinies are lost in immensity; whose cognizance of ourselves is akin with our own cognizance of the *animalculae* which infest the brain—a being which we, in consequence, regard as purely inanimate and material, much in the same manner as these *animalculae* must thus regard us. . . .

This fragment, as alien from the usual influence of his presence in his work as daybreak is different from the last of dusk, is by Edgar Allan Poe. And here is a passage, brimming with light, taken from Professor R. K. Gordon's translation of *The Phoenix*, an Anglo-Saxon poem, the source of which was the *Carmen de Phenice* of Lactantius; it has been attributed to Cynewulf:

I have heard that far hence in the east is the noblest of lands, famous among men. The face of the land is not to be found across the world by many of earth's dwellers, but by God's might it is set afar off from evil-doers. Lovely is all the land, dowered with delights, with earth's sweetest scents; matchless is that water-land, noble its Maker, proud, rich in power; He created the country. There often to the blessed the delight of harmonies, the door of heaven is set open and revealed. That is a fair field, green forests spread beneath the skies. There neither rain, nor snow, nor the breath of frost, nor the blast of fire, nor the fall of hail, nor the dropping of rime, nor the heat of the sun, nor unbroken cold, nor warm weather, nor wintry shower shall do any hurt; but the land lies happy and unharmed. That noble land is abloom with flowers. No hills or mountains stand there steeply, nor do stone-cliffs rise aloft, as here with us; nor are there valleys, or dales, or hill-caves, mounds or rising ground; nor are there any rough slopes there at all. But the noble field is fruitful under the sky, blossoming in beauty.

Gentle is that plain of victory; the sunny grove gleams; pleasant is the forest. Fruits fall not, bright are the blooms; but the trees stand ever green as God bade them. Winter and summer alike the forest is hung with fruits; the leaves under the sky shall never wither away, nor the fire ever do them hurt, before a change comes over the world. When long ago the torrent of water, the sea-flood whelmed all the world, the circuit of the earth, then by God's grace the noble field stood secure from the rush of wild waves, no whit harmed, happy, undefiled. Thus it shall bide in blossom till the coming of the fire, the judgement of God, when the graves, the tombs of men, shall be torn open. There is no foe in the land, nor weeping nor woe, nor sign of grief, nor old age, nor sorrow, nor cruel death, nor loss of life, nor the coming of a hateful thing, nor sin, nor strife, nor sad grief, nor the struggle of poverty, nor lack of wealth, nor sorrow, nor sleep, nor heavy illness, nor wintry storm, nor change of weather fierce under the heavens; nor does hard frost with chill icicles beat upon anyone. Neither hail nor rime falls on the ground there; nor is there a windy cloud; nor does water come down there, driven by the gust; but there the streams, wondrously splendid, gush welling forth; they water the land with fair fountains; winsome waters from the midst of the forests, which spring ocean-cold from the soil, sometimes go gloriously through the whole grove.

A bird wondrous fair, mighty in its wings, which is called the Phoenix, dwells in that wood. Alone there it holds its abode. its brave way of life; never shall death do it hurt in that pleasant place while the world endures. There it is said to gaze on the sun's going and to come face to face with God's candle, the gracious jewel, to watch eagerly till the noblest of heavenly bodies rises gleaming over the waves of the sea from the east, the ancient work of the Father, radiant sign of God, shining in its adornments. The stars are hidden, whelmed under the waves in the west, quenched in the dawn; and the dark night departs with its gloom. Then the bird, mighty in flight, proud of its pinions, gazes eagerly at the ocean, across the waters under the sky, till the light of the firmament comes gliding up from the east over the vast sea.

So the noble bird in its changeless beauty by the water-spring dwells by the surging streams. There the glorious creature bathes twelve times in the brook before the coming of the beacon, heaven's candle; and even as many times, at every bath, cold as the sea, it tastes the pleasant waters of the spring. Then after its sport in the water it rises proudly to a lofty tree, whence most easily it can see the movement in the east when the taper of the sky, the gleaming light, shines clearly over the tossing waters.

As soon as the sun towers high over the salt streams the grey bird goes in its brightness from the tree in the grove; swift in its wings, it flies aloft, pours forth harmony and song to the sky. Then so fair is the way of the bird, its heart uplifted, exulting in gladness, it sings a varied song with clear voice more wondrously than ever a son of man heard under the heavens since the mighty King, the Creator of glory, established the world, heaven and earth. The harmony of that song is sweeter and fairer than all music, and more pleasant than any melody. Neither trumpets, nor horns, nor the sound of the harp, nor the voice of any man on earth, nor the peal of the organ, nor the sweetness of song, nor the swan's plumage, nor any of the delights which God hath devised to gladden men in this dreary world can equal that outpouring. Thus it sings and chants, blissfully glad, till the sun has sunk in the southern sky. Then it is silent and falls to listening; it lifts up its head, bold, sage in thought; and thrice it shakes its feathers swift in flight; the bird is mute.

Page 60²—We thought we were alone:

❡ In other words, some self of the imagination has intruded upon this imaginary scene. That *self*, too, may become objectively visible. For just as Scrooge, even from a front view, could count his spectral friend Marley's back buttons, so in imagination we can watch our own phantasmal actions and antics even from behind—

an experience otherwise usual, and then unpleasing, only with the aid of a tailor's looking-glasses.

Here, again, individuals differ. Some apparently never objectify themselves even in memory. Others habitually do so, and particularly when that memoried self has been retrieved from childhood. One of my own earliest memories is of this kind. I am standing, aged about three, on a little footstool at a lamp-lit table, and, spoon in hand, am doing my utmost to conceal the horror I feel at the mere sight of the little plate of jelly that lies under my chin. It is of a delicious transparent amber colour, yet every morsel of it seems to stick in my throat and threaten to choke me. The room of this winter evening is small and lofty and rather dimly lit, and on either side of its Victorian chimney-piece sits a benevolent and incredibly old lady, calmly and graciously watching me at my feast. I am shy, shiveringly hot and cold, in torment; and at this moment the door opens, a capped head appears, and a maid announces that I have been called for. Transportation in one instant from utter misery to ecstatic bliss! What seems however a little queer in these circumstances is that I actually see my-*self* on that footstool. I am looking in, that is, at the complete scene, with myself (for this unusual occasion) full in the limelight. A simple explanation of the problem is that at some time or other I must have reconstructed the scene and visualized the memory of *that*. None the less, this objectification of self appears with some people to be more or less habitual.

There is a delightful example of it in *David Copperfield*. When David, ten years old, was still a bottle-washer at Murdstone and Grinby's rat-infested warehouse, he strays one hot summer evening into the bar of a little public-house and orders a glass of the landlord's famous 'Genuine Stunning' ale—'with a good head to it'. This mite of a customer so much impresses the landlord that he calls his wife to come and have a look at him.

She came out from behind the screen, with her work in her hand. . . . *Here we stand, all three, before me now.* The landlord in his shirt sleeves, leaning against the bar window-frame; his wife looking over the little half-door; and I, in some confusion, looking up at them from outside the partition. . . .

This may be memory; it may be pure fiction. But such was Dickens's genius that he could be either inside or outside of his characters, or both together, as the need of the moment dictated.

Whatever kind of entity, again, Crusoe's island may be for us now, it was once upon a time an island undiscovered by man. There is a curious fascination in that thought. How does 'nature' go on without man at all? Not even the philosophers can tell us; it is one of the secrets. And one may become acutely conscious of that secret on emerging, say, from a wintry wood at twilight, or when pacing at nightfall the deck of an Atlantic hotel as it goes plunging on into the vast solitudes of mid ocean —the garish light, the blaring music, the thump of the screws, the human cargo; and beyond—the sublime, immense, indifferent, watery sea! We may assume, at any rate, that in any such island, wheresoever it may be, neither fowl nor brute, any more than valley or rock, positively pines for 'the sound of the church-going bell'. Their natural tameness shocks nobody. And how rich, various and joyous a company even of winged things alone may disport their generations therein—themselves unshocked by the presence of that two-legged lord of creation, man.

The Norfolk and Lord Howe Islands alone, for example, cherish their own particular species of pigeon, rail, owl, kingfisher, robin, fly-eater, thick-head (a gimp, black, yellow, olive and white little creature about seven inches long which by no means appears to live down to its name), their fantail (not a pigeon), their caterpillar-catcher, white-eye, starling and crow-shrike; and all these share the circumambient air, skies and sea with swamp-hens, petrels (called, it is said, after St. Peter who could not, like them, step fearlessly along upon the water), shearwaters, terns, noddies, parrots, vinous-tinted blackbirds and the long-tailed cuckoo—whose egg, like that of the shorter tailed, is 'deposited in another bird's nest'— though no naturalist, apart from many sagacious hypotheses, is as yet certain why. May it be that the she-cuckoo refuses to build one by herself, and, being polyandrous, there is none to help her?

Page 60³—And start:

¶ Of all English writers Defoe was perhaps the furthest removed from the prig and the prude, unless a very lively sense of the prudery of his fellow-mortals makes him so. It may then startle the reader (of some of the earlier editions of the *Adventures*) to discover how fastidious Crusoe is when he is preparing for his swimming expeditions to the wreck. In the first he is wearing linen open-kneed breeches and stockings, his coat, shirt and waistcoat having been discarded because 'the weather was hot to extremity'. For the second he strips before leaving his hut, and enters the sea in a chequered shirt, a pair of linen drawers, and with a pair of pumps on his feet.

But this was not exactly the situation in the first edition. In his *Epistle* Gildon recounts the absurdities in the *Adventures*, among them being the *three* English Bibles in a Portuguese ship and Robinson's assertion that he had 'no cloaths' to cover him—'a downright Lie' since he had salved from the wreck a large quantity of 'Linnen & Woolen'. But apart from this (and a niggardly harvest it is over so wide a field), the above Breeches also appear in the indictment: 'I shall not take notice of his [Robinson's] stripping himself to swim on Board, and then filling his Pockets with Bisket, because that is already taken Notice of in Publick; and in the last Edition, at least, of the Book, you have endeavour'd to solve this Difficulty, by making him keep his Breeches on; tho' why he should do so I can see no reason; and tho' he did do so, I don't find how the Pocket of a Seaman's *Breeches* could receive any Biskets, that being generally no bigger than to contain a Tobacco Pouch, or the like'. In the *Everyman* edition

Crusoe discards the breeches but still pockets the biscuits. Mere midge-bites, but they can cause immoderate discomfort in a sensitive skin. And Defoe's was not invulnerable. In 1723 he admitted that *Crusoe* was mere Romance; but when, three years afterwards, a critic agreed with him, he denounced the statement as 'a most palpable Lie'.

Page 60[4]—The voice:
¶ Having, that is, built up a scene in the 'little nowhere of the mind' out of the effects produced by a series of words, we then, with inward ear intent, share not only the sea-like murmur of the wind, but its faintest whistle in the coral-coloured twigs of the tamarisks, the high inarticulate cries of the sea-birds, and the remoter—

> . . . grating roar
> Of pebbles which the waves draw back, and fling,
> At their return, up the high strand.

We may even feel the hot sunlight on our cheek, smell the spices in the air and faintly taste the salt. But all these phantom pleasures vary in intensity with individual faculty, and enquiries have proved that some men cannot 'visualize' at all. What, then, exactly happens in the non-visualizer's consciousness at mention, say, of the word appletree or lighthouse; or when reading, for instance, Cowper's 'The Poplar Field'? But, then, what exactly happens in consciousness at instant challenge of such a word as *to-morrow*, or *me*, or *abstraction*, or *Tuesday*, or *British Empire?* The picture evoked may be a very personal one—and misleading. What of the small examinee of eight who, being bidden write out the Lord's Prayer, wrote (and doubtless he had solemnly explained the phrases to his complete satisfaction), 'Harold be thy name' —apart from other words in it that had proved too 'hard' for him? But even the soberest of grown-ups might be a little startled to discover what some of *his* most impressive words positively *mean* to him.

The imaginary island, however, need not be constructed out of words. Lovely, aloof, it may unbidden float into the mind as if like a cornucopian raft it were being drawn dulcetly on by invisible dolphins. You watch it, and 'things', seemingly of their own volition, begin perhaps to 'take place'. It is as though, behind the proscenium of consciousness and across its 'heavens' and its inner stage, there moved continually a panorama of daydream.

Page 61[1]—¶ His parrot—
not borrowed from Selkirk, though lent with the utmost satisfaction to Stevenson, and as inseparable in memory from Crusoe as Puck now is from Bottom the weaver. Crusoe mentions by name many more trees and plants than birds—aloes, sugar-cane, grape, orange, lemon, citron, cedar and cocoa among them. But when *choosing* a desert island to be wrecked on, it is as well to consider its birds; in case the forlorn and menacing mewings of the sea-gulls and the mocking laughter of the oyster-catchers should prove oppressive.

Among the sea-birds of the Lagoon Islands of the Cocos Group, Darwin mentions the 'stupid and angry gannet', the 'silly noddy', and then a small snow-white tern, which, he says, 'smoothly hovers at the distance of a few feet above one's head, its large black eyes scanning, with quiet curiosity, your expression. Little imagination is required to fancy that so light and delicate a body must be tenanted by some wandering fairy spirit'. Could there be happier company than that?

One hardly knows which to (lovingly) smile at first, man or bird. In *The Book of a Naturalist* W. H. Hudson speaks with a like ardour of the humming-birds and of the hawk-moth, and concludes: 'Unless the soul goes out to meet what we see we do not see it; nothing do we see, not a beetle, not a blade of grass'.

Page 61[2]—Brazenly imitated:
¶ The first 'paltry imitation' of Robinson Crusoe, printed 'upon coarse paper for the common people', appeared in 1727, with the following title:

The Hermit: or the unparalleled Sufferings and surprising Adventures of Mr. Philip Quarll, an Englishman; who was lately discovered by Mr. Dorrington, a British Merchant, upon an uninhabited Island in the South Sea; where he has lived above Fifty years without any human assistance, still continues to reside, and will not come away.

Though 'Mr. Dorrington' boasts that the narrative which follows is 'not so replete with vulgar stories as *Robinson Crusoe, Moll Flanders* and the like', even his own emphasis must have been upon the *so*, and Quarll is a dull dog by comparison with Crusoe. At their first meeting the Hermit explains that his island is 'inhabited with monkeys and myself; but nobody else, thank God'. Monkeys, indeed, are his chief island novelty, and his account of the gifted life and tragic death of Beaufidelle, his first monkey servant, is the happiest thing in the book. It would have delighted William Cowper, and perhaps it did.

Having welcomed his unexpected visitors, the old gentleman sits them down in his arbour to a banquet—served elegantly in mother-of-pearl—and of no fewer than four courses: soup (thick); boiled meat—'that eat as delicious as house-lamb'—with oyster sauce; a roast, with mushrooms and pickles; and antelope cheese. He then shows them over his island, pointing out with a natural pride its grottoes, fountains, echoes and the like; but he talks like Polonius, and the story of his life (on parchment) which he then hands over is eighteenth century in kind and in that kind tedious.

The Thrilling Adventures of a Somersetshire Lad, my copy of which I owe to the kindness of my friend, Mr. R. N. Green-Armytage, was so much the delight of Walter Scott in his young days that in later years he reprinted it at his own expense for the entertainment of his friends. One's early loves both in life and in books may wear a glamour it is not always easy for others to share. So it may have been with Scott and this Somersetshire Lad—Richard Falconer.

He sets sail in the *Albion* frigate on May 2nd, 1699, and falls overboard on the way to Jamaica. After swimming, as he thinks, for four hours, he touches bottom on a low sandy island, one of many, and all bare. Its only growths are burton trees (? elders). For two or three days he keeps body and soul together with raw eggs and sea-water, 'which made my skin come off like the peel of a broiled codlin'—a reassuring symptom since other travellers have led the novice to suppose that a couple of quarts of sea-water in one athirst brings on almost instantaneous insanity.

Rain descends, and the castaway having made a cistern of shells for a reservoir then succeeds in getting a fire to burn, and that by the old two-sticks method—as simple on paper as it must be difficult in practice. And as he sits warming his bones at its blaze he amuses himself with an Elzevir Ovid, damp but still legible! Survivors of shipwreck at length invade his solitude on Makeshift island, and then, in spite of a few pages of pirates and cannibalism, the interest languishes. 'How rejoiced I was to see my native country, let them judge that have been placed in the same condition that I have.' But as few of his readers can have shared this condition, it is tantalizing that he was not a little more explicit.

A pirates' hoard of treasure, a massive family Bible whose covers prove to be packed tight with moidores, many pages of entertaining but rather old-fashioned 'natural history', a tamed hawk, called Yellow Bill, and a fawn, Miss Doe, that is no less natural and charming a creature than Llewellin's dark-skinned Luta, the first of his 'fair ribs'—*these* are the chief features of *The Journal of Llewellin Penrose* (1815). Unfortunately he is wrecked not on a desert island but on the Spanish Main, and he has in consequence far too many visitors. Discretion and 'manly fortitude' are his principal virtues, but in one respect he is perhaps a little *too* explicit, death being his favourite theme. Indeed he dies himself; and I hardly know which is the more afflicting—the last hours of his Dutch friend

Somer, 'whenever he drank, we could hear the liquid rattle within him', or his dissection of the vulture that came and perched near at hand to keep watch. But, as with nearly all the heroes of these bygone island romances, though Llewellin may make most things, he doesn't make love.

Island stories still abound. Blue lagoons continue to glass Pacific skies. Members of 'Mr. Fortune's' family continue to set sail for the remote and lone—and, apart from other delights, one may occasionally share the experience of a consummate tempest or earthquake. All such tales have at least the charm of their theme. Mr. Frank Morley's richly islanded *East South East*, with its buried treasure of ryders and ducatoons, has much else besides. Otherwise, not many, like *The Island of Dr. Moreau*, show striking originality or invention.

One nevertheless suspects that in the world of fiction there must somewhere be an island of the Bermoothes pattern, but one wherein the wauling demons are *not* wild pigs and where the ghost that begins to chatter as dusk descends is *not* a parrot. And there, it may be, forsaken divinities resort; or the sirens still make their haunt, their voices crying and dying in its rocky hollows. Islands of such beauty these that only dreams can offer any semblance to them in hours 'when the slumber of the body seems to be but the waking of the soul'. Islands where living creatures of unknown shapes, habits and faculties —after some old ruination of the world—may have been left in peace; where unfathomable abysses tempt to the unknown; where the spirits of the air are of so potent an influence that wisdom unconceived of is made manifest, and questions seemingly unanswerable here and now are so answered that one may question on. The realm of fantasy at any rate lies ever open to any adventurer who cares to set foot on it, nor is there a tittle of evidence to suggest that its potentialities are any more restricted, to say the least of it, than those of the great globe itself.

Page 61[3]—It was put into French:

¶ Thirty translations at least of the *Adventures* into as many foreign tongues have appeared, including Yiddish, Gaelic, Turkish, Persian and Polynesian—the last intended for the Maoris by an indulgent British Government. And apart from the *Robinsonaden* there is the complete series entitled *Voyages Imaginaires, Songes, Visions, et Romans Cabalistiques,* which was published towards the end of the eighteenth century and appears to be well worth hoarding for future exploration.

An abridged *Robinson Crusoe,* translated into Latin by F. J. Goffaux and entitled *Robinson Crusoeus,* appeared as far back as 1820. It was intended for use in schools and was 'liberally encouraged'. And I know of one small boy —now no longer eligible—who I am sure would have enjoyed its company rather more than he enjoyed wrecking the eloquent *De Senectute* or the Odes of that exquisite and worldly minded poet Horace. Still, the taste of the powder sometimes penetrates *through* the jam, and then the jam itself may never recover its pristine sweetness. Thus to have wasted Crusoe would have been a lamentable issue. Nor, perhaps, might Mr. Goffaux succeed in persuading to-day's small boy to appreciate the felicities of the urbaner language. 'Vocem audivit veluti coelo demissam haec verba articulatè proferentem: *Ave, Robinson*'. *That* is actually the voice of the most famous parrot in fiction, though it may suggest a bishop in lawn sleeves and with a nose like a toucan. Worse, the story in Latin is not told in the first person, and the continual use in consequence of Crusoe's remarkable Christian name is disillusioning.

It was hardly a pretty piece of craftsmanship, too, to condense the discovery of the footprint and of the cannibal's feast into two paragraphs. Here they are:

Primam noctem *Robinson* in arbore egit, ut tutus a feris esset; et posterà die iter persecutus est. Nec multum viae confecerat, cùm extremam insulae partem versùs meridiem attigit. Solum nonnullis in locis erat arenosum. Dum autem tendit ad tractum terrae in mare procurrentem, ecce pedem fert retrò; tum pallescere, contremiscere, oculos circumferre, et subito haerere quasi fulmine repentino ictus. Vidit nimirùm quod hic visurum se nunquàm speraverat, vestigia hominum arenae impressa! Tum ille territus undique circumspicit; audito vel levissimo foliorum strepitu stupet, sensusque adeo perturbantur ut stet inops consilii; tandem collectis viribus fugam corripit, quasi instarent a tergo, nec prae terrore respicere ausus est. At ecce repentè substitit. Metus in horrorem vertitur. Videt nimirùm fossam rotundam atque in medio ignis extincti focum. Quem circà, horresco referens, crania, manus, pedes, aliaque corporis ossa aspicit, execrandas reliquias convivii a quo natura abhorret; scilicet tunc temporis in insulis *Caraibicis* feri homines degebant, cannibales vocati aut anthropophagi; quibus solemnis erat consuetudo captivis mactatis assatisque immanes epulas celebrare, in quibus laetitiâ atrociùs debacchabantur, saltantes, canentes, aut potiùs, satiatâ feritate, ululantes. *Robinson* oculos ab horribili spetaculo avertit.

In 1884 appeared *Rebilius Cruso*—a work also intended 'to lighten tedium to a learner'—by Francis W. Newman, the brother of the great Cardinal and the author of *The Soul*. He finished his translation before he discovered that Goffaux's version was in existence. He then stopped the printing of his own book and secured a copy. He liked Goffaux's Latin but found his principles of remodelling the tale the opposite of his own, so bade the presses proceed. His view was that one should learn a language and *then* study its characteristic literature. One difficulty at a time. Also that it is *modern* Latin that should be taught in schools, and with a vocabulary that includes all familiar objects. He found that *Crusoe* far excelled the classics in this, but, alas, that when the tale is faithfully abridged its impossibilities become too glaring. So he borrowed only the general idea from Defoe.

Here is his Rebilius's balance sheet of 'goods' and 'evils'; but it has been severely edited and moralized, two items of Defoe's list having been omitted and three new ones inserted:

MALA MEA

1. In insulâ solitariâ sum pro- jectus.
2. Ego unus e sodalibus enecor aegrimoniâ.
3. Exsulo e societate hominum.
4. Vi bestiarum sum planē obnoxius.
5. Laboriosissimē victum quo- tidianum quaero.
6. Servio hic servitutem per- petuam.
7. Nĭsĭ prius solitariē moriar, ad solitariam senectutem reservor.

LEVAMINA MALORUM

1. At non es demersus, sicut ceteri.
2. At tibi uni restat spes aliqua effugii.
3. At non servĭs hominibus scelestis.
4. At non in belluosam Africam projectus.
5. At magnam tu habes ex nave opem.
6. At alios tu in servitutem non redigis.
7. At non tua magis quàm parentum senectus erit solitaria.

And this is the original—in Dutch:

KWAAD

Ik ben op een onbekend en onbewoond eiland geworpen, zonder eenige hoop op redding.

Ik Ben van 't overige mensch- dom gescheiden, eenzaam, een banneling.

Ik heb weinig kleeren tot bedekking en geen middel om 't vers etene door nieuw te ver- vangen.

Ik ben wel niet geheel zonder verdedigingsmiddelen; toch zou ik noch tegen wilde beesten, noch tegen een aanval van wilden opgewassen zijn.

Ik heb niemand om mee te spreken niemand om mij te troosten of te helpen.

GOED

Maar ik leef en ben niet ver- dronken, zooals mijn medes- chepelingen.

Maar ik behoef geen gebrek te lijden; mijn eiland is geen dorre woestenij.

Maar ik ben in een heet kli- maat, waar weinig kleeren voldoende zijn en genoeg dieren leven, waarvan ik de huid als kleeding kan gebruiken.

Maar op mijn eiland schijnen geen wilde beesten en geen wilde volksstammen aanwezig te zijn; wat zou mijn lot geweest zijn, als ik b.v. op de Afrikaansche kust schipbreuk geleden had?

Maar ik vond op het schip een trouwen kameraad, mijn hond; ik vond er, behalve al het andere, kijn katten, die mij op haar ma- nier vriendschap betuigen, en bovenal, ik vond er een bijbel, die mij van een liefderijk God sprak; ook andere boeken, die mij tot nut en genoegen strekten.

The first Italian version of the Adventures—*La Vita e le Avventure di Robinson Crusoe Storia Galante. . . . Traduzione dal Francesse*—was published in Venice in 1745. A fragment will suffice:

Questo fu l' anno nel quale ho goduto nell' Isola il maggior contento. *Venerdi* incominciava a parlare; sapeva i nomi di quasi tutte le cose delle quali potessi aver di bisogno, e di tutti i luoghi ove potessi inviarlo, ciò che mi rendeva l' uso della lingua che mi era stata per tanto tempo inutile; non solamente la sua conversazione mi faceva piacere, ma la fua probità mi dava un estrema consolazione, ed incominciavo a teneramente amarlo, vedendo che aveva per me tutta la tenerezza possibile.

Un giorno ebbi voglia di saper da lui se gli dispiaceva d' avere abbandonato la sua patria, se la sua nazione era mai vittoriosa contra i suoi nemici: *si*, mi rispose, *Io, mia compagni combattre meglio nemici;* cioè a dire che ottenevano la vittoria e non credo che dispiacerà al lettore che io gli racconti il dialogo che facemmo su questo particolare.

Se la vostra nazione combatte sempre meglio che le altre, d' onde viene dunque che siete stato fatto prigioniere?

Venerdi. *Io, nazione, e mia compagna combatre molto.*

Perchè dunque siete stato preso?

Venerdi. *Essi molto che mio nazion dove io stare. Essi prendeveun, due, tre, e io, ma mio nazion battere essi altro luoca dove io no stare, e la mio nazion prendre un due uh gran mille!*

Perchè dunque i vostri compagni non vi hanno ripreso sopra i nemici?

Venerdi. *Essi portar un, due, tre, e io dentro Canot, e mio nazion non aver Canot grand ora.*

La vostra nazione mangia ella i prigionieri che fa sopra i suoi nemici?

Venerdi. *Si mio nazion mangiar omini, e mangiar tutto tutto.*

Dove li conduce allora?

Venerdi. *Tutte parti dove facer bon.*

Gli conduce giammai in quest' Isola?

Venerdi. *Si qua, e portare molt' altro luogo.*

Siete stato voi qui colla vostra gente?

Venerdi. *Si me stare qua a quelle parte:* (indicando l' occaso dell' Isola).

My son-in-law, Mr. Rupert Thompson, has kindly translated this passage for me and as literally as possible. Difficulties abound—e.g. to put into English such Friday-talk as *Si mio nazion mangiar omini,* which, he tells me, in genteel Italian, should run *Si mia nazione mangia uomini.*

This was the year in which I enjoyed most content on the island. Friday was beginning to speak; he knew the names of nearly all the things I needed and of all the places to which I could send him, and this gave me the use of my tongue which had for so long been useless to me; not only did his conversation give me pleasure, but his probity was an extreme consolation to me, and I began to love him tenderly, seeing that he had the greatest possible tenderness for me.

One day I wanted to learn from him whether he was sorry to have abandoned his country, whether his nation were never victorious against their enemies: 'Yes,' he answered me, 'I, my companions fight better enemies'; that is to say, that they were victorious, and I do not think it will displease the reader if I tell him in detail the dialogue we had on this subject.

'If your nation always fights better than the others, how comes it, then, that you were made prisoner?'

Friday. 'I, nation, and companions fight much.'

'Then why were you captured?'

Friday. 'They much than my nation where I be. They took one, two, three, and I, but my nation beat they other place where I no be, and my nation take one, two, oh, great thousand!'

'Then why haven't your companions recaptured you from the enemy?'

Friday. 'They carry one, two, three and I inside Canoe, and my nation not have Canoe great time.'

'Do your nation eat the prisoners they take from their enemies?'

Friday. 'Yes my nation eat men, and eat everything, everything.'

'Where do they take them to?'

Friday. 'All parts where make good' [?].

'They never take them to this island?'

Friday. 'Yes here, and carry much other place.'

'Have you been here with your people?'

Friday. 'Yes me be here in those parts' (indicating the west of the island).

And here for comparison—after having survived three translations, French, Italian, then into English again—is the same passage as it appears in Defoe's own words.

One ponders over Friday's endearing idioms with the keenest interest: comparing 'We always fight the better' with 'come other else place'. The problem is complicated: Crusoe's English must have fallen into grave disrepair before Friday's arrival. Friday's talk, then, is the broken English he was taught by Crusoe, which he in turn must have broken again, and which Crusoe recalls long after the colloquy between them is over:

This was the pleasantest year of all the life I led in this place. Friday began to talk pretty well, and understand the names of almost everything I had occasion to call for, and of every place I had to send him to, and talk a great deal to me; so that, in short, I began now to have some use for my tongue again, which, indeed, I had very little occasion for before, that is to say, about speech. [A characteristically any-how order of sentence.] Besides the pleasure of talking to him, I had a singular satisfaction in the fellow himself. His simple, unfeigned honesty appeared to me more and more every day, and I began really to love the creature; and, on his side, I believe he loved me more than it was possible for him ever to love anything before.

I had a mind once to try if he had any hankering inclinations to his own country again; and having learned him English so well that he could answer me almost any questions, I asked him whether the nation that he belonged to never conquered in battle? At which he smiled, and said, 'Yes, yes, we always fight the better'; that is, he meant, we always get the better in fight; and so we began the following discourse: 'You always fight the better,' said I. 'How came you to be taken prisoner then, Friday?'

Friday. My nation beat much for all that.

Master. How beat? If your nation beat them, how came you to be taken?

Friday. They more many than my nation in the place where me was; they take one, two, three, and me. My nation overbeat them in the yonder place, where me no was; there my nation take one, two, great thousand.

Master. But why did not your side recover you from the hands of your enemies then?

Friday. They run one, two, three, and me, and make go in the canoe; my nation have no canoe that time.

Master. Well, Friday, and what does your nation do with the men they take? Do they carry them away and eat them, as these did?

Friday. Yes, my nation eats man too; eat all up.

Master. Where do they carry them?

Friday. Go to other place, where they think.

Master. Do they come hither?

Friday. Yes, yes, they come hither; come other else place.

Master. Have you been here with them?

Friday. Yes, I been here. (*Points to the N.W. side of the island which, it seems, was their side.*)

The name of the Italian translator does not appear on his title-page. But in a prefatory note 'to the Reader' he refers to the astonishing success of the *Adventures* in England, France and Holland. It does not surprise him. Never before in the life of a single man, runs his generous tribute, has there been so stupendous a series of marvellous adventures or such a variety of extraordinary happenings. And it is in this combination that the human mind delights. Since, however, the lover of truth can only perfectly enjoy such impressions if they are founded on reality, it would be in the translator's interest to persuade his reader that the *Adventures* are a History and not a Romance. 'My integrity', he says, and he does not appear to realize how little his author would enjoy the pleasantry, 'my integrity forbids me to act as frivolously as that!' All he can assert is that the *Adventures* seem to him to be probable, and particularly the thoughts and sentiments in them excited by the events.

As for the moral reflections and Robinson Crusoe's resignation—these 'are exemplary, and could not be surpassed by a Roman Catholic grown old in a monastery and worn out with acts of penitence'.

In translating the book his aim as a stylist had been first to avoid repetitions and to abridge superfluities, and next, to produce the very flavour of the English original —'which is artless and crude'. 'In the whole tale', he assures his reader, 'you cannot discover a single sign that the author was a cultivated man, but rather, on the contrary, a very simple person indeed who is often scarcely able to communicate his ideas to his readers. . . . There reigns in the whole work a naturalness which in tales of this kind is worth infinitely more than the spirit and the language of culture'. Defoe had been fourteen years in his grave when this subtle and apparently unintentional compliment was paid him, and it must have fallen like dew from heaven upon his resting-place.

Page 61⁴—¶ Oddly enough—
at least so it seems to me, though the oddity may be on
my side. A comma, or the word *of* inserted after Family
might help; or alternatively, The Swiss Robinsons; or
better, The Swiss Crusoes. As for the quality of the English,
there have been many translations, and mine perhaps was
not the best of them. Open that where one may, the influence of the translator is at once apparent. Mr. Robinson,
for example, has a charm whereby he tames wild pigeons:

> It is to a pigeon-merchant that I owe the secret which I am about
> to put into practice. . . . It consists in perfuming a new dove-cote
> with anise. The pigeons, it is said, are so fond of the odour of this
> plant that they will return, themselves, every night to respire its
> perfume. . . .

Alter that last sentence to, The pigeons, it is said, are so
fond of the smell of it that they will return every night of
their own accord to enjoy it; and that slight fine artificiality
to which even the *character* of Mr. Robinson himself owes
so much immediately evaporates.

Page 61⁵—There is a wreck:
¶ At first peep of day next morning Mr. Robinson and
his family set out from the wreck, his wife attired, though
reluctantly, in sailor clothes that best suited her size. Their
boat is heavily laden with a cargo resembling the combined effects of an arsenal and an ironmonger's shop.
Pursued by their geese and ducks and by their two dogs,
Turk and Flora, which Mr. Robinson had brusquely
intended to abandon, and which, when fatigued with
swimming, 'rested their forepaws on one of the paddles
and thus with little effort proceeded', they rowed gently
on: Mr. Robinson, Mrs. Robinson, 'the most tender and
exemplary of her sex', lovely little six-year-old Francis
(remarkable not only for his sweet temper but for his
affection to his parents), curly-pated Fritz, aged 14,
audacious Jack, 10, and reflective Ernest, 12—'well informed,' like his father, 'for his age'.

> But the nearer we approached the land, the more gloomy and
> unpromising its aspect appeared. The coast was clothed with barren

rocks, which seemed to offer nothing but hunger and distress. . . .
Now that we were close on land, its rude outline was much soft-
ened; the rocks no longer appeared one undivided chain; Fritz,
with his hawk's eye, already descried some trees, and exclaimed
that they were palm-trees. . . . By and by we perceived a little
opening between the rocks, near the mouth of a creek, towards
which all our geese and ducks betook themselves; and I, relying on
their sagacity, followed in the same course. This opening formed a
little bay; the water was tranquil, and neither too deep nor too
shallow to receive our boat. . . . The shore extended inland, in
something of the form of an isosceles triangle, the upper angle of
which terminated among the rocks, while the margin of the sea
formed the basis. . . .

They land, a gay, populous and noisy party, for the
human chorus is swelled not only by the poultry but by
the screams of penguin and flamingo—screams annoying
and discordant to Mr. Robinson after 'the harmony of
the feathered musicians' of his own country.

He is speedily at his best, and he seldom descends thence,
as guide, philosopher and friend.

 . . . We next entered a forest to the right, and soon observed that
some of the trees were of a singular kind. Fritz, whose sharp eye was
continually on a journey of discovery, went up to examine them
closely.

'O heavens! father, what odd trees, with wens growing all about
their trunks!'

I had soon the surprise and satisfaction of assuring him that they
were bottle gourds, the trunks of which bear fruit. Fritz, who had
never heard of such a plant, could not conceive the meaning of what
he saw, and asked me if the fruit was a sponge or a wen. 'We will
see,' I replied, 'if I cannot unravel the mystery. Try to get down one
of them, and we will examine it minutely.'

'I have got one,' cried Fritz, 'and it is exactly like a gourd, only
the rind is thicker and harder.'

'It then, like the rind of that fruit, can be used for making various
utensils,' observed I; 'plates, dishes, basins, flasks. We will give it the
name of the gourd-tree.'

Fritz jumped for joy. 'How happy my mother will be!' cried he in
ecstasy; 'she will no longer have the vexation of thinking, when she
makes soup, that we shall all scald our fingers.'

And so *ad infinitum*.

There is a neat little reversal of situation at the end
of the *Family* as compared with the *Adventures*, for while

Crusoe at last returns home (full of paternal longings, as we *hoped*) to rejoin his children, by this time well into their teens, Mr. and Mrs. Robinson see two of theirs off to Europe and themselves remain behind. Cannon other than their own have been heard by Fritz. The little commutiny is thrilled. Mr. Robinson sets out to investigate, little realizing, perhaps, that the Swiss mountain song with which he and his family entertain the English sailors would go yodelling down the centuries:

When we had finished, I cried out through my speaking-trumpet these three words, *Englishmen, good men!* But no answer was returned: our song, our cajack, and more than all our costume, I expect, marked us for savages, from the officer making signs to us to approach, and holding up knives, scissors, and glass beads, of which the savages of the New World are generally so desirous. This mistake made us laugh; but we did not approach, as we wished to present ourselves before them in better trim. We contented ourselves with exclaiming once more, *Englishmen*, and then darted off as fast as our boat could carry us. . . . My wife . . . praised us exceedingly for not presenting ourselves before people in such a machine as a miserable cajack. . . .

'We set off at sunrise; the weather was magnificent, and we sailed gallantly along, Fritz preceding us as pilot. My wife and Emily were dressed as sailors. Ernest, Jack, and Francis managed the boat, while I attended to the tiller. As a precaution we loaded our cannons and guns. . . .

'Hoist the English flag,' cried I in the voice of a Stentor. . . .

Page 64[1]—Francis Bacon:

❡ But the *New Atlantis*, though self-contained in every respect, is an island so extensive that it is hardly deserving of the name. Its inhabitants are as erudite as they are exclusive; and if poor Robin Crusoe had been wrecked on their shores he would have had a very cold welcome.

Nor are the voyagers in Bacon's (unfinished) romance wrecked. They set sail from Peru for China, after five months encounter 'strong and great winds from the south, with a point east', and find themselves 'in the midst of the greatest wilderness of waters in the world':

. . . The next day about evening we saw, within a kenning before us, towards the north, as it were thick clouds, which did put us in some hope of land: knowing how that part of the South Sea was utterly unknown: and might have islands or continents, that hitherto were not come to light. Wherefore we bent our course thither, where we saw the appearance of land, all that night: and in the dawning of next day, we might plainly discern that it was a land flat to our sight, and full of boscage, which made it show the more dark. And after an hour and a half's sailing, we entered into a good haven, being the port of a fair city. Not great indeed, but well built, and that gave a pleasant view from the sea. . . .

Bacon's account of the ark of cedar wood, with its small green branch of palm, which was discovered floating in the waters of the harbour of Renfusa about A.D. 30, and on being opened was found to contain 'all the canonical books of the Old and New Testament . . . and some other books of the New Testament which were not at that time written'; his concise historical description of the state of America about 1600 B.C., from which Joseph Smith (rather more than two centuries after Bacon finished the *New Atlantis*) may well have borrowed a hint or two when he translated the Book of Mormon out of its 'Reformed Egyptian'—all this is undeniably a feat of the imagination. And yet—well, the *Essays* are dew and roses by comparison.

As for the marvels of 'Salomon's House', containing that king's lost natural history, 'which he wrote of all plants, from the cedar of Lebanon to the moss that groweth out of the wall, and of all things that have life and motion', there is scarcely any scientific device of to-day (and maybe of to-morrow) that is not clearly or vaguely predicted, from beef-juice and prize parsnips to strawberries in January, from vivisection, the Science Museum and the *séance* to machine-guns, gramophones and celanese. The catalogue is impressive and it is good for us to realize how much in material things we now have to be grateful for and how little we notice it; but why Bacon's astonishing foresight should be so much less animating than Crusoe's immovable periagua or his broken pots is a problem that even the sage himself might find it difficult to expound. One of the fathers of the 'House' consents to give audience to the travellers, and the description of his entry into the city reveals Bacon's intense delight in colour, costume, ceremony and ritual. He proceeds:

. . . The end of our foundation is the knowledge of causes, and secret motions of things; and the enlarging of the bounds of human empire, to the effecting of all things possible. . . .

We have high towers, the highest about half a mile in height, and some of them likewise set upon high mountains, so that the vantage of the hill with the tower is in the highest of them three miles at least. And these places we call the upper region, account the air between the high places and the low as a middle region. We use these towers, according to their several heights and situations, for insulation, refrigeration, conservation, and for the view of divers meteors—as winds, rain, snow, hail; and some of the fiery meteors also. And upon them, in some places, are dwellings of hermits, whom we visit sometimes, and instruct what to observe.

We have great lakes, both salt and fresh, whereof we have use for the fish and fowl. We use them also for burials of some natural bodies, for we find a difference in things buried in earth, or in air below the earth, and things buried in water. We have also pools, of which some do strain fresh water out of salt, and others by art do turn fresh water into salt. We have also some rocks in the midst of the sea, and some bays upon the shore for some works, wherein is required the air and vapour of the sea. We have likewise violent streams and cataracts, which serve us for many motions; and likewise engines for multiplying and enforcing of winds to set also on divers motions.

We have also a number of artificial wells and fountains, made in imitation of the natural sources and baths, as tincted upon vitriol, sulphur, steel, brass, lead, nitre, and other minerals; and again, we have little wells for infusions of many things, where the waters take the virtue quicker and better than in vessels or basins. And amongst them we have a water, which we call water of Paradise, being by that we do it made very sovereign for health and prolongation of life. . . .

We have also large and various orchards and gardens, wherein we do not so much respect beauty as variety of ground and soil, proper for divers trees and herbs, and some very spacious, where trees and berries are set, whereof we make divers kinds of drinks, besides the vineyards. In these we practise likewise all conclusions of grafting, and innoculating, as well of wild-trees as fruit-trees, which produceth many effects. And we make by art, in the same orchards and gardens, trees and flowers, to come earlier or later than their seasons, and to come up and bear more speedily than by their natural course they do. We make them also by art greater much than their nature; and their fruit greater and sweeter, and of differing taste, smell, colour, and figure, from their nature. And many of them we so order, as that they become of medicinal use.

We have also means to make divers plants rise by mixture of earths without seeds, and likewise to make divers new plants, differing from the vulgar, and to make one tree or plant turn into another.

We have also parks and enclosures of all sorts, of beasts and birds; which we use not only for view or rareness, but likewise for dissections and trials, that thereby may take light what may be wrought upon the body of man. Wherein we find many strange effects: as continuing life in them, though divers parts, which you account vital, be perished and taken forth; resuscitating of some that seem dead in appearance, and the like. We try also all poisons, and other medicines upon them, as well of chirurgery as physic. By art likewise we make them greater or smaller than their kind is, and contrariwise dwarf them and stay their growth; we make them more fruitful and bearing than their kind is, and contrariwise barren and not generative. Also we make them differ in colour, shape, activity, many ways. We find means to make commixtures and copulations of diverse kinds, which have produced many new kinds, and them not barren, as the general opinion is. We make a number of kinds of serpents, worms, flies, fishes, of putrefaction, whereof some are advanced (in effect) to be perfect creatures, like beasts or birds, and have sexes, and do propagate. Neither do we this by chance, but we know beforehand of what matter and commixture, what kind of those creatures will arise. . . .

We have drinks also brewed with several herbs and roots and spices; yea, with several fleshes, and white-meats; whereof some of the drinks are such as they are in effect meat and drink both, so that divers, especially in age, do desire to live with them with little or no meat or bread. And above all we strive to have drinks of extreme thin parts, to insinuate into the body, and yet without all biting, sharpness, or fretting; insomuch as some of them put upon the back of your hand will, with a little stay, pass through to the palm, and yet taste mild to the mouth. . . .

We have also divers mechanical arts, which you have not; and stuffs made by them, as papers, linen, silks, tissues, dainty works of feathers of wonderful lustre, excellent dyes, and many others, and shops likewise as well for such as are not brought into vulgar use amongst us, as for those that are. For you must know, that of the things before recited, many are grown into use through the kingdom; but yet, if they did flow from our invention, we have of them also for patterns and principals.

We represent also all multiplications of light, which we carry to great distance, and make so sharp, as to discern small points and lines. Also all colourations of light: all delusions and deceits of the sight, in figures, magnitudes, motions, colours. All demonstrations of shadows. We find also divers means, yet unknown to you, of producing of light, originally from divers bodies. We procure means of seeing objects afar off, as in the heavens and remote places; and represent things near as afar off, and things afar off as near; making feigned distances. We have also helps for the sight far above spectacles and glasses in use; we have also glasses and means to see small and minute bodies, perfectly and distinctly; as the shapes and colours of small flies and worms, grains, and flaws in gems which cannot otherwise be seen, observations in urine and blood not otherwise to be seen.

We have also sound-houses, where we practise and demonstrate all sounds and their generation. We have harmony which you have not, of quarter-sounds and lesser slides of sounds. Divers instruments of music likewise to you unknown, some sweeter than any you have; with bells and rings that are dainty and sweet. We represent small sounds as great and deep, likewise great sounds, extenuate and sharp; we make divers tremblings and warbling of sounds, which in their original are entire. We represent and imitate all articulate sounds and letters, and the voices and notes of beasts and birds. We have certain helps, which set to the ear do further the hearing greatly; we have also divers strange and artificial echoes reflecting the voice many times, and as it were tossing it; and some that give back the voice louder than it came, some shriller and some deeper; yea, some rendering the voice, differing in the letters or articulate sound from that they receive. We have all means to convey sounds in trunks and pipes, in strange lines and distances.

We have also perfume-houses, wherewith we join also practices of taste. We multiply smells which may seem strange; we imitate smells, making all smells to breathe out of other mixtures than those that give them. We make divers imitations of taste likewise, so that they will deceive any man's taste. And in this house we contain also a confiture-house, where we make all sweetmeats, dry and moist, and divers pleasant wines, milks, broths, and salads, far in greater variety than you have.

We have also engine-houses, where are prepared engines and instruments for all sorts of motions. There we imitate and practise to make swifter motions than any you have, either out of your muskets, or any engine that you have; and to make them and multiply them more easily and with small force, by wheels and other means, and to make them stronger and more violent than yours are, exceeding your greatest cannons and basilisks. We represent also ordnance and instruments of war and engines of all kinds; and likewise new mixtures and compositions of gunpowder, wild fires burning in water and unquenchable, also fire-works of all variety both for pleasure and use. We have ships and boats for going under water and brooking of seas, also swimming-girdles and supporters. We have divers curious clocks and other like motions of return, and some perpetual motions. We imitate also motions of living creatures by images of men, beasts, birds, fishes, and serpents; we have also a great number of other various motions, strange for quality, fineness and subtility.

We have also a mathematical-house, where are represented all instruments, as well of geometry as astronomy, exquisitely made.

We have also houses of deceits of the senses, where we represent all manner of feats of juggling, false apparitions, impostures, and illusions and their fallacies. And surely you will easily believe that we, that have so many things truly natural which induce admiration, could in a world of particulars deceive the senses if we would disguise those things, and labour to make them more miraculous. But we do hate all impostures and lies, insomuch as we have severely forbidden it to all our fellows, under pain of ignominy and fines, that they do not show any natural work or thing adorned or swelling, but only pure as it is, and without all affectation of strangeness.

These are, my son, the riches of Salomon's House. . . .

As for the *old* fabulous Atlantis, in greatness infinite and unmeasurable, surrounded by seas impassable and impenetrable, and with its insular labyrinth of alternate zones of sea and land—*that*, with Lyonesse, long since foundered beneath the ocean that still bears its name. Nevertheless, an American writer, Colonel James Churchyard, with the assistance of 'certain ancient Naacal tablets discovered in India'—'the Naacals left Burma more than 15,000 years ago'—has recently given an account of his adventures in quest of it in a volume entitled *The Lost Continent of Mu.*

Page 64²—A flying chariot:
¶ Here he had in mind a lively fantasy, *The Man in the Moon*, which is as full of invention as an egg is of meat. It was published in 1638, five years after the death of its author, Francis Godwin, who also was a bishop. His hero, Domingo Gonzales, of a noble Andalusian family, after prosperous voyagings, lands on the island of St. Helena. He refers to a 'pretty Chappel' he finds there, beautified with a Tower, and Bell therein. In this there lay a com-

modious Room with a fair Window well glazed, its walls plaistered white. Here Gonzales amuses himself sending messages by means of a light, now screened, now exposed, to his Black-moor servant, Diego, who, for his private quarters, occupies a cave at the west end of the island. Wearying of this pastime, Gonzales at last tames the island's wild swans, or gansa's, as he calls them, to such perfection that by means of rods, little pulleys of cork and a sort of kite, a squadron of twenty-five of them can hoist him safely and easily into the air. A lively cut in the 1728 edition shows him in full career—ruff, doublet, breeches, cork-heeled shoon, Baconian hat and moustachios all complete; but only ten gansa's are attached to his 'engine'. This lapse on the part of the artist, however, may have been due not to want of accuracy but of space; and as if to make up for it, the welkin around the traveller fairly burns with light and colour.

With boundless satisfaction Gonzales then embarks on shipboard for Spain, his gansa's stowed safely away in hutches. At threat of shipwreck he harnesses them to his engine and lands on the very summit of the volcanic and forested 'Pike of Tenariff', one of the loveliest natural objects in the world, as I have been told, but not, as the author states, 'fifteen miles high'.

Thence, now unmanageable in this rarer, purer air, his elated gansa's strike 'bolt upright', and in a trice he finds himself on the way to—the Moon. He is troubled awhile on his journey by Illusions of Devils who give him food he does not need—capons and a bottle of canary. As the shining earth he has left behind him diminishes in magnitude, the blur of Africa, a spot like a pear with a morsel bit out of one side, gives place to the unflecked brightness of the vast Atlantic Ocean, and that to 'a Spot almost Oval, just as we see America described in our Maps'. Thus fantasy pays heed to passing fact.

He lands, 'extream hungry', only to find his Devils' meat corrupted into hair and dung and feathers in his pockets, while his 'canary-wine is turned and stinks like

Hors-piss . . . these cursed Spirits!' Everything about him in Moonland—trees, beasts, herbs, houses—is gigantic in size; and he is presently surrounded by 'a strange kind of people', some of whom are five times the stature of a man, while all are habited in a curious tissue of a colour past human conception for glory and delight. These 'Lunars' live in love and peace and amity to an immense age (the most excellent of them far out-rivalling Methuselah), and after an existence *sans* sickness, vice or crime, 'they die merry', without sadness or repining, and they die ungrieved for. 'With us in the like case all seem to mourn, when many of them do oft but laugh in their Sleeves, or under a Vizard'. Since also after death Lunar bodies do not putrefy, on the moon one can not only boast of one's ancestors but exhibit them. Another pretty addition to this life is that the dwarf Lunars, of whom Gonzales is now one, fall drowsy as the sun begins to rise, and sleep throughout the moon's day, an earthly fortnight long. That sun once set, and they aroused again, our own great looking-glass of a planet, through all its changes, affords them light in abundance.

'Their Females are all absolute Beauties', and to love there once, is to love always. Not that, even so, this is the best *possible* of worlds. For unpromising little Lunars at times make their appearance, and these are despatched —by means undiscovered by Gonzales—to the earth, the usual vent for them there being 'a certain high hill in the North of *America*'.

He is presented to the supreme monarch of the moon, Irdonozur, who of his royal bounty bestows on him nine precious stones of three kinds and of incredible virtues. One, like jet, when laid in a fire, produces an extreme fervent heat that can be cooled again and again; another, like a topaz, is of such a splendour that in a large church it will make 'all as light as if an hundred lamps were hanged round'; the third, of a colour ineffably beautiful, will—according to which side of it is laid on the naked skin—so add to or diminish the weight of the human body as to counteract the pull of gravitation. Gonzales then enquires if the Lunars have a 'jem' that will make its wearer invisible. But no.

He becomes homesick at last, and pines to see his wife and children again. So he trims up his engine, harnesses his gansa's, and departs earthward in March 1601. He lands in China, at Pequin. There, he tells us, the Mandarins use a language which, like that of the Lunars, 'consists chiefly of tunes'.

Gonzales' island of St. Helena has been in latter times the abode of many exiles—Napoleon, Piet Cronje, the Sultan of Zanzibar. But centuries before them it was the peaceful refuge for no less than thirty solitary years of an outcast named Fernão Lopez. His full story has been retold by Sir Hugh Clifford in *Heroes of Exile*, from which the following brief particulars have been taken.

In 1512 the Portuguese Viceroy, Alfonso Dalboquerque, made terms for the surrender by its Mohammedan defenders of the fortress of Benastarim which then dominated 'Golden Goa'—once a market for all the splendours of the East, now naked, deserted and in decay. He promised to spare the lives of certain renegade Christians who had cast in their lot with the infidels; but he spared little else. To avenge their treason and treachery, he lopped off their right hands, the thumbs of their left, their ears and their noses, and, apart from other excesses, he had their heads and chaps plucked bald and smeared with mud.

Fernandez Lopez was the leader of these renegades. In 1515 his enemy died. Lopez then stowed himself away in a vessel bound for Lisbon, where, as he hoped, still awaited him his wife and children. But courage failed him when the ship put in to water at St. Helena, then uninhabited. He escaped into the woods. His shipmates sought him in vain, and so left him, leaving behind them a barrel of biscuit, some pieces of hung beef and dried fish, salt, a fire and some old clothes.

The blessed Isle of St. Hellens, as one of its devotees

calls it, 'the only Paradice I believe on Earth', is volcanic and mountainous. It is 'about 16 Leagues in Compass'— one-third the area of the Isle of Wight, and because of its conveniency was once known as the Sea Town. The Directors of the East India Company having decided in 1709 that the goats on the island which were destroying the young trees were more valuable than its ebony, its appearance, once luxuriant, is now barren and forbidding.

When, however, Lopez was its only human inhabitant, it resembled the gardens of the Hesperides. Its Portuguese discoverers had planted it with oranges, lemons, pomegranates, with figs and almonds and rose trees, and among its wild birds were partridges and peacocks and the swan. With the stump of his right arm and his four-fingered left, Lopez scooped himself out a cave wherein to keep his precious fire burning, and this he fortified with prickly thorn bushes. For a year he was left in peace and comparative plenty, and then a Portuguese ship came up over the sea. He hid himself in terror. The crew left him some cheeses, some biscuits and other food, and, no less welcome, a message of reassurance. As their ship sailed away a farmyard cock escaped from its crate and flew overboard. Lopez rescued it from the sea, carried it home and it became his Crusoe's parrot.

Ten years passed, and the King of Portugal himself sent him a letter promising his protection if Lopez would return to his fatherland. About this time a Javanese slave boy escaped from a passing ship into the woods, but his company was unwelcome to the recluse. The fugitive gave himself up to the next crew that landed, and at the same time betrayed Lopez. But their captain treated him kindly, and gave him an assurance of safety in the king's name, signed and sealed.

It was, however, Fernão Lopez's conscience that at length drew him home. He craved permission of the King to go to Rome. There in the ear of the Pope himself, and mounted up on a high platform in St. Peter's, he confessed his sins. He was absolved on a Maundy Thursday, the white mantle of the Pope concealing him from view of the great congregation. In a private audience afterwards he confided to the Pope—being pressed to do so—the only wish he now had left in him, that he might return to his island. It was granted. So he went back. He had his ducks and his hens, his sows and his tame goats, good company all: his plantations also of pomegranates and palm-trees and gourds. And there at last, in 1546, he died.

Page 67[1]—After my new love had been with me a fortnight:
⁊ Peter's Youwarkee, his *Madam*, his *lady*, his *fair*, his *charming creature*, is a virginal isle within a virgin island, and far more original in effect than that island itself, though the picture would have been less delightful without its frame. Again and again when alone in his mud-and-earth hut in the dark season, Peter had heard strange voices and at length 'felt such a thump upon the roof' of his 'anti-chamber as shook the whole fabric and set him all over into a tremor':

I then heard a sort of shriek and a rustle near the door of my apartment; all which together seemed very terrible. But I having before determined to see what and who it was, resolutely opened my door, and leaped out. I saw nobody; all was quite silent, and nothing that I could perceive but my own fears a moving. I went then softly to the corner of my building, and there looking down, by the glimmer of my lamp, which stood in the window, I saw something in human shape lying at my feet. I asked, 'Who's there?' No one answering, I was induced to take a nearer view of the object. But judge of my astonishment when I discovered the face of the most lovely and beautiful woman eyes ever beheld! I stood for a few seconds transfixed with astonishment, and my heart was ready to force its way through my sides. At length somewhat recovering, I viewed her more minutely. But if I was puzzled at beholding a woman alone in this lonely place, how much more was I surprised at her appearance and dress. She had a sort of brown chaplet, like lace, round her head, under and about which her hair was tucked up and twined; and she seemed to me to be clothed in a thin hair-colored silk garment, which upon trying to raise her, I found to be quite warm, and therefore hoped there was life in the body it contained. I then took her into my arms, and conveyed her through the door-way into my grotto; where I laid her upon my bed.

When I lay her down, I thought, on laying my hand on her breast, I perceived the fountain of life had some motion. This gave me infinite pleasure; so warming a drop of wine, I dipped my finger in it, and moistened her lips two or three times, and I imagined they opened a little. Upon this I bethought me, and taking a tea-spoon, I gently poured a few drops of the wine by that means into her mouth. Finding she swallowed it, I poured in another spoonful, and another, till I brought her to herself so well as to be able to sit up.

I then spoke to her and asked divers questions as if she had understood me; in return of which she uttered a language I had no idea of, though in the most musical tone and with the sweetest accent I ever heard.

You may imagine we stared heartily at each other, and I doubted not but she wondered as much as I by what means we came so near each other.

Like Julia in Herrick's eyes, 'her grace and motion' perfectly charmed Peter, and 'her shape was incomparable'. 'Well, we supped together, and I set the best of every thing I had before her'.

And so the narrative proceeds. Peter, scrupulous and considerate on the one side; Youwarkee, very woman in spite of her wings, on the other. Nothing could be more domestic, homely and peaceable. Indeed the solitude of their island and their (rather sophisticated) idyll withstand every shock, including even the discovery of 'an old crape hat-band'—until Youwarkee's relatives begin to arrive.

In the year *Peter Wilkins* was published *A Narrative of the Life and astonishing Adventures of John Daniel* also appeared. Its ostensible author, 'Mr. Ralph Morris', who may be apocryphal, seems at any rate to be untraceable. His book shows clearly that Crusoe was no stranger to him, that he may have read *The Isle of Pines* and probably also *The Man in the Moone*. In style he is rather heavyhanded, his spelling is occasionally his own, and some of the words he uses seem to be local—*dripple*, *sobby* and the like.

His hero runs away from an amorous and violent young stepmother and is wrecked on a desert island sixty miles in circuit, its deep woods frequented by droves of wild cattle and wild swine. Only one shipmate shares his solitude, and he discovers by chance—when she falls and wounds herself—that this shipmate is a woman. He had noticed how docile 'Thomas' was, and how 'slack in invention', and had been surprised to see the poor fellow wipe his eye, with tears trickling down his cheeks, over the sorrows of a captive motherless calf.

From master to wooer proves an easy step: 'O! mr. Daniel', says she, 'I may now say you have saved my life'. They wed; a charming little ceremony, with a piece of catgut for a ring and some beef and water for a wedding breakfast. Their children multiply, and 'mr Daniel', naively winning his Ruth over to his views by asking where Adam's sons found *their* wives, marries them off and settles them in various parts of his dominions, now called *The Isle of Providence*. The customary wreck supplies them with all that they need, and in particular with a glut of calico. The years go by, and at length one of the younger sons, Jacob, a confirmed bachelor and a natural mechanic, constructs out of pig-fatted calico and slender iron ribs a flying machine, which he calls the Eagle. It is worked by a hand-pump. In this *Eagle* he and his father sail off—unintentionally—to the moon. Unconscious of their whereabouts they set out to explore it.

. . . Having traversed this plain about two days, we lost the moon [i.e. the brightly shining earth] entirely, but in lieu thereof, found what was much more grateful to us, the light of the sun approaching; and the third day it rose up above the hills.

Its presence gave us such a flow of spirits, that we even forgot our toils and hardships. It gave us from the mountain we afterwards climbed up, a prospect of the most romantick country I had ever beheld; there were prodigious mountains, extensive plains, and immense lakes, interspersed with the vastest plantations of trees that can be imagined, to lie within the compass of the eye at once; and then the air was so serene, thin and transparent, that we could see distinctly, to a distance beyond comparison, to what we ever could before; and what aggravated our extasies was, that we were now in hopes of not losing the sun again, for it seemed not, visibly, to alter its position at all.

The moon-men they find there are volatile creatures of a bright copper colour all over that shines like gold in the sun. They are clad in a mantle of hair, thick and long; and there are little round eyes in their small faces. They are preternaturally nimble, and their language is of 'short and broken aspirates' with little variety even at that. These beings faintly recall the exquisite effete 'upper' classes of Mr. Wells's romance, *The Time Machine*.

On their return to earth, Jacob's plane is nearly wrecked at the bottom of a precipitous gully of the sea, where, with their family of thirty descendants, live 'mr. and mrs. Anderson', two monsters, part human, part marine, and of a very genteel address, though they are shapes of veritable nightmare—with their fish-scale skins and hooked talons—as they are depicted in the cut in the book. Their father and mother had also been castaways—and that mother, who has left a *MS.* behind her which John Daniel reads, was a castaway indeed. So much so that he fails to finish her record—'it was so shocking to human nature'.

Once again wafted on their way, Jacob and his father descend upon Lapland, whose inhabitants, with their 'rain deer', are adepts in the second-sight. Mr. Daniel, who is now an old gentleman upwards of ninety, is told that his wife grievously mourns for him, but he makes no effort to return to her; and when Jacob is drowned at sea he is afflicted at the moment with so many other cares that he can give no room to his grief for this!

The patriarch returns at last to Royston, his native place, and there meets a remarkable parson, aged seventy-five:

Upon our chariot stopping at the door, before we had knocked, we saw him returning from his garden, in a black cap over a white linen one, a neckcloth loose about his neck, with an almost black night-gown, flowing behind him; he was of a tall stature, at least six feet, with hair as white as milk, and a complexion clear as alabaster, seamed with the furrows of time in it; but he had a good set of teeth, and a very bright eye, and to my thinking, had something angelick in his aspect.

Having thus conducted his reader through a 'series of uncommon adventures' Mr. Adams bids him remember 'that life is but a journey and the grave a home'. About five years afterwards, now long become 'quite childish', he expires: *Sistit viator fatigatus Johannes Daniel, ob. 13 Aprilis 1711. Aetat 97.*

Page 68¹—Incensed by Mr. Robinson's seamanship:
❡ It is easy (and especially for a child in these matters) to forgive Mr. Robinson such little deficiencies and excesses as these, if only for the sake of auld lang syne. But, unhappy man, he even scorned his great prototype. When Ernest jocundly declares how happy he would be to live *à la Crusoe* on the little island which the family have discovered harbouring the prodigious carcase of the Greenland whale, his father positively scoffs:

The idea made me smile and I instantly replied, 'You foolish boy. Do[n't] you know that the life of Robinson is but a finely-wrought fiction and that your romantic project has a thousand obstacles attending it? You would not be there long before you would grow tired of your solitude; sickness would come and some fine morning we should find the poor hermit dead upon the beach'.

After which horrid and irrefutable little sermon Mr. Robinson persuades Madam to accompany him with her tubs to bring in the blubber.

Yet another discourse follows when, having examined the deceased mammal's narrow throat, Ernest remembers the prophet Jonah. But Mr. Robinson is equal to all difficulties, all problems, all crises, all occasions, and having disposed of this one, cries rapidly and blithely, 'To work, gentlemen—to work!' Whereupon he 'literally' swims in grease amidst walls of solid fat, a situation that seems to fit his temperament like a glove. Next day, having determined to make his way into the interior of the whale, he leaves Mrs. Robinson at home. And rightly so; for he must needs strip to his pantaloons. A memorable picture, and of a 'true butcher.'

Page 68²—Defoe's pattern:
❡ And a very ancient pattern it was, for Crusoe's island is after all only the scene of a prolonged episode in the record of his wanderings, just as for Ulysses the island of

Calypso is in the *Odyssey;* indeed, in Book V, with Hermes for guide, Crusoe might have found the originals of his cavern and his stockade! And in what lovely English.

> This took, he stoopt Pieria, and thence
> Glid through the air, and Neptune's confluence
> Kist as he flew, and checkt the waves as light
> As any sea-mew in her fishing flight,
> Her thick wings sousing in the savory seas.
> Like her, he past a world of wilderness;
> But when the far-off isle he toucht, he went
> Up from the blue sea to the continent,
> And reacht the ample cavern of the Queen,
> Whom he within found, without seldom seen.
> A sun-like fire upon the hearth did flame,
> The matter precious, and divine the frame,
> Of cedar cleft and incense was the pile,
> That breath'd an odour round about the isle.
> Her self was seated in an inner room,
> Whom sweetly sing he heard, and at her loom,
> About a curious web, whose yarn she threw
> In with a golden shittle. A grove grew
> In endless spring about her cavern round,
> With odorous cypress, pines, and poplars crown'd,
> Where haulks, sea-owls, and long-tongued bittours bred,
> And other birds their shady pinions spread;
> All fowls maritimal; none roosted there,
> But those whose labours in the waters were,
> A vine did all the hollow cave embrace,
> Still green, yet still ripe bunches gave it grace.
> Four fountains, one against another, pour'd
> Their silver streams; and meadows all enflower'd
> With sweet balm-gentle, and blue-violets hid,
> That deckt the soft breasts of each fragrant mead.

For comparison (though this is far beyond the scope of this rambling commentary) there follows a further fragment from Book IX, in three forms, (a) Professor A. T. Murray's translation in prose, (b) Pope's, and (c) Chapman's—both in verse. It is interesting to compare these three versions word by word—and then, it may be, return to the original if, like Defoe, one can 'read' Greek —a joy beyond me. The Pope version slightly *civilizes* its original, patronizes the hunters and views that murmuring main from afar. Chapman rejoices in the proud-liv'd Cyclops, himself scales the mountain-tops with the hunters and exults in every salty breath his sea-meadows yield.

(a) . . . Thence we sailed on, grieved at heart, and we came to the land of the Cyclops, an overweening and lawless folk, who, trusting in the immortal gods, plant nothing with their hands nor plough; but all these things spring up for them without sowing or ploughing, wheat, and barley, and vines, which bear the rich clusters of wine, and the ram of Zeus gives them increase. . . .
Now there is a level isle that stretches aslant outside the harbour, neither close to the shore of the land of the Cyclopes, nor yet far off, a wooded isle. Therein live wild goats innumerable, for the tread of men scares them not away, nor are hunters wont to come thither, men who endure toils in the woodland as they course over the peaks of the mountains. Neither with flocks is it held, or with ploughed lands, but unsown and untilled all the days it knows naught of men, but feeds the bleating goats. . . . In it are meadows by the shores of the grey sea, well-watered meadows and soft, where vines would never fail, and in it level ploughland, whence they might reap from season to season harvests exceeding deep, so rich is the soil beneath. . . .

(b) . . . With heavy hearts we labour through the tide,
To coasts unknown, and oceans yet untried.

The land of Cyclopes first, a savage kind,
Nor tamed by manners, nor by laws confined:
Untaught to plant, to turn the glebe, and sow,
They all their products to free nature owe:
The soil, untill'd, a ready harvest yields,
With wheat and barley wave the golden fields:
Spontaneous wines from weighty clusters pour,
And Jove descends in each prolific shower. . . .

Opposed to the Cyclopean coast, there lay
An isle, whose hills their subject fields survey;
Its name Lachaea, crown'd with many a grove,
Where savage goats through pathless thickets rove:
No needy mortals here, with hunger bold,
Or wretched hunters through the wintry cold
Pursue their flight; but leave them safe to bound
From hill to hill, o'er all the desert ground.
Nor knows the soil to feed the fleecy care,
Or feels the labours of the crooked share;
But uninhabited, untill'd, unsown,
It lies, and breeds the bleating goat alone. . . .

244

Fields waving high with heavy crops are seen,
And vines that flourish in eternal green,
Refreshing meads along the murmuring main,
And fountains streaming down the fruitful plain. . . .
   (c) All then aboard, we beat the sea with oars,
And still with sad hearts sail'd by out-way shores,
Till th' out-law'd Cyclops' land we fecht; a race
Of proud-liv'd loiterers, that never sow,
Nor put a plant in earth, nor use a plow,
But trust in God for all things; and their earth,
Unsown, unplow'd, gives every offspring birth
That other lands have; wheat, and barley, vines
That bear in goodly grapes delicious wines;
And Jove sends showers for all. . . .
                        . . . But there stood
Another little isle, well stor'd with wood,
Betwixt this and the entry; neither nigh
The Cyclops' isle, nor yet far off doth lie.
Men's want it suffered, but the men's supplies
The goats made with their inarticulate cries.
Goats beyond number this small island breeds,
So tame, that no access disturbs their feeds,
No hunters, that the tops of mountains scale,
And rub through woods with toil, seek them at all.
Nor is the soil with flocks fed down, nor plow'd,
Nor ever in it any seed was sow'd. . . .
There, close upon the sea, sweet meadows spring,
That yet of fresh streams want no watering
To their soft burthens, but of special yield.
Your vines would be there; and your common field
But gentle work make for your plow, yet bear
A lofty harvest when you came to shear. . . .

Page 69¹—Its supremacy:
¶ 'Altogether I don't like him', was Macaulay's summary
of Defoe; and it is amusing to observe how sufficient
even lesser men than Macaulay suppose this particular
judgement to be. It *may* imply a pretty compliment. On
the other hand, 'Nobody ever laid down the book of
Robinson Crusoe without wishing it longer', was Dr. Johnson's verdict, one equalled in vigour only by his tribute
to the *Anatomy of Melancholy* and the *Pilgrim's Progress.*
The first real book, thumbed and beloved, of one's early

245

childhood has too as happy and serene a place in one's remembrance as one's first sweetheart; and *Crusoe* can have few rivals for this willow-shaded niche. Take, first, George Borrow's rhapsody. When he was a little boy he was given a copy of *Crusoe*, not by his own but by his brother's young godmother. It became, he says, a bridge between the unconsciousness of childhood and the world of sensation and ideas. He tells us how he was simply transmogrified with wonder and rapture by the pictures he found in the book—that rocky shore, the moon peering; that sandy beach and furious sea, overcast with leaden-like cloud and rack, and that one small half-smothered wretch stumbling beneath the crest of a gigantic toppling billow; and last, hairy-hatted Crusoe himself gazing in amazement at the footprint; and then—

The true chord had now been touched; a raging curiosity with respect to the contents of the volume, whose engravings had fascinated my eye, burned within me, and I never rested until I had fully satisfied it; weeks succeeded weeks, months followed months, and the wondrous volume was my only study and principal source of amusement. For hours together I would sit poring over a page till I had become acquainted with the import of every line. My progress, slow enough at first, became by degrees more rapid, till at last, under 'a shoulder of mutton sail', I found myself cantering before a steady breeze over an ocean of enchantment, so well pleased with my voyage that I cared not how long it might be ere it reached its termination.

And he returns thanks:

Hail to thee, spirit of De Foe! What does not my own poor self owe to thee? England has better bards than either Greece or Rome, yet I could spare them easier far than De Foe, 'unabashed De Foe', as the hunch-backed rhymer styled him.

And this is Dr. L. P. Jacks's tribute, taken from the volume entitled *Among the Idol Makers*, which contains also that other signally memorable short story, *The Magic Formula*.

The critical moment of my history may be assigned to a certain date in March 1868, when my Father, according to an entry in his Journal, bought me a copy of *Robinson Crusoe* for four-and-six.

Little did my Father dream what he was doing. As he walked home that night my Destiny was in his pocket.

A book absorbed by an imaginative child can give a lifelong climate to the soul, lending its colours to the experience of the coming years, tempering the quality of moods, laying all values under debt to its influence. The atmosphere of the author's mind, which critics may never discover, is the first element the child appropriates, becoming thereby a visionary on his own account. In reading the letter he catches the spirit rather than the meaning, the sense rather than the idea; he pierces to the secret springs of imagery; he sees, hears, touches, tastes; and so, following the innermost impulse of the written word, his own imagination becomes creative, and a new world is woven out of the living tissue of his sympathies. The book may sow no seed, neither of wheat nor of tares; but air and weather are created for Sowings that are to come; broad limits drawn within which the spirit may wander and beyond which it cannot pass; the region assigned which is to be the nursery of dreams, and the firmament stored with visions waiting to be born—Delectable Mountains hung in air, and far-seen Islands that shine like jewels in the circumambient waste.

Had the eye of my Father chanced upon some other book, all would have been different. Had he bought me the *Fairchild Family*, or *Sandford and Merton*, or Miss Edgeworth's *Tales*, or *Tom Brown*, then the lady who is now my wife would have belonged to another; my present children would not have been born, my strange life would not have been lived; and these lines would not have been written. If you find me a bore, a nuisance, or a liar—remember my Father's act.

Robinson Crusoe was the first book I read; nor have I ever read another with faith so complete, with imagination so on fire. The sources of thought were tapped; the waters of fancy were unsealed, and the channel cut in which they are doomed to flow until they are lost for ever in the sea. Like a stone dropped into the mouth of a geyser, the reading of that book let loose the floods that boil around the central fires; and a way was made for spirits that haunt the secret springs of life to come and go from that day to this.

No philosopher has ever had a clearer conception of the true end of man than I had at the age of twelve. All forms of self-realisation were false save one; and that was, to get oneself cast away, by hook or by crook, upon a Desolate Island. Nothing else would satisfy. Let others go to Heaven if they would; let others be good, or great; but let me be cast on some lonely palm-strewn shore in the uttermost parts of the earth. It was the foolish ship that came to port; it was the wise ship that was wrecked. Not for all the kingdoms of this world would I have exchanged my keg of powder, my cap of goatskin, my fortification, and my raft.

247

Fundamentally I have never changed that creed. All has been of a piece; there has been no breach in my continuity; the child was father of the man, and my old madness, if madness it was, is with me yet. Before I was twelve years old my fate was sealed; and the gods have kept their bond. It was written that I should explore no Great Continents nor lift up a voice in any City; that the call should come from afar; that I should shun the mainlands where men grow fat and live at ease; that I should stand out into great waters, follow the albatross in her lonely flight, and dwell on the sounding rocks where she makes her nest. O ye Universal Histories and Views of the World, O ye Perfect Satisfactions and Summum Bonums ready-made, what have I to do with you? A pin-point of time in the wide wastes of eternity, whereon some god had flung me, was all the dwelling-place I ever had. Of broad cities paved with gold I have had no vision; yet have I seen and handled many a shining grain washed down by the River of Life. Good in its Totality I have not known; but hands unseen, held out to save me, have drawn the spent swimmer from the billows of death. Standpoint for viewing, the universe has never been mine; but often, when sinking in deep waters, I have felt a sudden standpoint beneath my feet. With Men in the Mass I have had no traffic. None but lonely souls have I ever met; all were exceptions; Desolate Islands in Time; and with no chart to guide me I have sailed among them, sounding as I went.

Wordsworth speaks of a far-off day when the cataract haunted him like a passion. My haunting passion was the Island. I ransacked libraries for the literature of Islands, and the more desolate they were the better I was pleased. I pored over great maps till Polynesia and Melanesia were more familiar than the geography of the county in which I lived. I found that men who had written of Utopia and other impossible things were as mad as I was about Islands, and I loved them all and read their books over and over again. I knew the Hebrides by heart, I was at home in the archipelagos of the Pacific, I could thread my way among the smallest groups of the Indies, East and West, and a navigator of the Cyclades might almost have used me for a pilot. Columbus, Magellan, Drake, Dampier, Anson, Cook—these were the names of my familiar spirits; and had I not sailed with Odysseus of many devices over leagues and leagues of the unharvested sea?

It was always the little islands I loved the best, and if they were not only small but very remote, like St. Kilda, Kerguelen, or Juan Fernandez, so that a mariner shipwrecked on their shores might have reasonable chance of being unrescued for years, I rejoiced like the man who discovered a treasure hid in a field. Australia interested me not the least—it was too big. No castaway of twelve years could be expected to manage such a place. The Channel Islands were contemptible; they were too near. They suggested the odious possibility of being rescued by a steamer! But the Isles of Aru, Tinian and Tidore, the Dampier Group, the Solomons, the Celebes—these were the places where a castaway of merit might make his mark. . . .

One night [years afterwards] I sat disconsolate by a sounding shore; the sea-birds screamed; the waves bellowed in the caverns; and through all and over all I heard the tick, tock of the everlasting pendulum—like an endless note of doom. The memory of vanished youth lay heavy on my heart; I was thinking of my many dead; their wan faces haunted me, and they whispered that I too must die; old fancies came back, but they came like gibbering ghosts and mocked me; I visited old scenes and, lo, they were disenchanted; I clothed me in Crusoe's skins, and they hung upon me like a shroud; all the islands of the sea were empty as the eye-sockets of a skull; the gates of dreams were barred, and 'nevermore' was written over every one. The very order of the world appalled me; for what was I but a cog on its wheels? 'Is there aught so wearisome as knowledge,' I cried; 'is there aught so unlovely as the known? . . .'

Then it was that Truth fell towards me like a meteor out of the sky. . . .

Such were my new voyages; yet, even in the furthest I never passed beyond the limits of the common day. Plain men were my companions; familiar faces were around me; my body passed to and fro among streets of brick houses, or wandered in old pastures where tame oxen stood knee-deep in the grass. But all day long I was breaking the barriers and peering into secrets that lie beyond the flaming walls. I went through Wonderland in evening-dress; I made strange land-falls in a drawing-room; I was blown 'ten thousand leagues awry' while listening to a modern play; I saw ships foundering in a drop of rain; I picnicked with the Anthropophagi, and dined at restaurants with 'men whose heads do grow beneath their shoulders'. I met a tramp—and we two passed a day and a night in the deep; I talked with an old shepherd on the Downs—and heard the surf fall thundering on an unknown shore. I opened the books I had read in childhood, and the wind Euroclydon blew out from the printed page and carried me away; ancient saws burst upon me with the shock of great explosions; the black ship staggered and plunged; I drove under the lee of dark continents; strange fires lit up the headlands; hands mightier than mine grasped the rudder, and I saw One riding on the wings of the storm.

Desolate Islands, more than I could ever explore, more than I could count or name, I found in the men and women who press upon me every day. Nay, my own life was full of them; the flying moment was one; they rose out of the deep with the ticking of the clock. And once came the rushing of a mighty wind; and the waves fled backward till the sea was no more. Then I saw that the islands were great mountains uplifted from everlasting foundations, their basis one beneath the ocean floor, their summits many above the sundering waters—most marvellous of all the works of God.

Page 69²—'Treasure Island':

¶ The appearance of the island when I came on deck next morning was altogether changed. Although the breeze had now utterly failed, we had made a great deal of way during the night, and were now lying becalmed about half a mile to the south-east of the low eastern coast. Grey-coloured woods covered a large part of the surface. This even tint was indeed broken up by streaks of yellow sandbreak in the lower lands, and by many tall trees of the pine family, out-topping the others—some singly, some in clumps; but the general colouring was uniform and sad. The hills ran up clear above the vegetation in spires of naked rock. All were strangely shaped, and the Spy-glass, which was by three or four hundred feet the tallest on the island, was likewise the strangest in configuration, running up sheer from almost every side, and then suddenly cut off at the top like a pedestal to put a statue on. . . .

. . . Perhaps it was the look of the island, with its grey, melancholy woods, and wild stone spires, and the surf that we could both see and hear foaming and thundering on the steep beach—at least, although the sun shone bright and hot, and the shore birds were fishing and crying all around us, and you would have thought any one would have been glad to get to land after being so long at sea, my heart sank, as the saying is, into my boots; and from that first look onward, I hated the very thought of Treasure Island. . . .

We brought up just where the anchor was in the chart, about a third of a mile from either shore, the mainland on one side, and Skeleton Island on the other. The bottom was clean sand. The plunge of our anchor sent up clouds of birds wheeling and crying over the woods; but in less than a minute they were down again, and all was once more silent.

The place was entirely land-locked, buried in woods, the trees coming right down to high-water mark, the shores mostly flat, and the hilltops standing round at a distance in a sort of amphitheatre, one here, one there. Two little rivers, or, rather, two swamps, emptied out into this pond, as you might call it; and the foliage round that part of the shore had a kind of poisonous brightness. . . . There was not a breath of air moving, nor a sound but that of the surf booming half a mile away along the beaches and against the rocks outside. A peculiar stagnant smell hung over the anchorage—a smell of sodden leaves and rotting tree trunks.

It is a lovely and vivid piece of writing: certain master

words sound out like hitherto unheard instruments in an orchestra—*uniform and sad, spires, plunge, down again, poisonous brightness.* Most effective, too, that seeming afterthought—*the bottom was clean sand;* and how admirably contrived the illusion of the interior of the island, the sea never out of *mind.*

Page 69³—'Lost Endeavour':

¶ Mr. Masefield's *Boca Del Drago* will not be found (at least under that name) in any gazetteer, and the Gulf of Honduras is a pretty wide space of sea in which to search for it, however ample a survey may be obtained from the Cockscomb Mountains:

> The island is an irregular cone, sloping up, not very gently, to the hill-top which is called Sombrero Hill, because it is like one of those Don's peaked hats. . . . The whole island is four miles long, and about half as broad. In that compass is contained nearly every variety of landscape, from impassable cliff to impassable swamp. There are no roads nor native tracks into the interior from the coast. It is just a tangle of forest, often extremely dense, and so full of poison ivy and manchineels that a man must be careful how he cuts his way there lest the juices poison his face and hands. . . .
>
> I entered the wood as carefully as an Indian, stepping lightly, and covering my tracks, as one learns to do when one lives in the wilds. When I was well inside the wood I had to cut my way with my machete, in a sort of gloom which chilled me. There was not much visible reassuring life in the woods. No life of man, at any rate. The birds were not song-birds, the noises were not friendly noises. I would hear quavering, cracking noises from branches, rotted through, slowly giving way, and strange booming noises from the sea. Very strangely the noises came to me. There must be something dense in the air of forests, so that sound gets checked or softened in its passage. Another thing was strange, the silence of the live things. That part of the island seemed almost deserted. Now and then a rustle told me where a snake vanished. Sometimes a snake would drop from a branch like a rope flung down from its pin. Then, in some chance opening of the trees, I would see a blue patch of sky, and a silent bird would waver across it into the blackness of the gloom beyond.

There follows a passage of music (in words) which once it has fallen on the reader's ear will never cease to haunt him with its cadences. And then:

> When that temple was laid bare before me I did not think of the

secrets of the water-pots. I thought only of what lay beyond, down in the dimness there, in the open space of the floor. The floor sloped down between an array of carven figures, kings and queens of the dead, who stood on each side solemn as Egyptian figures, grander than living figures, with brows crushed back and lips protruding and their tongues transfixed by briers. There was a glimmer upon all these carvings. They were hung with golden plaques made of the very soft pure gold, which can be bent by the fingers. There was more gold there on those carvings than any man has seen at one time since Cortes saw the Mexican treasure, or Pizarro the ransom of Atahualpa. There was gold enough there to build a navy. It glinted all down the temple, a marvel of gold-worker's art, the worth of a kingdom. . . .

That 'very soft pure gold'—it melts like butter in the mouth, it is like honey to the senses, it would seduce the guards even of the innermost citadel!

And the ancient temple? 'All houses wherein man has lived and died,' says Longfellow, 'are haunted houses', and assuredly if the deserted house ever follows the 'solitary horseman' into the oblivion of the old-fashioned, fiction will have been deprived of one more of its hoarily romantic objects. Two such houses not of fiction but of actuality, and three or four thousand arctic miles apart, shared three whole centuries of solitude. One of these, built by William Brants in 1597 on the north-east coast of Nova Zembla, was never apparently seen again by human eye until it was discovered by Captain Carlsen in 1871. The other was built by Martin Frobisher twenty years earlier near the bay that bears his name in Meta Incognita. And there in its icy winter wastes it remained —as solitary in the eye of fancy as the island of the Incas in the high lake of Titicaca—until it was chanced on by the American explorer Captain Charles Hall in 1862. At thought of them some phantom within hies away to peer at their tenantless walls. But why his deserted hermitage should be an even more romantic object than the hermit himself is something of a mystery. So too with the imagination of a man-abandoned world. So too with a flint arrow-head—or even a Victorian bead mat.

Page 69⁴—William Morris:

❡ It is not easy to make choice between the *Isles* in William Morris's 'Wondrous' archipelago. But here is 'the Isle of Nothing':

. . . Deepened then the dusk, and became night, and she floated on through it, and was asleep alone on the bosom of the water. . . . Long before sunrise, in the very morn-dusk, she awoke and found that her ferry had taken land again. Little might she see what the said land was like; so she sat patiently and abode the day in the boat; but when day was come, little more was to see than erst. For flat was the isle, and scarce raised above the wash of the leeward ripple on a fair day; nor was it either timbered or bushed or grassed, and, so far as Birdalone might see, no one foot of it differed in aught from another. Natheless she deemed that she was bound to go ashore and seek out the adventure, or spoil her errand else.

Out of the boat she stepped then, and found the earth all paved of a middling gravel, and nought at all growing there, not even the smallest of herbs; and she stooped down and searched the gravel, and found neither worm nor beetle therein, nay nor any one of the sharp and slimy creatures which are wont in such ground.

A little further she went, and yet a little further, and no change there was in the land; and yet she went on and found nothing; and she wended her ways southward by the sun, and the day was windless.

Page 69⁵—'Enoch Arden':

❡ The *Good Fortune* is wrecked on her journey home from the Orient:

. . . Less lucky her home-voyage: at first indeed
Thro' many a fair sea-circle, day by day,
Scarce-rocking, her full-busted figure-head
Stared o'er the ripple feathering from her bows:
Then follow'd calms, and then winds variable,
Then baffling, a long course of them; and last
Storm, such as drove her under moonless heavens
Till hard upon the cry of 'breakers' came
The crash of ruin, and the loss of all
But Enoch and two others. Half the night,
Buoy'd upon floating tackle and broken spars,
These drifted, stranding on an isle at morn
Rich, but the loneliest in a lonely sea. . . .

Goats, coconuts, palms and palm-thatched huts follow. The youngest of the three survivors after the wreck of the

Good Fortune perishes after 'five years' death-in-life', another of sunstroke, and Enoch lives on alone. In these deaths he read God's warning, 'Wait'. And here is the description of his island, full of vivid and lovely natural (and verbal) detail which yet perhaps does not quite succeed in transporting us into it. It seems to have been woven together of different kinds of threads. How curiously small the figure of Enoch Arden looks, sitting there—like a speck in a picture. Indeed, imagine the island, so described, *as* a picture in paint, and qualities both of conception and craftsmanship not hitherto so perceptible reveal themselves.

> The mountain wooded to the peak, the lawns
> And winding glades high up like ways to Heaven,
> The slender coco's drooping crown of plumes,
> The lightning flash of insect and of bird,
> The lustre of the long convolvuluses
> That coil'd around the stately stems, and ran
> Ev'n to the limit of the land, the glows
> And glories of the broad belt of the world,
> And these he saw; but what he fain had seen
> He could not see, the kindly human face,
> Nor ever hear a kindly voice, but heard
> The myriad shriek of wheeling ocean-fowl,
> The league-long roller thundering on the reef,
> The moving whisper of huge trees that branch'd
> And blossom'd in the zenith, or the sweep
> Of some precipitous rivulet to the wave,
> As down the shore he ranged, or all day long
> Sat often in the seaward-gazing gorge,
> A shipwreck'd sailor, waiting for a sail:
> No sail from day to day, but every day
> The sunrise broken into scarlet shafts
> Among the palms and ferns and precipices;
> The blaze upon the waters to the east;
> The blaze upon his island overhead;
> The blaze upon the waters to the west;
> Then the great stars that globed themselves in Heaven,
> The hollower-bellowing ocean, and again
> The scarlet shafts of sunrise—but no sail. . . .

There is, too, in the *Faërie Queene*, an island, in 'a wide Inland sea', 'hight by name' *The Idle Lake*. Cymochles, husband of the enchantress Acracia, sets out to wreak his wrath on Sir Guyon—and to his death. He comes to a river and sees as swift as glance of eye a little Gondolay decked like an arbour—'That like a litle forrest seemèd outwardly', and that steers itself:

> . . . And therein sate a Ladie fresh and faire,
> Making sweet solace to her selfe alone;
> Sometimes she sung, as loud as larke in aire,
> Sometimes she laught, that nigh her breth was gone,
> Yet was there not with her else any one,
> That might to her move cause of meriment:
> Matter of merth enough, though there were none,
> She could devise, and thousand waies invent,
> To feede her foolish humour, and vaine jolliment. . . .

> Eftsoones her shallow ship away did slide,
> More swift, then swallow sheres the liquid skie,
> Withouten oare or Pilot it to guide,
> Or winged canvas with the wind to flie,
> Only she turn'd a pin, and by and by
> It cut away upon the yielding wave,
> Ne carèd she her course for to apply:
> For it was taught the way, which she would have,
> And both from rocks and flats it selfe could wisely save. . . .

> Her light behaviour, and loose dalliaunce
> Gave wondrous great contentment to the knight,
> That of his way he had no sovenaunce,
> Nor care of vow'd revenge, and cruell fight,
> But to weake wench did yeeld his martiall might.
> So easie was to quench his flamèd mind
> With one sweet drop of sensuall delight,
> So easie is, t'appease the stormie wind
> Of malice in the calme of pleasant womankind. . . .

> Whiles thus she talkèd, and whiles thus she toyd,
> They were farre past the passage, which he spake,
> And come unto an Island, waste and voyd,
> That floted in the midst of that great lake,
> There her small Gondelay her port did make,
> And that gay paire issuing on the shore
> Disburdned her. Their way they forward take
> Into the land, that lay them faire before,
> Whose pleasaunce she him shew'd, and plentifull great store.

255

It was a chosen plot of fertile land,
 Emongst wide waves set, like a litle nest,
 As if it had by Natures cunning hand
 Bene choisely pickèd out from all the rest,
 And laid forth for ensample of the best:
 No daintie flowre or herbe, that growes on ground,
 No arboret with painted blossomes drest,
 And smelling sweet, but there it might be found
To bud out faire, and her sweet smels throw all around.

No tree, whose braunches did not bravely spring;
 No braunch, whereon a fine bird did not sit:
 No bird, but did her shrill notes sweetly sing;
 No song but did containe a lovely dit:
 Trees, braunches, birds, and songs were framed fit,
 For to allure fraile mind to carelesse ease.
 Carelesse the man soone woxe, and his weake wit
 Was overcome of thing, that did him please;
So pleasèd, did his wrathfull purpose faire appease.

Thus when she had his eyes and senses fed
 With false delights, and fild with pleasures vaine,
 Into a shadie dale she soft him led,
 And laide him downe upon a grassie plaine;
 And her sweet selfe without dread, or disdaine,
 She set beside, laying his head disarm'd
 In her loose lap, it softly to sustaine,
 Where soone he slumbred, fearing not be harm'd,
The whiles with a loud lay she thus him sweetly charm'd. . . .

By this she had him lullèd fast a sleepe,
 That of no worldly thing he care did take;
 Then she with liquors strong his eyes did steepe,
 That nothing should him hastily awake:
 So she him left, and did her selfe betake
 Unto her boat againe, with which she cleft
 The slouthfull wave of that great griesly lake;
 Soone she that Island farre behind her left,
And now is come to that same place, where first she weft. . . .

The languorous rhythms soon lull the reader into a
daydream, and that is akin to sleep. Indeed, all that we
look on is dreamlike and clear in this still scene, but it is
curious one should *hear* so little; neither the clap of the
oars, nor the birds in the branches, however shrill the
notes of their lovely 'dit', nor the false lady's own loud

lay. Even the gentle clashing of the rhymes as one reads the verse to oneself is more audible.

Such is Spenser's island, as much the creation of fancy, expressed in verse, as Poe's *Island of the Fay* is, expressed in prose—and how easily we forget that the first is allegorical. Which of the two holds in solution the purer 'poetry' is a question which must remain a personal one. In any case Poe's island is his and no other man's. Its air has a faint exotic flavour. The words produce not merely a scene but a mood of the mind, though one not to all tastes pleasing. Here and there are phrases as estranging as the 'rich anger' in Keats's ode *On Melancholy*, but the epicure will linger over the cadence even of that one word *clambered,* of *Are these green tombs theirs?* and of *While the sun rushed down to his slumbers.*

My position enabled me to include in a single view both the eastern and western extremities of the islet; and I observed a singularly marked difference in their aspects. The latter was all one radiant harem of garden beauties. It glowed and blushed beneath the eye of the slant sunlight, and fairly laughed with flowers. The grass was short, springy, sweet-scented, and Asphodel-interspersed. The trees were light, mirthful, erect—bright, slender, and graceful—of eastern figure and foliage, with bark smooth, glossy, and particolored. There seemed a deep sense of life and joy about all; and although no airs blew from out the Heavens, yet every thing had motion through the gentle sweepings to and fro of innumerable butterflies, that might have been mistaken for tulips with wings.

The other or eastern end of the isle was whelmed in the blackest shade. A sombre, yet beautiful and peaceful gloom here pervaded all things. The trees were dark in colour and mournful in form and attitude—wreathing themselves into sad, solemn, and spectral shapes, that conveyed ideas of mortal sorrow and untimely death. The grass wore the deep tint of the cypress, and the heads of its blades hung droopingly, and, hither and thither among it, were many small unsightly hillocks, low and narrow, and not very long, that had the aspect of graves, but were not; although over and all about them the rue and the rosemary clambered. The shade of the trees fell heavily upon the water, and seemed to bury itself therein, impregnating the depths of the element with darkness. I fancied that each shadow, as the sun descended lower and lower, separated itself sullenly from the trunk that gave it birth, and thus became absorbed by the stream; while other shadows issued momently from the trees, taking the place of their predecessors thus entombed.

This idea, having once seized upon my fancy, greatly excited it, and I lost myself forthwith in revery. 'If ever island were enchanted,' said I to myself, 'this is it. This is the haunt of the few gentle Fays who remain from the wreck of the race. Are these green tombs theirs? —or do they yield up their sweet lives as mankind yield up their own? In dying, do they not rather waste away mournfully; rendering unto God little by little their existence, as these trees render up shadow after shadow, exhausting their substance unto dissolution? What the wasting tree is to the water that imbibes its shade, growing thus blacker by what it preys upon, may not the life of the Fay be to the death which ingulfs it?'

As I thus mused, with half-shut eyes, while the sun sank rapidly to rest, and eddying currents careered round and round the island, bearing upon their bosom large, dazzling, white flakes, of the bark of the sycamore—flakes which, in their multiform positions upon the water, a quick imagination might have converted into any thing it pleased—while I thus mused, it appeared to me that the form of one of those very Fays about whom I had been pondering, made its way slowly into the darkness from out the light at the western end of the island. She stood erect in a singularly fragile canoe, and urged it with the mere phantom of an oar. While within the influence of the lingering sunbeams, her attitude seemed indicative of joy—but sorrow deformed it as she passed within the shade. Slowly she glided along, and at length rounded the islet and re-entered the region of light. 'The revolution which has just been made by the Fay,' continued I, musingly, 'is the cycle of the brief year of her life. She has floated through her winter and through her summer. She is a year nearer unto Death: for I did not fail to see that as she came into the shade, her shadow fell from her, and was swallowed up in the dark water, making its blackness more black.'

And again the boat appeared, and the Fay; but about the attitude of the latter there was more of care and uncertainty, and less of elastic joy. She floated again from out the light, and into the gloom (which deepened momently) and again her shadow fell from her into the ebony water, and became absorbed into its blackness. And again and again she made the circuit of the island, (while the sun rushed down to his slumbers) and at each issuing into the light, there was more sorrow about her person, while it grew feebler, and far fainter, and more indistinct; and at each passage into the gloom, there fell from her a darker shade, which became whelmed in a shadow more black. But at length, when the sun had utterly departed, the Fay, now the mere ghost of her former self, went disconsolately with her boat into the region of the ebony flood—and that she issued thence at all I cannot say,—for darkness fell over all things, and I beheld her magical figure no more.

Spenser's island resembles the islands of the Celts—very different in substance and effect from those in the lost Atlantis, the Hesperides, or that island mentioned by Rabelais where Pantagruel bought 'three fine young Unicorns; one of them a Male of a Chesnut colour, and two grey dappled Females':

> . . . That Day and the two following, they neither discovered Land nor any thing new . . . but on the fourth they made an Island call'd Medamothy, of a fine and delightful Prospect, by reason of the vast number of Light-houses and high Marble Towers in its Circuit.

Maeldun's, for example, of the eighth century, whose adventures are recorded in a manuscript written about 1100, entitled *The Book of the Dun Cow*. Many were the islands he saw or skirted or landed on during his long voyage to avenge the murder of his father, Ailil of the Owens of Arran. Heedless of the bidding laid upon him by the wizard who sent him on his way, he had turned back in his great curragh, which was manned by sixty seamen, to save from drowning his three foster-brothers—so eager to accompany him that in despair they had dived into the sea and swum out after him. So it chances that when, drawing landward, he actually sets eyes on the reaver he is in pursuit of, a wind of wizardry begins to blow and sweeps him out to sea.

There seems to be some inward meaning in the wild fantasy of this romance. But what? Whether this is so or not, its islands belong to a world of which at times we are clearly aware and wherein we are at home though it is assuredly not the world of our workaday senses:—the isle of the prodigious ants active as goats upon its sands; the isle of the gigantic horses swifter than the wind; of the house with the stone door into the sea; of the magic apples; of the fiery swine in their subterranean sties; of the miller of hell at his mill door; of the spouting fountain whose waters, arched like a rainbow, stretch east to west from strand to strand; and, in particular, the isle of the eagles and the isle of the little cat that leaps in sublime heedlessness of these sea-strangers from one to the other of the four pillars in the vast hall of the greatest of the cloud-capped enormous houses, white as snow, its walls hung round with the bright weapons and armour and quilts and raiment of warriors who have apparently been feasting there—all these, though of another day and another mind and of another state of being, are still not alien to us:

The sea laments
The livelong day
Fringing its waste of sand;
Cries back the wind from the whispering shore—
No words I understand:

Yet echoes in my heart a voice,
As far, as near, as these—
The wind that weeps,
The solemn surge
Of strange and lonely seas.

The hundred treeless Shetlands too—Unst, Fetla, Foula, Yell and the rest—are not wholly of the earth earthy. They harbour their own species of fairy; while on Pomona of the Orkneys lurk Tang, and Luridan, its *genius Astral*, who in the days of Solomon was in Jerusalem. The island of Rügen, again. It is mounded with nine hills, and therein flourish the three orders of the dwarfs, the white, the brown and the black, also the little Troll people of the dunes.

Like the Islands of the Blessed, like the Fortunate Isles, these islands of fantasy lie amid seas not only distant in time and space, but of a water that resembles ichor, it being a something between the material and the immaterial. It is not so wet to the touch as common seawater, and is of the temperature of new milk. They are islands without longitude or latitude. They may be 'there' when one's age is seven, or even three times seven, and gone when it is forty-nine. And to those who have never raised visionary eyes in their direction they are as obscure and mysterious as the 'Yd laman Satanaxio', and as little like actuality as that O'Brasile in search of which Spain sent her galleons (and the Indians their braves), in hope to discover the waters of the Fountain of Perpetual Youth. Captain Rich sailed so near this O'Brasile that he sighted a harbour, but a mist came down on him and he failed to make the land.

Once, all such islands—a corrupt word which should not in this connection, at any rate, be so spelt, but a choice be made between *eland, ealond, ilond, illond, yllonde, ylond, ylande* and *hylyn*—however perilous they might be to track down, were believed to be truly terrestrial and real. To-day only one's ghost stares out of its ivory tower in their direction. What, then, and where is that 'inward eye' with which we regard, for example, Avilion?

> Where falls not hail, or rain, or any snow,
> Nor ever wind blows loudly; but it lies
> Deep-meadow'd, happy, fair with orchard lawns
> And bowery hollows crown'd with summer sea . . .

Those bowery hollows seem—though individual seers may differ—to be more easily discernible (either voluntarily or involuntarily) when one's *outward* eyes are open rather than shut. But whether this seeing involves a change of focus in the outward eye it is difficult to decide. It certainly involves a withdrawal of the mind's attention from the objects reflected on the retina, a withdrawal which may be momentary or protracted.

What, again, is the difference between the object visible to the inward eye (a) when it has been retrieved from memory, and (b) when it is purely imaginary? In dream, too, which eyes are we using? But whatever psychology has to say on these and similar questions, Sancho Panza's Barataria is more after most men's hearts than any hylyn of those mentioned above, though Barataria too is no less fabulous than the rest.

Page 69[6]—I dare not go back:
¶ Nor can I remember the name or even the sex of the author of this amiable story. My impression is that it was of feminine workmanship; and the possibility of that sets

one speculating whether small *girls* and their elders ever share the odd infatuation of small boys and *their* elders for desert islands and Crusoes. One cannot escape the misgiving that really 'sensible' women at any rate might deal with all this truck about islands much as if it were the rubbish left behind him by a schoolboy gone back to school. Women are not only less solitary beings than men, but far less likely to see any use in the useless. And yet when I think of these mothers and sisters and wives neglecting Crusoe, a voice within me cries in despair, Oh that there had been one—but one soul saved!

Yet another saddening reflection arises. What does the small boy of our own day, glutted with talkies and 'comics' and a literary diet minced as fine as mince will mince, feel about Crusoe? I should tremble to enquire.

Page 70¹—Unbroken solitude:
❡ What *is* this being alone, this condition we call solitude? It is a state of many degrees, affecting both mind and spirit, of which one must be conscious and aware, for bodily sleep however isolated is not a condition of solitude.

We enter a room and shut the door; all other inmates of the house being out of sight, if not of hearing. There let us sit awhile as motionlessly as life permits, and let us die away into ourselves and be as passive as a glass-clear pool of water reflecting only the mantling swans and the flowers and the trees on its margin and the blue overhead. Leaving all comparison, all association and memories aside, let us then keep open house to all around us—these objects, as if we had never set eyes on them before, a sparrow chirping, a cock crowing, a horse's hoofs, a distant motor-horn. This is one degree of solitude.

Now let us shut our eyes and seal our ears as near as may be; and let the whole house around us, every room of it, every nook, corner and shadowy corridor, moon-lit, or by Sirius gazed upon, become a mere shadowland, silent, vacant—no sound, not even a clock's ticking, or the *wowgh* of a distant dog. All vacant, empty—and the self a mere conscious phantasm, sensible only of an irreducible minimum of physical contacts, and of that internal spangly gloom described by Keats. Then darkness and an intense awareness. This is another degree of solitude. 'When', says Prof. Eddington, in *The Nature of the Physical World*, 'I close my eyes and retreat into my inner mind, I feel myself *enduring*, I do not feel myself *extensive*. It is difficult to make sure, and still more difficult to protract the experiment: Something unknown is doing we don't know what'.

There is, too, a state of the mind (all else normal), at the coming on of which and with no warning, the demon of the egocentric may skulk in and cross his shank bones at the hearthside. Then we are alone indeed, for everything in the world of the now, the hitherto solidly actual, the alive and responsive, the near and dear, has faded away into mere shades and appearances, become unreal, untrustworthy, a 'set piece'. Then north, south, east and west, the past and the future, are only directions for the gaze of the I.

What degrees of sensitiveness most intensify solitude? That wretched man in Joseph Conrad's *Nostromo* hanging strappadoed from the roof-beam in the great gallery was left alone; and he was in pain. Jane Eyre in her childhood was left alone in Mrs. Reed's great bedroom; and she was frenzied with fear. But even when alone on the verge of the grave, not yet blind or deaf, but dumb and almost touch-proof, a man may be vividly and nicely observant. For still the little flame of consciousness may burn clear and small in the bony lantern.

Indeed, how—with all memory's old voices, reminders, warnings, evocations, callings, fragments of music, siren voices, the past years' birds and one's childhood—how is it possible, is it conceivable, ever to be quite alone at all, ever to be a complete and yet all-hospitable nought? A sort of nought, but one which, even at that, could not but still be pining for some other strange, inscrutable presence to slip in before that cipher, and make of its nothing all.

'Solitarinesse, mee seemeth,' says Montaigne, 'hath more appar-ance and reason in those which have given their most active and flourishing age into the world, in imitation of Thales. We have lived long enough for others, live we the remainder of our life unto our selves; let us bring home our cogitations and inventions unto our selves and unto our ease. It is no easie matter to make a safe retreit: it doth over-much trouble us with joyning other enterprises unto it; since God gives us leasure to dispose of our dislodging. Let us prepare ourselves unto it, packe wee up our baggage. Let us betimes bid our companie farewell. Shake we off these violent holdfasts which else-where engage us, and estrange us from our selves. These so strong bonds must be untied, and a man must eftsoones love this or that, but wed nothing but himselfe; That is to say, let the rest be our owne: yet not so combined and glued together that it may not be sundred without fleaing us, and therewithall pull away some peece of our owne. The greatest thing of the world is for a man to know how to be his owne. It is high time to shake of societie, since we can bring nothing to it. And he that cannot lend, let him take heed of borrow-ing. Our forces faile us: retire we then, and shut them up into our selves. He that can suppresse and confound in himselfe the offices of so many amities, and of the company, let him doe it. In this fall, which makes us inutile, irkesome, and importunate to others, let him take heed he be not importunate, irkesome, and unprofitable to himselfe. Let him flatter, court, and cherish himselfe, and above all let him governe himselfe, respecting his reason and fearing his conscience, so that he may not without shame stumble or trip in their pre-sence. . . .'

Page 70²—Four years' silence:
❡ Nothing outrageous seems to have edged into the mind of Henry Welby, who solely on account of his solitary habits has found a niche in the Dictionary of National Biography.

Henry Welby, a native of Lincolnshire, was born in 1552, and in-herited a clear estate of more than 1,000l. a year. He was regularly bred at the University, and studied some time in one of the Inns of Court. He afterwards spent several years in the Low Countries, Germany, France, and Spain. When he returned he settled on his paternal estate, and lived with great hospitality, respected by the rich, prayed for by the poor, and honoured and beloved by all. Here he married, and had a daughter, who was afterwards led to the hymeneal altar by Sir Christopher Hilliard, a baronet in Yorkshire.

At the age of forty, a younger brother, with whom he had some difference of opinion, meeting him in the field, snapped a pistol at him, which fortunately, however, flashed in the pan. Thinking this was only done to frighten him, he coolly disarmed the ruffian, and putting the weapon carelessly into his pocket, thoughtfully returned home; on examination, he discovered that the pistol was charged with more than one bullet, and this circumstance had such an effect upon his mind, that he instantly formed the extraordinary resolution of retiring entirely from the world, in which he inflexibly persisted till the end of his life.

In the year 1592 he accordingly came to London, and took a neat house at the lower end of Grub Street, near Cripplegate. This house he prepared for the purpose, and contracting a numerous retinue into a small family, he selected [not unlike Alexander Selkirk] three chambers for himself, one for eating, another for sleeping, and the other for a study. As they were one within another, while his repast was set on the table by an old maid, he retired into his bedchamber, when his bed was making, into his study, till the rooms were clear. From these chambers he never issued till he was carried out, forty-four years afterwards, to his grave; during which time, no person ever saw him, except his servant Elizabeth, and she only in cases of necessity, although she cleaned his rooms and provided his food.

During the whole of his retirement, his chief food was oatmeal gruel, or occasionally in summer a salad of cool herbs, or the yolk of a hen's egg, but not the white, and what bread he ate he cut out of the middle, never tasting the crust. His constant drink was beer, excepting at times his servant Elizabeth fetched him some milk hot from the cow; yet he kept a bountiful table for his servants, and sufficient entertainment for any stranger or tenant who had business at his house. Every book that was printed was bought for him, but such as related to controversy he laid aside and never read.

At Christmas, Easter, and other holidays, he had all dishes in season provided and served up in his own chamber, when, having returned thanks to God, he would put a clean napkin before him, and putting on a pair of white holland sleeves, which reached to his elbows, and cutting them up dish after dish, would send them to different poor neighbours, till the table was quite empty; and then, without tasting any thing whatever himself, caused the cloth to be taken away. This formality he invariably practised, with both dinner and supper, on those days. He kept a kind of perpetual fast, and devoted himself to continual prayer and study. He was both a scholar and a linguist, and left behind him some collections and translations of philosophy. . . .

This singular, but benevolent and exemplary character, died while sitting in a chair, at his house in Grub Street, after a confinement of forty-four years, October the 29th, 1636, aged eighty-four years. At his death, his hair and beard were so overgrown, that he appeared

265

rather like a hermit of the wilderness, than the inhabitant of one of the first cities in the world. His remains were interred in St. Giles's Church, Cripplegate.

This relapse into the hairy appears to be one of the distressing but inevitable consequences of becoming a hermit —either in life or in literature. When even the passing of time becomes unnoticeable, so must much else. I remember being impressed as a child by the gloomy information that one's hair and nails may continue to grow even in one's coffin. It was, then, perhaps for his readers' sake that Defoe supplied Crusoe with scissors and razors to keep his moustachios trimmed. Man's proper vanity wages a livelong conflict with nature's prodigality in this respect; and woman's too. But solitude frets away at last even vanity.

Sarah Bishop, for example—'a young Salem lady of considerable beauty'—disgusted with man, retired in the eighteenth century into complete solitude at the age of twenty-seven. She lived for three-and-twenty years without even the company of hen or cat or dog—and in a cave or rocky cleft in the mountains, near which she had a little plantation of peach trees, beans, cucumbers, potatoes and vines.

There, in November, 1804, 'we found this wonderful woman, whose appearance it is rather difficult to describe; indeed, like nature in its first state, she was without form—that is, she appeared in no form or position I had ever seen before; her dress appeared little else but one confused and shapeless mass of rags, patched together without any order, obscuring all appearance of human shape, excepting her head, which was clothed with a luxuriancy of lank grey hair, depending on every side just as nature and time had formed it, without any kind of artificial covering or ornament whatever'.

At sight of strangers this lonely soul scuttled off like a wild and timid animal into her cave. None the less her visitors talked

'with her a considerable time, found her to be of a sound mind, a religious turn of thought, and entirely happy and contented with her situation. . . . We saw no utensil, either for labour or cookery, except an old pewter bason, and a gourd-shell; no bed but the solid rock, unless it were a few old rags, scattered here and there upon it;

on bed-clothes of any kind; nor the least appearance of any sort of food, and no fire.

'She had, indeed, a place in one corner of her cell, where she kindled a fire at times, but it did not appear that any fire had been kindled there that year. To confirm this opinion, a gentleman said that he passed her cell five or six days after a great fall of snow in the beginning of March, that she had no fire then, and had not been out of her cave since the snow had fallen. . . .

'She kept a Bible with her, and said she took much satisfaction, and spent much time in reading and meditating on its pages. It may be this woman was a sincere worshipper of God; if so, she was yet more rich, wise, and happy, than thousands in affluence and honour, who beheld her with astonishment and scorn. . . .'

Robert Burton first beautifies the prospect, and then:

Voluntary solitariness is that which is familiar with melancholy, and gently brings on like a syren, a shoeing-horn, or some sphinx to this irrevocable gulf—a primary cause, Piso calls it. Most pleasant it is at first, to such as are melancholy given, to lie in bed whole days, and keep their chambers, to walk alone in some solitary grove, betwixt wood and water, by a brook side, to meditate upon some delightsome and pleasant subject, which shall affect them most; *amabilis insania, et mentis gratissimus error:* a most incomparable delight it is so to melancholize, and build castles in the air, to go smiling to themselves, acting an infinite variety of parts, which they suppose and strongly imagine they represent, or that they see acted or done. . . .

So delightsome these toys are at first, they could spend whole days and nights without sleep, even whole years alone in such contemplations, and fantastical meditations, which are like unto dreams, and they will hardly be drawn from them, or willingly interrupt, so pleasant their vain conceits are, that they hinder their ordinary tasks and necessary business, they cannot address themselves to them, or almost to any study or employment, these fantastical and bewitching thoughts so covertly, so feelingly, so urgently, so continually set upon, creep in, insinuate, possess, overcome, distract, and detain them, they cannot, I say, go about their more necessary business, stave off or extricate themselves, but are ever musing, melancholizing, and carried along . . . winding and unwinding themselves, as so many clocks, and still pleasing their humours, until at last the scene is turned upon a sudden. . . .

Fear, sorrow, suspicion, *subrusticus pudor,* discontent, cares, and weariness of life surprise them in a moment, and they can think of nothing else, continually suspecting, no sooner are their eyes open, but this infernal plague of melancholy seizeth on them, and terrifies their souls. . . .

267

Burton actually ends, too, his great book on melancholy (and everything else) with a piece of counsel so grave in tone that it amounts to a solemn warning:

I can say no more or give better advice. . . . Only take this for a corollary and conclusion, as thou tenderest thine own welfare in this ['religious'] and all other melancholy, thy good health of body and mind, observe this short precept, Give not way to solitariness and idleness. 'Be not solitary, be not idle.' . . . 'Be penitent whilst rational:' by so doing I assert that you are safe. . . .

Page 71[1]—There are islands of many kinds:
¶ This one, for example, taken from Mr. Visiak's *Medusa*.

There was in farthest antiquity a very large and fertile island lying in those parts of the ocean which are off the south side of the island of Ceylon; the inhabitants whereof, like to those of the huge island of *Atlantis*, of which Plato writes in his *Timaeus*, were in the first times exceeding prosperous and wise, and of an upright and noble mind, but afterwards fell off from virtue and declined from wisdom.

They enjoyed at first such a divine infusion of super-eminent vision as cannot be imagined, having converse with that bright world whereof this is but a shadow. They did behold the forms, or bodies of things through their essential irradiations; thus much more gloriously substantial. They looked not outwards upon the infinite one way, as from a window, but every way, inwards, as from an aereal sphere; and the utterless sweet fragrance and lively, fair, glowing colours of things were the raiment and element of their enchanted souls.

Love they knew, one with another, without obstacle of corporeal bars: they mingled soul with soul in virtual union, total harmony. Their affections were of the sun; they knew not, nor had occasion to know, its terrestrial and corrosive compound, fire.

But, in the process of time, this pure and original temper of their souls began to change. Their direct vision with which they enjoyed felicity (for true perception is meeting and union), was turned outwards, and their senses, become mortal, presented to them, instead of real things, but their false and finite shadows. They grew into the likeness of their hearts' imagination. . . .

Page 71[2]—Solitudes of sundry degrees:
¶ E.g. this of the man of science, as it is described in Prof. A. S. Eddington's *The Nature of the Physical World:*

I am standing on the threshold about to enter a room. It is a complicated business. In the first place I must shove against an atmosphere pressing with a force of fourteen pounds on every square inch of my body. I must make sure of landing on a plank travelling at twenty miles a second round the sun—a fraction of a second too early or too late, the plank, would be miles away. I must do this whilst hanging from a round planet head outward into space, and with a wind of aether blowing at no one knows how many miles a second through every interstice of my body. The plank has no solidity of substance. To step on it is like stepping on a swarm of flies. Shall I not slip through? No, if I make the venture one of the flies hits me and gives a boost up again; I fall again and am knocked upwards by another fly; and so on. I may hope that the net result will be that I remain about steady; but if unfortunately I should slip through the floor or be boosted too violently up to the ceiling, the occurrence would be, not a violation of the laws of Nature, but a rare coincidence. These are some of the minor difficulties. I ought really to look at the problem four-dimensionally as concerning the intersection of my world-line with that of the plank. Then again it is necessary to determine in which direction the entropy of the world is increasing in order to make sure that my passage over the threshold is an entrance, not an exit.

Verily, it is easier for a camel to pass through the eye of a needle than for a scientific man to pass through a door. And whether the door be barn door or church door it might be wiser that he should consent to be an ordinary man and walk in rather than wait till all the difficulties involved in a really scientific ingress are resolved.

There is the solitude of the self within when news comes—as it did without warning to John Keats—that life on earth is nearing its end. Dr. Johnson was alone on the night of June 16th, 1783, when he was aroused out of sleep by a 'dreadful stroke of the palsy'. On the following morning he sent a brief message to Edmund Allen, the landlord of his house in Bow Court—'a worthy obliging man and his very old acquaintance'—who 'though he was of a very diminutive size used, even in Johnson's presence, to imitate the stately periods and slow and solemn utterance of the great man':

Dear Sir,

It has pleased God, this morning, to deprive me of the powers of speech; and as I do not know but that it may be his farther good pleasure to deprive me soon of my senses, I request you will, on the receipt of this note, come to me, and act for me, as the exigencies of my case may require.

I am, sincerely yours,

Sam. Johnson.

Two days afterwards he wrote to Mrs. Thrale:

On Monday, the 16th, I sat for my picture, and walked a considerable way with little inconvenience. In the afternoon and evening I
felt myself light and easy, and began to plan schemes of life. Thus I
went to bed, and in a short time waked and sat up, as has been long
my custom, when I felt a confusion and indistinctness in my head,
which lasted, I suppose, about half a minute. I was alarmed, and
prayed God, that however he might afflict my body, he would spare
my understanding. This prayer, that I might try the integrity of my
faculties, I made in Latin verse. The lines were not very good, but
I knew them not to be very good: I made them easily, and concluded
myself to be unimpaired in my faculties.

Soon after I perceived that I had suffered a paralytic stroke, and
that my speech was taken from me. I had no pain, and so little
dejection in this dreadful state, that I wondered at my own apathy,
and considered that perhaps death itself, when it should come,
would excite less horrour than seems now to attend it.

In order to rouse the vocal organs, I took two drams. Wine has
been celebrated for the production of eloquence. I put myself into
violent motion, and I think repeated it; but all was in vain. I then
went to bed, and strange as it may seem, I think slept. When I saw
light, it was time to contrive what I should do. Though God stopped
my speech, he left me my hand; I enjoyed a mercy which was not
granted to my dear friend Lawrence, who now perhaps overlooks
me as I am writing, and rejoices that I have what he wanted. My
first note was necessarily to my servant, who came in talking, and
could not immediately comprehend why he should read what I put
into his hands.

I then wrote a card to Mr. Allen, that I might have a discreet
friend at hand, to act as occasion should require. In penning this
note, I had some difficulty; my hand, I knew not how nor why,
made wrong letters. I then wrote to Dr. Taylor to come to me, and
bring Dr. Heberden; and I sent to Dr. Brocklesby, who is my neighbour. My physicians are very friendly, and give me great hopes; but
you may imagine my situation. I have so far recovered my vocal
powers as to repeat the Lord's Prayer with no very imperfect articu-
lation. My memory, I hope, yet remains as it was: but such an attack
produces solicitude for the safety of every faculty.

Cowper's poem, *The Castaway*, with its tragic last two
stanzas, was written when, after the death of Mrs. Un-
win, and with his two nearest friends too ill to see him,
his solitude of mind and spirit was at an even sharper
extreme. He had been reading Anson's *Voyages*, and had

270

found his theme in its pages. Throughout the poem there is not a thought or word—except of his despair—distorted or amiss. Yet at this time 'he firmly believed that good and evil spirits haunted his couch every night, and that the latter had the mastery'. He suspected those around him, and for dreadful reasons. He affirmed of a young kinsman of his that he was not one being, but two: one the real man, the other an evil spirit in his shape. And when Cowper came out of his room in the morning, this friend confessed, 'he used to look me full in the face enquiringly, and turn off with a look of benevolence or anguish, as he thought me a man or a devil'.

Jude—'the obscure'—was alone when he died:

It was a warm, cloudless, enticing day. She shut the front door and hastened round into Chief Street, and when near the Theatre could hear the notes of the organ, a rehearsal for a coming concert being in progress. . . .

The powerful notes of that concert rolled forth through the swinging yellow blinds of the open windows, over the housetops, and into the still air of the lanes. They reached far as to the room in which Jude lay; and it was about this time that his cough began again and awakened him.

As soon as he could speak he murmured, his eyes still closed: 'A little water, please.'

Nothing but the deserted room received his appeal, and he coughed to exhaustion again—saying still more feebly: 'Water—some water —Sue—darling—drop of water—please—O please!'

No water came, and the organ notes, faint as a bee's hum, rolled in as before.

While he remained, his face changing, shouts and hurrahs came from somewhere in the direction of the river.

'Ah—yes! The Remembrance games,' he murmured. 'And I here. And Sue defiled!'

The hurrahs were repeated, drowning the faint organ notes. Jude's face changed more: he whispered slowly, his lips scarcely moving:

'*Let the day perish wherein I was born, and the night in which it was said, There is a man child conceived.*'

('Hurrah!')

'*Let that day be darkness; let not God regard it from above, neither let the light shine upon it. Lo, let that night be solitary; let no joyful voice come therein.*'

('Hurrah!')

271

'Why died I not from the womb? Why did I not give up the ghost when I came out of the belly? . . . For now should I have lain still and been quiet. I should have slept: then had I been at rest!'

('Hurrah!')

And John Clare was alone when, a 'harmless lunatic' —'I am very weary of being here'—he wrote his last poems in the asylum at Northampton:

> I AM: yet what I am none cares or knows,
>   My friends forsake me like a memory lost;
> I am the self-consumer of my woes,
>   They rise and vanish in oblivious host,
> Like shades in love and death's oblivion lost;
> And yet I am, and live with shadows tost
>
> Into the nothingness of scorn and noise,
>   Into the living sea of waking dreams,
> Where there is neither sense of life nor joys,
>   But the vast shipwreck of my life's esteems;
> And een the dearest—that I loved the best—
> Are strange—nay, they are stranger than the rest.
>
> I long for scenes where man has never trod;
>   A place where woman never smiled or wept;
> There to abide with my Creator, God,
>   And sleep as I in childhood sweetly slept:
> Untroubling and untroubled where I lie;
> The grass below—above the vaulted sky.

Page 71³—❡ The self within hovers over the envied ashes:

Because I do not hope to turn again
Because I do not hope
Because I do not hope to turn
Desiring this man's gift and that man's scope
I no longer strive to strive towards such things
(Why should the agèd eagle stretch its wings?)
Why should I mourn
The vanished power of the usual reign?

Because I do not hope to know again
The infirm glory of the positive hour
Because I do not think
Because I know I shall not know
The one veritable transitory power
Because I cannot drink
There, where trees flower, and springs flow, for there is nothing again
Because I know that time is always time

And place is always and only place
And what is actual is actual only for one time
And only for one place
I rejoice that things are as they are and
I renounce the blessèd face
And renounce the voice
Because I cannot hope to turn again
Consequently I rejoice, having to construct something
Upon which to rejoice

And pray to God to have mercy upon us
And I pray that I may forget
These matters that with myself I too much discuss
Too much explain
Because I do not hope to turn again
Let these words answer
For what is done, not to be done again
May the judgement not be too heavy upon us

Because these wings are no longer wings to fly
But merely vans to beat the air
The air which is now thoroughly small and dry
Smaller and dryer than the will
Teach us to care and not to care
Teach us to sit still.

Pray for us sinners now and at the hour of our death
Pray for us now and at the hour of our death. . . . T. S. Eliot.

Page 71⁴—St. Anthony:

¶ In his life of this saint, St. Athanasius records:

He was not terrified at the devils, he was not wearied by the desert, and his soul had no fear of the wild beasts which were therein; but Satan suffered torture from all these things. And one day he came to the blessed man who was singing the Psalms of David, and he gnashed his teeth upon him loudly; but the blessed Anthony ceased not to sing, and he was comforted and helped by the grace of our Lord. One night whilst he was standing up and was watching in prayer, Satan gathered together all the wild beasts of the desert, and brought them against him, and they were so many in number that he can hardly have left one beast in its den; and as they compassed him about on every side, and with threatening looks were ready to leap upon him, he looked at them boldly and said unto them, 'If ye have received power over me from the Lord, draw nigh, and delay not, for I am ready for you; but if ye have made ready and come at the command of Satan, get ye back to your places and tarry not, for

I am a servant of Jesus the Conqueror.' And when the blessed man had spoken these words, Satan was straightway driven away by the mention of the Name of Christ like a sparrow before a hawk.

When St. Anthony had become famous throughout Egypt a multitude of people came to him and besought him to reveal himself to them and to hear their petitions:

And he having gone forth to them even like a man who goeth forth from the depths of the earth, they saw that his appearance was like unto that of an angel of light, and they marvelled why it was that his body had not been weakened by all his confinement, and why it was that his understanding had not become feeble, and why, on the contrary, his appearance, and his bodily stature, and his countenance were then as they had known them always to have been in the times which were past.

When the governor of the country in which he dwelt

did homage to him, and begged him to remain with him for a day or two, the old man entreated him courteously to be allowed to depart, saying, 'This thing is impossible, for as fish die if a man lift them out of the water, so, if we monks prolong our stay with men, do our minds become perverted and troubled; therefore it is meet that as fish pass their lives beneath the waters we also should let our lives and works be buried in the wilderness'.

At his death when he had given directions that his body should not be embalmed but hidden under the earth,

he straightway stretched out his legs, whereupon the brethren began to cry out [to him], and to kiss him; now his face was full of joy unspeakable at the meeting of those who had come for him, and it resembled that of a man when he seeth a friend whom it rejoiceth him to meet. So the blessed man held his peace and died, and was gathered to his fathers.

That strange and uninvited guests are likely to intrude on any protracted human solitude there seems to be little doubt. What stuff they are made on is another matter. Not that by any means what is most 'real' to us is necessarily either substantial or substantiable.

Among the hermits in the sands of Egypt there was a man of Palestine named Valens. He dwelt in the desert many years and grew arrogant. One day as he was working in the dark with the labour of his hands the needle wherewith he was sewing together the palm leaves fell down on the ground, and although he searched for it he could not find it; and a devil lit a fire for him until he found it, and because of this thing he became the more proud, and having reached the summit of his pride,

that devil, who had completely led him astray, went and made unto himself a form wherein he resembled our Redeemer; and he came unto him by night, together with phantoms of angels in great numbers who marched along bearing lamps and wax candles, and they advanced with chariots and carriages of fire, as if that devil were Christ Himself. Then one of the angels came forward unto him, and said unto him, 'Christ loveth greatly thy life and deeds, and thy boldness of speech, and He hath come to see thee. Get thee forth from thy cell, and do nothing whatsoever except such things as I shall tell thee. When thou seest Him afar off fall down and worship Him, and go back to thy cell.' Now therefore when Valens had gone forth and seen the ranks of phantoms bearing lamps of fire, and Antichrist himself sitting upon a chariot of fire—now he was distant from him about a mile—he fell down and worshipped him. And Valens was so much injured in his mind that at the turn of the day he was sufficiently mad to come into the church and to say before all the brotherhood who were assembled therein, 'I have no need to become a partaker in the offering, for this day I have seen Christ Himself'. Then the fathers tied him up and put iron fetters upon him for about the space of one year, and in this way they made him whole; and he was praying continually, and they humbled him and brought him down from the exalted conception which he held concerning himself by means of sundry and divers works of a lovely and humble character, and thus they rooted out from him pride, even as it is written, 'Each opposing sickness must be healed by medicines which are contrary and opposite thereto'.

Eustathius, too, drank to the dregs the cup of solitude.

This man followed so strenuously after the acquisition of impassibility, and made his body so dry (i.e. emaciated) by the labours of vigilant prayer, that the light of the sun could be seen between his ribs. And of him the following story is told by the brethren who were continually with him, that is to say his disciples: he never turned himself towards the west, because close by the side of the door of his cave was a mountain which, because of its mighty bulk, was very hard to ascend; and he never looked at the sun after the sixth hour of the day, because the door of his cell was hidden by the shadow of the mountain so long as the sun was declining towards its place of setting. And moreover he could never see those stars which appear in the western part of the sky, and for five and twenty years from the time when he entered the cave wherein he dwelt he never went down from the mountain.

But the same end awaited all:

And a certain brother came to the monks who lived in that spot wherein there were twelve wells of water, and seventy palm trees, where Moses and the people of Israel encamped when they went forth from Egypt, and that brother told them the following story, saying: 'I once had it in my mind to go into the inner desert and see if there was any man living therein, and I went a journey of four days and four nights, and found a certain cave; and having approached it I looked inside and saw a man sitting therein, and I knocked at the door according to the custom of the monks, so that he might come out to me, and I might salute him, but he never moved, for he was dead. Now I did not hesitate or draw back, but I went in and laid my hand upon his shoulders, and he crumbled into dust and became nothing at all; and in wonderment I came out of that place and journeyed on again in the desert.'

As for the visions, apart from the apparitions, which may enlighten extreme solitude, we know a little but not much. But the vision of the *Revelation* came to a recluse upon an island:

. . . And I beheld when he had opened the sixth seal, and, lo, there was a great earthquake; and the sun became black as sackcloth of hair, and the moon became as blood; and the stars of heaven fell unto the earth, even as a fig tree casteth her untimely figs, when she is shaken of a mighty wind.

And the heaven departed as a scroll when it is rolled together; and every mountain and island were moved out of their places.

And the kings of the earth, and the great men, and the rich men, and the chief captains, and the mighty men, and every bondman, and every free man, hid themselves in the dens and in the rocks of the mountains; and said to the mountains and rocks, Fall on us, and hide us from the face of him that sitteth on the throne, and from the wrath of the Lamb: For the great day of his wrath is come; and who shall be able to stand? . . .

Page 71⁵—Crusoe came back:

¶ *His* island constituted for its inmate solitude, but hardly solitary confinement. For fifteen years, before Friday joined him, he had shared the company of living things though not of man—fish and seal, goat, insect and bird, and of that peculiar kind of bird, too, which, pert and docile of tongue, intimates even more than most of us by its natural appearance the possession of the wisdom of Solomon himself. And no one who has ever been alone will deny what the companionship of *any* living creature can mean. A sleeping cat—even a ticking clock. That insanity or savagery is likely to be the exit of a wild and prolonged solitude seems to have been definitely proved. But in wholesome surroundings why should this dreadful pining continue? Selkirk grew accustomed to solitude, 'without seeing the face of Man'. The frenzied desire for human companionship dwindled and vanished. He 'looked' wild when found, but Steele suggests nothing insane.

Perhaps the majority of us nowadays spend most of our time on the conscious surface of our minds; we even reason about our instincts, and taste everything before we eat of it. Yet one can conceive of an existence without much active thought in it, yet not without joy in the passing hour and not without inward company; an existence wherein body and mind might be in a rare and beautiful accord, and the spirit at peace with Him who made it. This might not be the kind of life which would be approved of by our masters of industry, our censors or our newspapers, or that which is aimed at by our public schools, but it might nevertheless be harmless and even useful, serene and at times enraptured.

Page 72[1]—*In Ropemaker's Alley:*

⁋ It suggests a dark and sinister lodging in which to die. But this was not so. Moorfields was then in open country, and in 1710 a house—neither dark nor sinister—was advertised to be let in this very alley:

In Rope-Maker's Alley . . . is a very sweet and large house to be lett. The Drawing Room and Parlour well Wainscotted to the Top. A good Wash-house and Chamber over it in case of Sickness, or other Occasions. With a very large Garden Wall'd in and well Planted, the Walks well Gravell'd; the house stands alone by itself, in the midst of pleasant Gardens. 'Tis fit for a Gentleman of a considerable Family.
. . .

May such a chamber as this have been the last to fade from out of Defoe's eyes?

His last days had been full of affliction. On August 12th, 1730, he wrote to his son-in-law, Henry Baker, his 'dearest Sophia's' husband:

Dear Mr. Baker,

I have yor very kind and affecc'onate Letter of the 1st: . . . it would be a greater comfort to me than any I now enjoy, that I could have yor agreeable visits wth safety, and could see both you and my dearest Sophia, could it be without giving her ye grief of seeing her father *in tenebris*, and under ye load of insupportable sorrows. I am sorry I must open my griefs so far as to tell her, it is not ye blow I rec^d from a wicked, perjur'd, and contemptible enemy, that has broken in upon my spirit; wch as she well knows, has carryed me on thro' greater disasters than these. But it has been the injustice, unkindness, and, I must say, inhuman dealing of my own son, wch has both ruined my family, and, in a word, has broken my heart; and as I am at this time under a weight of very heavy illness, wch I think will be a fever, I take this occasion to vent my grief in ye breasts who I know will make a prudent use of it, and tell you, that nothing but this has conquered or could conquer me. *Et tu! Brute.* I depended upon him, I trusted him, I gave up my two dear unprovided children into his hands; but he has no compassion, and suffers them and their poor dying mother to beg their bread at his door, and to crave, as if it were an alms, what he is bound under hand and seal, besides the most sacred promises, to supply them with; himself, at ye same time, living in a profusion of plenty. It is too much for me. Excuse my infirmity, I can say no more; my heart is too full. I only ask one thing of you as a dying request. Stand by them when I am gone, and let them not be wrong'd. . . .

I have not seen son or daughter, wife or child, many weeks, and kno' not which way to see them. They dare not come by water, and by land here is no coach, and I kno' not what to do.

It is not possible for me to come to Enfield, unless you could find a retired lodging for me, where I might not be known, and might have the comfort of seeing you both now and then; upon such a circumstance, I could gladly give the days to solitude, to have the comfort of half an hour now and then, with you both, for two or three weeks. But just to come and look at you, and retire immediately, 'tis a burden too heavy. The parting will be a price beyond the enjoyment.

I would say, (I hope) with comfort, that 'tis yet well. I am so near my journey's end, and am hastening to the place where ye weary are at rest, and where the wicked cease to trouble; be it that the passage is rough, and the day stormy, by what way soever He please to bring me to the end of it, I desire to finish life with this temper of soul in all cases: *Te Deum laudamus*. . . .

It adds to my grief that I must never see the pledge of your mutual love, my little grandson. Give him my blessing, and may he be to you both your joy in youth, and your comfort in age, and never add a sigh to your sorrow. But, alas! that is not to be expected. Kiss my dear Sophy once more for me; and if I must see her no more, tell her this is from a father that loved her above all his comforts, to his last breath.

Yo^r unhappy,

D.F.

Even Defoe's enemies might have been moved by that. There were qualities in his mind and character that are not considered to be among those most appropriate to the typical John Bull, but in genius he was a signally English *writer*. And though, in his day, the antithesis between London and the country had not reached the absurd extreme it has in ours, he was also a true Londoner. He was born (? 1661) within hearing of Bow Bells, at Moorfields, in the parish of St. Giles's, Cripplegate, 'once the resort of archers, washerwomen and (later) of booksellers'. In the church of St. Giles's Oliver Cromwell was married, and there lie John Milton, John Speed and John Foxe. There, too, rests Thomas Stagg, whose epitaph closes, as all epitomes of life must, with 'That is all'.

In Bunhill Fields (originally called Tindall's Burial Ground), under an obelisk bought and paid for in 1870 by the boys and girls of England, Defoe shares the same soil with John Bunyan, Dr. Watts and the mother of Charles Wesley, while the bones of George Fox lie not very far distant.

In Stoke Newington—and Thomas Day of *Sandford & Merton* and John Howard are among its other literary associations—Defoe as a small boy went to school, 'a dissenting academy'. So did Edgar Allan Poe about a century and a half after him. Now 'mainly occupied by small villas', it was in Poe's childhood

279

a misty-looking village of England, where were a vast number of gigantic and gnarled trees, and where all the houses were excessively ancient. In truth, it was a dream-like and spirit-soothing place, that venerable old town. At this moment, in fancy, I feel the refreshing chilliness of its deeply shadowed avenues, inhale the fragrance of its thousand shrubberies, and thrill anew with undefinable delight, at the deep hollow note of the church-bell, breaking, each hour, with sullen and sudden roar, upon the stillness of the dusky atmosphere in which the fretted Gothic steeple lay imbedded and asleep.

These are Poe's own words, from *William Wilson*, and how curiously the veils of his imaginative atmosphere colour this English scene. The tale itself echoes with the music of muffled bells rung in some half-dismantled belfry by a scarcely human agency, and this, like many other of his stories, is concerned with states of the spirit.

The school, he tells us, was a large rambling Elizabethan house

. . . old and irregular. The grounds were extensive, and a high and solid brick wall, topped with a bed of mortar and broken glass, encompassed the whole. . . . To me how veritably a palace of enchantment! There was really no end to its windings—to its incomprehensible subdivisions. It was difficult, at any given time, to say with certainty upon which of its two stories one happened to be. From each room to every other there were sure to be found three or four steps either in ascent or descent. Then the lateral branches were innumerable—inconceivable—and so returning in upon themselves, that our most exact ideas in regard to the whole mansion were not very far different from those with which we pondered upon infinity. During the five years of my residence here, I was never able to ascertain with precision in what remote locality lay the little sleeping apartment assigned to myself and some eighteen or twenty other scholars.
The school-room was the largest in the house—I could not help thinking, in the world. It was very long, narrow, and dismally low, with pointed Gothic windows and a ceiling of oak.

But that, too, with the gigantic and gnarled trees and the excessively ancient houses, has vanished.

Defoe spoke well of his 'Newington Green Academy'. 'Though,' he said, 'the Scholars from this Place were not Destitute in the Languages,' (he himself was more or less conversant with French, Latin, Spanish, Italian and could 'read' Greek), 'yet it is observed of them, they were by this made Masters of the English Tongue, and more of them excelled in that Particular, than of any School at that Time.'

It is a tribute well worth pondering over, an exercise that may be assisted by an essay on 'Thought and Language', by Samuel Butler, included in *The Humour of Homer*.

Defoe's headmaster, Charles Morton, weary of persecution, finally set sail for America, and became 'vice-president of Harvard College', and among Defoe's schoolfellows at Stoke Newington was a boy, about five years older than himself, named Timothy Cruso, who in later years became a popular Presbyterian preacher and was known as 'the Golden'. 'He could pray two hours together in Scripture-language.'

It would not be surprising to hear that Defoe could do likewise. When, indeed, he was young and his father's sect was afraid of the activities of Charles II, he copied out the whole of the Pentateuch in shorthand—after which, he confesses, he grew so tired that he was willing to risk the rest. His prose is haunted by memories of the language of the *Authorized Version;* and *there* are to be found the record of two sea voyages which must surely have been shared by an immeasurably greater number of readers than any others in the history of the world—the voyage of Jonah from Joppa in his terrified and vain attempt to evade his mission to Nineveh; and that of St. Paul, a prisoner in the charge of Julius, the centurion, from Caesarea to Rome.

St. Paul's voyage, like all such ventures in these early days, was one, hugging the shore as far as possible, from island on to island. He embarked for Italy in a ship of Adramyttium, which touched at Sidon. Thence he sailed 'under Cyprus', and came to Myra, a city of Lycia. Thence, with adverse winds—

. . . We sailed under Crete, over against Salmone; and, hardly passing it, came unto a place which is called The fair havens; nigh whereunto was the city of Lasea.

Now when much time was spent, and when sailing was now dangerous, because the fast was now already past, Paul admonished them, and said unto them, Sirs, I perceive that this voyage will be with hurt and much damage, not only of the lading and ship, but also of our lives.

Nevertheless the centurion believed the master and the owner of the ship, more than those things which were spoken by Paul. And because the haven was not commodious to winter in, the more part advised to depart thence also, if by any means they might attain to Phenice, and there to winter; which is an haven of Crete, and lieth toward the south west and north west. And when the south wind blew softly, supposing that they had obtained their purpose, loosing thence, they sailed close by Crete.

But not long after there arose against it a tempestuous wind, called Euroclydon. And when the ship was caught, and could not bear up into the wind, we let her drive. And running under a certain island which is called Clauda, we had much work to come by the boat: which when they had taken up, they used helps, undergirding the ship; and, fearing lest they should fall into the quicksands, strake sail, and so were driven.

And we being exceedingly tossed with a tempest, the next day they lightened the ship; and the third day we cast out with our own hands the tackling of the ship. And when neither sun nor stars in many days appeared, and no small tempest lay on us, all hope that we should be saved was then taken away.

But after long abstinence Paul stood forth in the midst of them, and said, Sirs, ye should have hearkened unto me, and not have loosed from Crete, and to have gained this harm and loss. And now I exhort you to be of good cheer: for there shall be no loss of any man's life among you, but of the ship. For there stood by me this night the angel of God, whose I am, and whom I serve, saying, Fear not, Paul; thou must be brought before Caesar: and, lo, God hath given thee all them that sail with thee. Wherefore, sirs, be of good cheer: for I believe God, that it shall be even as it was told me. Howbeit, we must be cast upon a certain island.

But when the fourteenth night was come, as we were driven up and down in Adria [the expanse of sea between Crete and Malta], about midnight the shipmen [hearing breakers] deemed that they drew near to some country; and sounded, and found it twenty fathoms: and when they had gone a little further, they sounded again, and found it fifteen fathoms. Then fearing lest we should have fallen upon rocks, they cast four anchors out of the stern, and wished for the day.

And as the shipmen were about to flee out of the ship, when they had let down the boat into the sea, under colour as though they

282

would have cast anchors out of the foreship, Paul said to the centurion and to the soldiers, Except these abide in the ship, ye cannot be saved.

Then the soldiers cut off the ropes of the boat, and let her fall off.

And while the day was coming on, Paul besought them all to take meat, saying, This day is the fourteenth day that ye have tarried and continued fasting, having taken nothing. Wherefore I pray you to take some meat: for this is for your health: for there shall not an hair fall from the head of any of you. And when he had thus spoken, he took bread, and gave thanks to God in presence of them all: and when he had broken it, he began to eat. Then were they all of good cheer, and they also took some meat.

And we were in all in the ship two hundred threescore and sixteen souls. And when they had eaten enough, they lightened the ship, and cast out the wheat into the sea. And when it was day, they knew not the land: but they discovered a certain creek with a shore, into the which they were minded, if it were possible, to thrust in the ship. And when they had taken up the anchors, they committed themselves unto the sea, and loosed the rudder bands, and hoised up the mainsail to the wind, and made toward shore. And falling into a place where two seas [or cross currents] met, they ran the ship aground; and the forepart stuck fast, and remained unmoveable, but the hinder part was broken with the violence of the waves.

Defoe seldom achieved the natural verbal melody and the sensitive rhythms of this quiet, unlaboured prose. Every detail, every word, in it seems to be there solely for the sake of giving a truthful record, while Defoe's chief aim in form and method was to give the *appearance* of a truthful record—a different problem.

The narrative by St. Luke is also a delicate piece of portraiture. In his few spoken words St. Paul stands clear before us—courteous, far-seeing, serene, courageous. And apart from this a clear integrity and beauty of character is made evident in the mind of the narrator. Moreover, the writer of this passage seems to have no audience of any kind in his thoughts, except only the silent one of his own spirit; and this, in every author, great or small, affords him the light or dusk or obscurity in which he works.

Here, too, is evidence of that rare and profound condition of solitude known, it seems, to the true artist when the creative vision blots out for awhile the consciousness of all else besides; the solitude that Henry James tells of in those few pencilled pages which—intended only for his own eyes—were found among his papers after his death.

And last, after contemplating, even though only by way of books, so many 'scenes of silent life', we find ourselves face to face with a riddle that may seldom ask itself and may not require any answer. There are answers—and questions—that may be taken for granted. Why is it that the mere company of one's own kind, their talk, their changing faces, even their shared silence should be so natural, reassuring and close, and, as it would seem, so necessary to the peace and happiness of the self within? Any evidence of pattern, of design, sharply interests us. Evidence of *human* activity where it is wholly unexpected is curiously moving. It is a kind of company. We are sharing something. What?

We cannot say where either our thoughts or our dreams 'come from'. It may be that, like bees in a garden, we all partake of the same treasury, and that this nectar we so assiduously pursue and enjoy is no more individually our own than the honey should be. That being so, utter solitude for any man must be beyond achieving, even though all his world were to fall silent and he should find himself alone except for the memoried ghosts of the past. Like that inward communion recorded by Henry James, it would be for him a solitude thronged with the phantoms of the universe of the mind.

Additional Notes for the Second Edition

Some little time after the publication of the first edition of *Desert Islands*, I discovered, through the kindness of Mr. Arthur Rogers, that a preface more or less appropriate to it had long since been written by the author of *The Voyages, Dangerous Adventures and Imminent Escapes of Captain Richard Falconer*. . . . It is dated November 7th, 1719, and runs as follows:

I am told, that a Book without a Preface, is like a New Play without a Prologue, or a French Dinner without Soup; and tho' I cannot tell what to say, yet I am resolv'd to say something, tho' perhaps not any thing to the Purpose. So far I hope you'll allow me to be an Author. I shall give you, gentle Reader, (if you are so) Three of my Reasons why I publish these following Pages; which, I must confess, are not so well polish'd as I could wish, but Truth is amiable tho' in Rags. The first and chiefest, to get Money; for tho' I have a considerable Income, yet I can never bring both points together at the Year's End; but however, don't blame my economy, since I owe you nothing, and if I am beholden to any Body, it is to Honest Chetwood, my Bookseller; (I beg his Pardon if I miscall him, tho' I don't believe it will anger him in the least, for all Men love to be term'd so, whether they deserve it or no) being he will run the greatest Risque if my Book does not sell. Second, to save my Lungs, and a great deal of Trouble in repeating to my Friends these following Adventures, for now they may at a small Expence get 'em by Heart, if they will endeavour to stretch their Memories. Third and lastly, to appear in Print, which was, I assure you, a great Motive, with me as well as with a great many others of the same Rank, that make Work for many Printers, tho' as little to the Purpose as my self. I cou'd give a Catalogue of some of 'em, but that wou'd be making my Preface exceed the Bulk of my Book. Tho' I cou'd put the Booksellers in a Way to save Money in their Pockets, and that is to persuade a great many Authors to print their Lucubrations at their own Charge, and that might make some of the poorest to desist; but for the richer Sort of Authors, there's no Help, it's like the Itch, and they must write to be scratch'd tho' the Blood comes. The following Sheets, however extraordinary they appear, I assure you upon the Word of a Man are Truth, and I hope they will entertain you; but if they don't, and you should chance to slight 'em, you will not anger

Your Servant,
R. FALCONER

The author, as these remarks suggest (and I hope honest Chetwood enjoyed the handsome compliment he paid him), had a turn for literature, and in the course of his narrative quotes Shakespeare, Milton and Dryden. Was he, perhaps, of the same family as the poet of *The Shipwreck*? He tells us that on occasion he fed on dolphins —a rather unusual dish, I assume, for the castaway—and that they were not in his estimation so pleasing to the palate as herring or mackerel. He enticed them with the strains of 'an excellent Trumpet'. He mentions various fruits, e.g., 'the fair apple of the deadly *Mangineel* tree', and the '*Phisick-Nut*, much of the Taste of our Pig-nuts, but one or two of 'em will do your business . . . as well as Dr. *Annodyne-Necklace's* Sugar-Plumbs'. Fights, broadsides, pirates, Spaniards, 'hand-granados', waterspouts, and so forth bedeck his narrative, and, like that of most of his rivals, his style is far from the mealy-mouthed: 'After we had cleared our vessel of the blood and dead men, and refresh'd ourselves. . . .'

To Mr. Rogers I owe also the reading of yet another tale of solitary woe:

An Authentick Relation of the many Hardships and Sufferings of a Dutch Sailor, Who was put on Shore on the uninhabited Isle of *Ascension*, By Order of the Commadore of a Squadron of *Dutch* Ships. With a Remarkable Account of his Converse with Apparitions and Evil Spirits, during his Residence on the Island.

The Journal from which this 'Relation' was printed was found in the Dutch sailor's tent by some men of the *Compton* in January, 1725-6. The book itself is dated 1728, and its price was sixpence. It was printed, according to the epistle to the reader, 'exactly as it was wrote, by the miserable Wretch who is the Subject of it'. He was marooned for 'villainy', and after being furnished with a cask of water, two buckets, an old frying-pan and other comforts, including tea, the squadron of Dutch ships sailed away—vanished beneath the verge of the vast arc of his horizon. Ill fortune dogged him. He had a hatchet, and the helve of it at a critical moment broke in his hand.

He finds water in his treeless, desolate island, but its well-spring dries up. Evil spirits beset him, one of whom becomes embodied and on occasion converses with him—'voices'. These spirits engage also in a violent quarrel in the dark hours, with a din 'as though there had been a hundred Copper-Smiths at work with Beatings and Drummings'. They flood his mind with imprecations. He in reduced to the condition of the beseiged in Samaria.

Perhaps the strangest feature of his case is that he should have kept a journal at all, though it remains but the skeleton of the narrative it might have been. Life at such an extreme is the bleakest of monotonies, though this victim seems to have become incapable of detecting the difference between the within and the without—not always an entirely easy feat even for the sanest of the sane, and one apparently of increasing difficulty in a protracted solitude. The entries become very brief, and every word—*booby*—*Strand*—*dismal*—*Cloud*—*Light*—in such a context seems haunted, like those in which the chief Baker told his dream to Joseph in the prison house:

The 18th Ditto, after my usual custom of Praying, I caught two *Boobys*. The 19th Ditto, nothing worthy of Note. The 20th Ditto, caught one *Booby*. The 21st Ditto, nothing at all.

and again:

The 5th, 6th, 7th and 8th, I delayed no time to look for Water, unless when I prayed.

This is followed by:

The 9th Ditto, As I walked upon the Strand, I heard again a very dismal Noise of Cursing and Swearing in my own Language. During the time of this Noise, I never in all my Life saw so many Fowls together, they looking like a Cloud, and intercepting between me and the sky deprived me of some of its Light.

And last:

The 9th, 10th, 11th, 12th, 13th and 14th of *October*, All as before.

And then—'*FINIS*'.

How curious by comparison with the nakedness of such

a narrative—whatever its source—is the eloquence of Thomas de Quincey:

Oh, burden of solitude, that cleavest to man through every stage of his being! in his birth, which *has* been—in his life, which *is*—in his death, which *shall* be—mighty and essential solitude! that wast, and art, and art to be; thou broodest like the Spirit of God moving upon the surface of the deeps, over every heart that sleeps in the nurseries of Christendom. Like the vast laboratory of the air, which, seeming to be nothing, or less than the shadow of a shade, hides within itself the principle of all things, solitude for the meditating child is the Agrippa's mirror of the unseen universe. Deep is the solitude of millions who, with hearts welling forth love, have none to love them. Deep is the solitude of those who, under secret griefs, have none to pity them. Deep is the solitude of those who, fighting with doubts or darkness have none to counsel them. But deeper than the deepest of these solitudes is that which broods over childhood under the passion of sorrow—bringing with it at intervals the final solitude which watches for it, and is waiting for it within the gates of death. Oh mighty and essential solitude, that wast, and art, and art to be! thy kingdom is made perfect in the grave; but even over those that keep watch outside the grave, like myself, an infant of six years old, thou stretchest out a sceptre of fascination.

Of solitudes not hitherto mentioned in these pages a temporary one of a peculiar kind may be secured in a diving-suit or bell; more particularly, in that marvel of ingenuity from within which Dr. William Beebe has recently been surveying and photographing the fauna and flora of the submarine—and this at so many fathom that if his metal lodging sprang the minutest of leaks, its occupant would, I gather, be instantly annihilated. The account of a less dangerous diving 'engine' may be found, a friend tells me, on pages 411-412 of *The Gentleman's Magazine* for 1749, and on pages 568-569 of Volume VI of *Magna Britannia*. In this its inventor, John Lethbridge, recovered no less a sum than £100,000 from the bottom of the sea. When at intervals he returned to its surface he was refreshed with a pair of bellows.

Islands have been known to vanish and others have shared the fate that has recently overtaken Tristan da Cunha—that of being abandoned. Last year Robben

Island also went this way. My introduction to it—for until then even its name was strange to me—was accompanied by two odd coincidences. In January of that year a lady living in Cape Colony wrote to me as follows:

I am on a drought-stricken farm, everything is sun coloured, golden brown and khaki, the ground, the grass, the rocks and the ranges. The spring-buck are all down at the water holes with the sheep.

To read of islands in such circumstances is to share an inversion of one of the most vivid experiences recounted by the Ancient Mariner:

The waves foam and beat up on to the stoep and the thirsty cattle lowing in the kraal blend their plaintive voices with those of the sea-gulls as I read.

I want—this letter continued—to tell you about an island an hour's run from Cape Town in Table Bay, for years an asylum and more particularly a Leper Settlement. Robben Island. Here the lepers have their church, their padre, their doctor and small army of attendants. And the freedom of the islands. No iron bars or stone walls. But free to wander on the grassy uplands, and trap rabbits, or play, and explore the sandy coves. The mail boats marking the days of the week for them, and the storms of the sea lashing the waves on the rocks, even bringing them wrecks for excitement.

The last island wedding took place last week; the island will verily become a Desert Island. The poor lepers are going to Pretoria to be placed behind iron bars and enclosed by a stone wall. The well-built houses of island stone, the beautiful little church and the pretty gardens are all to be deserted. The government find it costs too much money to run a daily tug in this little bay of storms. The fiat has gone forth. The lepers already shifted write pathetic letters about the new prison and now realize the joys of the once hated Robben Island. Surely no Desert Island will ever be so sadly deserted as this little Robben Island of freedom. . . .

In an evening paper on the very day when I received this letter I chanced on a photograph of this 'new prison'. It had been burned to a shell; children were amusing themselves throwing stones at its dismantled walls.

Not long after this, at Easter, I visited an ancient church in Essex, the incumbent of which very kindly permitted me to see some of its treasures. As I went out into the churchyard again, the drizzling rain falling over its fresh spring moss and grasses, he hastened after me to say that he had forgotten to point out what was still detectable of the stone framework of the old leper hole in the north wall of the church. Naturally, this recalled to memory Robben Island; and I spoke of it. He had himself, for a period some years before this, held the office of chaplain there!

My correspondent in Colesburg also mentioned a translation of *Robinson Crusoe* in a 'very new language'—Afrikaans.

Yet another correspondent, Mr. Arthur B. Watkins, after, alas, disillusioning a remembrance of my childhood: 'Robina Crusoe, I fear, is merely lifeless clay', her only claim to glory being that she was 'a useful shot' with the bow and arrow—went on to refer to Eliot Warburton's *Darien*, wherein appears the description of a desert island 'compared with which Treasure Island was a health resort', while ' "Flint's Pointer" is no more than a baby's rattle compared with the bones that lie on its beach'.

'There's five of 'em (islands) stand thegither, like the pops on a die; and the sea rins in whirlpools a round the inner island; and the jagged coral gies it a bluidy look; and the deadly blue sharks, and the cruel cat fishes, and the slimy tangle, are a' shimmering in the welterin' waters. The centremost island isn't aboon' half a mile ower; it's shaped amaist like a coffin, and covered o'er wi't a ghastly gray sand, and a few stinted trees twisted all shapes, in agony like, by the hurricanes.

'One of them is a cedar tree; and just a dozen yards east of it there lies sic a skeleton as man never saw afore. That skeleton has neither leg banes nor arm banes . . . an' its gruesome teeth are clenched on the neck o' another skeleton lying crosswise by its side.'

Anglicize that *thegither, bluidy, aboon, amaist, sic, banes*—and how specific a flavour of the sinister thins off in the process! To Mr. Watkins I am also indebted for the following copy of a title-page:

God's Protecting Providence, Man's Surest Helps and Defence in times of Greatest Difficulty and Most Imminent Danger, Evidenced in the remarkable Deliverance of Robert Barrow, with divers other Persons, from the Devouring Waves of the Sea, amongst which they suffered Shipwreck; and also from the cruel devouring Jaws of the inhuman Cannibals of Florida. Faithfully related by one of the Persons concerned therein: Jonathan Dickenson.

and also for an account of George Varson of Nottingham:

One of the Troop of Missionaries first sent to the South Sea Islands by the London Missionary Society in the Ship Duff. Capt. Wilson in 1796.

'Missionary yarns are generally poor tack, but George Varson is in rather a different class.' He ' "went native", had two wives (at least), and regularly went to the dogs. . . . He was tattooed all over, and in four years'—to a greater degree than Selkirk, that is, though in the same space of time—'had practically lost all his English speech. The crew of the chance ship by which he escaped did not recognize him for a white man'. But then a white man in the imperial sense he assuredly was then *not*.

Apropos of the ingenuous young white man (referred to on p. 182) who was over-seen surveying himself in a looking-glass, and overheard suavely remarking to himself, 'Not handsome, perhaps, but distinguished!', a friend, who, alas, has forbidden me the privilege of giving her name, concluded from it that most good stories reach back to antiquity, and continued: 'He must, I think, be in the direct line of descent from a tutor' of two generations ago who had for rather intractable victims of his erudition two young men, C. and A.—one of whom, none the less (or otherwise) became a bishop. They delighted in plaguing one who meant them so well, and

always averred that, prying and peeping into his room one day, they overheard him saying to his looking-glass, 'Not exactly handsome, but *vastly spruce and genteel*'.

That a delight in the classics and a passion for *Robinson Crusoe* can be comfortably housed in the same young brains is proved by the following fragment which I owe to the same friend. It is taken from Dorothea Herbert's *Retrospections* of 1772:

When the Boys first returned from School it gave a new turn of affairs—They spouted to us and we stood gaping round till we were all book-mad—Dido and Aeneas—Hector and Paris fired our Brains, a Sixpenny Voyage of Lord Anson, and Old Robinson Crusoe's Tale completed our Mania—One time we fancied ourselves thrown on a Desert Island till a fight who sd. be Crusoe and who Fryday ended our play—Another time we were a set of Sailors thrown on the Delightful Island of Juan Fernandez—We spent whole weeks in an old Blue Bed under cure for the Sea-Scurvy and ate such quantities of Cabbage Stumps, Celery and other Anti-scorbutic Thrash that we really got scorbutic Disorder with worms and a variety of Complaint that obliged us to submit to Continual Doses of Physick which old Mary administered with tearswoln eyes to half a Dozen of us at Once.

But that castaways, however closely accustomed they may be to weevils and stinking water, do not expire within a week of consuming *their* 'Thrash' is one of the many marvels of their experiences to those who live at home at ease.

As for the cry of despair to be found on page 262, it was quickly followed by groans of remorse, though the ashes that accompanied them were fragrant as spices of the East. One curious fact, however, emerges from this blunder: namely that a statement intended as veracious but yet iridescent with error may be far more productive of benefits than one positively shining with the gold of truth. If the original comment had been, 'How pleasing and salutary it is that little girls and small boys should be equally devoted to desert islands, and that Robinson Crusoe's is one in which brother and sister can play as happily together as will some day lion and lamb!'—that would have been the end of the matter. Its converse evoked a paean of protest. 'Naturally I can only speak for myself', wrote Miss Marjorie J. F. Hett,

but I strongly suspect that many of my sex are well acquainted with that 'odd infatuation' for a small island (and preferably a desert one) of which you speak, and that you are mistaken in supposing that it belongs only to 'small boys and *their* elders.'

When I was a little girl, I ruled over a kingdom named North Bruno. I even made a map of it, and though it only truly existed in the realms of my imagination, yet, when we played out-of-doors, it was symbolized for me by a small plantation of fir trees which grew

292

in our field, ringed by an iron paling. The field was an ocean which I crossed to reach it, putting forth from the dark shores of the shrubbery. North Bruno must have lain, I think, too near the land altogether to satisfy me. There was yet another clump of firs, perhaps smaller and certainly sunnier, and further out on the green sea, which I loved far better and called 'The North Brunetic Isle'. You see, therefore, that I am not one of those women whom you call 'sensible', indeed, even now, the sight or the thought of a lonely isle has power to make my heart beat faster. In 1928 I saw my first coral island. From the liner, it appeared as nothing but a level band of bright verdure edged below with dazzling white and seemingly afloat on the endless blue of the Indian Ocean. I shall never forget it, and the words *Minikoi Atoll* will never lose their power to thrill me.

On that same voyage, I saw the Cocos Islands and their Lagoon, but I will not write about them because I could never say what I should like to say. Thinking of the *solitude* of such islands, I wonder whether you know a certain passage in W.H. Hudson's *Idle Days in Patagonia* which gives the most moving and perfect account of such a state that I know of (though it is not the solitude of an island). . . .

Lastly, I would remind you [astonishing oversight that made this necessary!] of that island, acquaintanceship with which may save the soul of even the small boy of our own day 'glutted with talkies and comics'. I cannot resist quoting from its creator's description of it:

'So . . . they drew near the Neverland; for after many moons they did reach it . . . because the island was out looking for them. It is only thus that anyone may sight those magic shores.

' "There it is," said Peter calmly.

' "Where, where?".'

Then, again, Miss Ida Bennett broke the silence of remote Uruguay:

. . . There was certainly *one* small girl with an infatuation for desert islands and Crusoes, and the infatuation still lives, although she herself is now a mother with a schoolgirl daughter. Probably there are thousands of other girls and women in the same category, but I can at least vouch for myself.

Before I was ten, I had written many tales with, as their subject, always a desert island and a castaway girl, thus living on paper what I should dearly have liked to happen to myself, and, although I was not so fortunate as to possess a *Robinson Crusoe* then, my first favourite (notwithstanding its many faults, of which I was aware, such as the smug, encyclopaedic knowledge of the father) was *Swiss Family Robinson*, the honour afterwards being shared by *Gulliver's Travels*, with Edgar Allan Poe's works and *King Solomon's Mines* also in the running. The love of travel and adventure led me first to Africa and afterwards to South America. . . .

I cannot now truthfully say I should like to be cast away on a desert island, having 'roughed it' too often, yet, whenever I see an island during a voyage (I have crossed the Equator eight times), I feel an unaccountable emotion stirring me. I once spent six months on the veldt, where I was alone from 7 a.m. to 5 p.m., and I felt that the quiet and the loneliness re-created me, whilst I spent most of my time watching ants. There were no birds to sing, and no sound of any sort, and, although I was 1,500 miles from the sea, I felt more as if I were on a desert island than at any time in my life. It is quite a different feeling from being alone in a house in London for there I felt the loneliness would drive me mad. . . .

And finally Miss Rose Macaulay, whose *Orphan Island* alone should have been warning enough, while most gently tempering the wind, settled this question. 'Talking of Everychild', she wrote, after making a plea for *Masterman Ready* ('To me it seems to have every merit: but, as it was the first book I ever read to myself, perhaps I don't see it quite in cool blood'); and also mentioning Ballantyne's *Coral Island*, without which no book even touching on the islands of romance could be excusable—'talking of Everychild, your note'—on Woman and the Island— 'rather grieved and shocked me. . . . Girls do like islands, you know—as much as boys, I am sure. I mean, the normal, average girl. Certainly all I have ever known have read of them, played at them, dreamed of them, and written of them, as much as—perhaps even more than— being more romantic creatures as a rule—their brothers. It was my own pet game and daydream always, and I know so many little females who always read island stories with delight. I wonder why gentlemen so often make such strange mistakes about ladies? I don't think ladies do it so much about gentlemen, for some reason— there must be some psychological reason, I suppose. You say "sensible women". But most women aren't, very; anyhow not throughout. The most sensible might have some island weakness, I think.' May I be forgiven then, and my blunder too; for this is final. And what of the past?

294

Sir W. N. M. Geary's refers to 'Painters' Wives Islands':

In the 16th century when a 'painter' was making a map; his wife would say to him, 'Dear, put me in one island all for myself!'

'For', not *to*, be it noted.

When (for example) Sir Francis Drake was returning to England, he was studying a Spanish chart he had taken and, thinking an island thereon would serve as a depot, began to put questions thereon to a Spanish prisoner. The Don smiled and replied, 'I don't think you will find that island; it was put in to please Señora.'

And as, one may assume, no master mariner who has ever heard the call of romance would resent the appearance of islands on his charts which he is neither in search of, nor would touch at if encountered (and no *ship* can be wrecked on the imaginary), it seems a pity that cartography should have become so exact an art. Sir Francis Drake at any rate, if he had been alive to-day, would have seen to it in his own summary fashion that one of his islands, whether real or otherwise, should be for ever known as *Amelia Earhart*, if only as a small remembrance of *her* icy, starless, and indomitable thirteen hours' solitude when she crossed his Atlantic but a season ago on the wings of a vessel far smaller even than the least of his own cockle shells, and with the phantom called Danger, whose surname is Imminent, continually at her elbow as she flew.

As for *sandy* solitudes—and there may be close copies of these in the world within—Mr. Bertram Thomas has recently explored what seems to be the last remaining tract of the world left by men of Europe, until his day, untraversed—Arabia Felix. And the photograph he has chosen for frontispiece to his record of that great journey is itself a symbol in design of what solitude means to the mind. And last, Major Bagnold with his companion adventurers not long since 'mapped nearly 100 miles west of Dalla, and then trekked 500 miles south to the oasis of Owenat through sand-dunes ranged at regular intervals "like an army".' Owenat, itself, an oasis discovered in 1923, 'is in a sheer rocky plateau 6,000 feet high'—like that, says Major Bagnold, 'described by Conan Doyle in *The Lost World.*' 'The expedition . . . climbed up the plateau, and found there a few people belonging to a negro tribe from Central Africa. . . .' North-east of Owenat they discovered a circle of stones three feet high and twenty-seven feet across, similar in formation to Stonehenge, and 150 miles from the nearest water; and later, they followed the old slave-trade route from Darfur to Assuit—a forty days' camel journey—that had been left unused for fifty years, every mile of which was marked out with the skeletons of more than two hundred camels.

And what solitude in space is more impressive than that which coincides with solitude in Time?

ACKNOWLEDGMENTS

FOR PERMISSION to include in this volume certain copyright material, to which particular reference has for the most part been made in the preceding pages, I am indebted to the following authors and publishers: To Dr. William Beebe and Messrs. George Putnam's Sons, for citations from *Galápagos: World's End;* to Sir Ernest A. T. Wallis Budge, for extracts from his *Palladius: The Paradise or Garden of the Holy Fathers;* to Professor A. S. Eddington, the Cambridge University Press and The Macmillan Company, for a passage from *The Nature of the Physical World;* to Mr. T. S. Eliot and to Messrs. Faber & Faber, Ltd., for his poem 'Because I do not hope to turn again'; to Professor R. K. Gordon, Messrs. J. M. Dent & Sons, Ltd., and Messrs. E. P. Dutton for an extract from *Anglo-Saxon Poetry;* to Mr. Ralph Hodgson, for his poem ' Reason has moons' and for a stanza from *Stupidity Street;* to Professor L. P. Jacks, for an extract from *The Castaway;* to Mr. John Masefield, for an extract from *Lost Endeavour;* to Messrs. The Hogarth Press, for an extract from Montaigne's *Diary;* to Mr. Scoresby Routledge, for an extract from *The Mystery of Easter Island;* to Mr. E. H. Visiak and Messrs. Victor Gollancz, Ltd., for an extract from *Medusa;* to Mr. J. Redwood Anderson, who has generously allowed me to print his note on *Cannabis Indica* for the first time; to many correspondents who have permitted me to include extracts from their letters in the 'additional notes'; and—for a host of kindnesses—to Mr. H. M. Tomlinson.

My thanks are also due to the Editor of *The Times*, for permission to reprint extracts from an article on Daniel Defoe contributed to the *Literary Supplement;* to Mrs. Hardy, for permission to include an extract from *Jude the Obscure;* to Miss May Morris, for an extract from *The Water of the Wondrous Isles;* to Mr. Lloyd Osbourne, Messrs. Chatto & Windus, and Messrs. Charles Scribner's Sons, for an extract from *Treasure Island;* to the Hakluyt Society; to the Controller of H.M. Stationery Office, for extracts from official publications; and to Mr. Pieter van Tienhoven.

For other generous help and kindness I am most grateful to Mr. Forrest Reid, Mr. R. N. Green-Armytage, Mr. F. P. Sprent, Mr. G. E. Manwaring, Mr. Elbridge Adams, to my nephew, Mr. J. de la Mare Rowley, and, in particular, to Miss Olive Jones.

INDEX

INDEX

INDEX

INDEX

INDEX

INDEX